MICHAEL ROSENBERG

ALAN LEWIS

SOCIAL DEVIANCE

AN INTEGRATED APPROACH

Prentice Hall Canada Inc.
Scarborough, Ontario

Canadian Cataloguing in Publication Data

Rosenberg, M. Michael
    Social deviance : an integrated approach

Includes index.
ISBN 0-13-205394-2

1. Deviant behavior.   I. Lewis, Alan, 1943-
II. Title.

HM291.R67 1992   302.5'42   C92-094780-8

Prentice-Hall Inc., Englewood Cliffs, New Jersey
Prentice-Hall International, Inc., London
Prentice-Hall of Australia, Pty., Sydney
Prentice-Hall of India Pvt., Ltd., New Delhi
Prentice-Hall of Japan, Inc., Tokyo
Prentice-Hall of Southeast Asia (Pte.) Ltd., Singapore
Editora Prentice-Hall do Brasil Ltda., Rio de Janeiro
Prentice-Hall Hispanoamericana, S.A., Mexico

ISBN 0-13-205394-2

Acquisitions Editor: Michael Bickerstaff
Developmental Editor: Maryrose O'Neill
Production Editor: William Booth
Production Coordinator: Anna Orodi
Cover Design: Olena Serbyn
Page Layout: Suzanne Boehler

1 2 3 4 5   RRD   97 96 95 94 93

Printed and bound in the United States of America
by R.R. Donnelley & Sons

Contents

7 Critical and Feminist Criminologies   159

8 Ethnomethodological and Phenomenological Approaches to Deviance   189

9 Conceiving Deviance   213

Preface

This book had its origins in the courses on social deviance taught by us at Dawson College and at Concordia University over the past few years. We would like to thank our many students in both institutions who helped us evolve the approach to teaching of deviance found in this book.

Our real joy in writing this book has been the ability to engage in a stimulating and exciting dialogue with our colleagues at Dawson College, in particular William Hanigsberg, William Moss, David Muhlstock, Sam Parkovnik, Fay Rogers and Peter Sawchuk. Deena White of l'Université de Montréal, Elizabeth Comak, H. Taylor Buckner and P.A. Saram also made many important suggestions which substantially helped to improve this book.

Special mention must also be made of Allan Turowetz. Originally, Allan was to have been one of the co-authors of this book and he contributed greatly to its initial planning. Unfortunately, Allan was unable to participate because of other commitments. Nevertheless, he never lost his interest in the project and throughout its writing continued to provide us with valuable guidance and ideas.

The staff of Prentice-Hall Canada, Pat Ferrier, Jean Ferrier and Maryrose O'Neill have been a pleasure to work with. They guided the book to its conclusion with encouragement, enthusiasm and extraordinary patience.

CHAPTER

1 What Is Deviance?

There are many ways in which people in our society differ from one another. There are the obvious physical differences: those of gender and age, of height and weight, of eye, hair, and skin colour. There are the subtle individual differences which emerge as we discover some to be brighter than others, some stronger or more aggressive, some more talented or more creative, some more emotional or more loving. There are the many social differences which have a profound impact on our lives: differences of social class, of status and reputation, of occupation, of language, religion and ethnicity. To Canadians, difference seems an obvious fact of life. Canada is a nation originally founded on group differences, a political union of two distinct ethnic, linguistic and religious groups. To these "founding groups" have been added people from every corner of the world, and many Canadians today proudly assert that Canada is a "multicultural" society. Moreover, as a modern industrial state promoting differential degrees of educational, occupational and economic achievement, Canada is also a nation that promotes individual differences. "Differentness" permeates our society, giving it much of its character, its energy and its flow. But there are some differences—moral differences—which are typically seen negatively. Such differences are those which fall under the term "deviance."

Even if it has not yet entered into common parlance, the term deviance refers to phenomena with which most people are familiar long before they may take a sociology course devoted to it. All of us have an understanding of what is meant by crime, or mental illness, or alcoholism. We have some conception of what sort of behaviour we would consider immoral, or "wrong," or "disgusting." We know when we have done something which we consider embarrassing or humiliating, and we know what we mean when we say of others that they are "strange," "weird," "nerds," "sick" or "gross." Our understanding of crime or the criminal may not be that of the lawyer, the judge or the policeman, but it is sufficient for our practical purposes in everyday life.

1

Nevertheless, the sociologist is not satisfied to let knowledge of deviance remain at this practical level. What is "good enough" for everyday life is inadequate—and sometimes simply wrong—when it comes to understanding how social phenomena such as deviance really work. While sociologists make use of everyday notions about deviance as data and as a foundation for their own concepts, they do not simply accept the common-sense explanations most people use to make sense of deviance. People often have a mistaken or confused understanding of social events, and when the subject matter with which we are dealing is deviance, they let their understanding be directed by biases, emotional reactions or ingrained beliefs. Moreover, given that a person's ideas or behaviours concerning deviance can lead to their being punished or condemned by others, people are very likely to conceal, distort or misrepresent their actions and views.

Sociologists, like other social scientists, attempt to generate systematic knowledge about the social world. They do this by constantly questioning their assumptions and data, and by subjecting their findings to the critiques of other social scientists. This is not to deny that common sense, everyday notions play a crucial role in sociology itself, particularly the sociology of deviance. These notions are the very stuff out of which deviance as a social phenomenon is constructed. Understanding these notions—without being subjected to them—is an essential first step in sociological analysis. "Debunking," "unmasking," and "engaging in critical thought" are among the terms sociologists use to describe this all-important step of getting past the appearance to uncover the whys and wherefores of what is really going on. It is one of the major advantages of sociology over the natural sciences that our subject matter—people—can talk to us, tell us what they think, react to our theories, and correct their evident flaws.

But there is a problem. Sociologists cannot seem to agree among themselves on how to define deviance or on how deviance works. This is in large part because different sociologists view deviance in terms of different perspectives. Each of these perspectives provides its own definition of deviance, because each directs attention to some elements of social reality over others. A second difficulty in developing a common definition is the relativity built into the very concept of deviance itself. People disagree on what is or is not deviant. A third relates to the general ambiguity prevalent in our society over what we consider to be deviance, what should be done about it, and by whom.

SOCIOLOGY AND SOCIOLOGICAL PERSPECTIVES

Sociology, as we just noted, is a social science, and while its subject matter is society, sociologists are united into a single discipline on the basis of a common set of fundamental assumptions rather than on the basis of a common set of theoretical propositions. Most of what we refer to as "theories" in sociology would better be characterized as "perspectives." Fleming and Goff (1983: 28) describe a perspective as composed of five interrelated components: purposes, assumptions, concepts, methods and implications for action. To this list one might well want to add a common body of data or set of research interests. In the sociology of deviance, in particular, different perspectives tend to focus on different forms of deviance, on which they typically do research and to which they frequently refer when giving examples.

Different perspectives develop because of differences in any one or more of these components. For example (Fleming and Goff, 1983: 30):

> Some sociologists claim as their purpose a straightforward desire to know. Others claim, or are accused of, an interest in understanding in order to maintain the existing order. Still others are explicitly motivated by a desire to understand in order to change the social order, in the name of such values as equality or freedom.

Despite all of these possible areas of difference, there is one crucial assumption which is shared by almost all sociologists. This key assumption, which has been referred to as the "basic sociological insight" (Fleming and Goff, 1983: 32), is that human beings are essentially *social* beings. The natural environment of human beings is other people. It is in the presence of others and together with others that we come to take on a self, learn appropriate social roles, act out social expectations, and come to experience the world in a shared, common way. Entering society from the very moment of birth, we are shaped into social objects to such a degree that even our biology is modified. Plastic surgery is an obvious example, but Ray Birdwhistell (1970) has argued that the socially approved gestures and body movements we learn from infancy set our muscles into patterns which alter our appearance and make all the members of a single culture quite literally look alike.

Using this common set of shared assumptions sociologists, have studied an extraordinarily diverse set of topics whose ties to one another may be tenuous at best: decision-making in the family; how pedestrians avoid collisions on sidewalks; how hospitals deal with the death of a patient; how prostitution helps to preserve the institution of marriage; the development of informal networks in bureaucracies; the impact of education on social mobility; the role of "distorted communication" in preserving systems of oppression; the ritual significance of shaking hands. The field of sociology is so broad that each socologist must specialize in a relatively narrow set of research interests such as the family, stratification, demography, education or religion in order to master all of the relevant data. If sociologists rarely agree on what they mean by sociology, it is in large part a consequence of the enormous conceptual and methodological differences that inevitably separate those who deal with such diverse topics.

In contrast, within some narrower area of study, such as the family, one is likely to find much more agreement as to just what it is that is being studied. Even, here, however, disagreements rage; though less so over what is being studied than over what to do about it: the implications for action. The sociologists' vision of the family is affected by their reasons for dealing with and attempting to understand the family.

With the study of deviance, however, the sociologist returns to a set of topics as broad as sociology itself. Indeed, it can be asserted that deviance is itself a widespread feature of all social life. If so, then (Rosenberg, Stebbins and Turowetz, 1982: 91):

> the study of deviance is at the heart of the study of society. In uncovering disorder, we discover the sources upon which order rests; in uncovering immorality, we discover the boundaries within which morality is contained. The study of deviance is on the cutting edge of the sociological debate on the nature of social order.

The sociology of deviance mirrors much of the controversy and disagreement found in sociology as a whole.

Almost any area of social life presents instances of deviance and provides opportunities for further deviance. We usually think of crime when we think of deviance, and more specifically of major crimes such as murder, armed robbery or rape. But deviance occurs as well in the minute interactions of everyday life (Denzin, 1971) in which we manipulate, lie, cover-up, seduce, disgust or simply irritate one another. There are the deviant organizations, not only organized crime, but "legitimate" organizations which bribe officials, cheat customers or knowingly produce hazardous or defective products. There is the multitude of subcultural groups, from religious cults to the homosexual community, which many or most people view as deviant. There are the daily news reports of deviance by public officials, such as Canadian immigration officials opening private mail, police entrapping criminals or Cabinet ministers cheating on conflict of interest guidelines. The study of deviance is inevitably the study of society itself, and it reproduces all of the controversies experienced by those engaged in that larger study.

THE RELATIVITY OF DEVIANCE

A second source of disagreement is a consequence of the fact that deviance is always socially and culturally relative. What this means is that no form of behaviour is intrinsically deviant; no form of behaviour has been considered deviant when committed by everyone in every society. Deviance is always relative to the particular group which defines that behaviour as deviant. That is, any particular form of behaviour will only be considered deviant in a particular cultural context. Cannibalism is decidedly deviant in our society; among the Aztec we are told that it was sacred and revered. Socio-cultural relativity means that the sociologist cannot treat deviance as if it were an intrinsic property of an act, the way the physicist can treat atomic bonding as an intrinsic property of matter. The sociologist must always view deviance as socially constructed and socially defined.

Another form of relativity in addition to social and cultural relativity is "situational relativity" (Goode, 1978: 35). Take the example of cannibalism just mentioned. Now think of different circumstances in which people in our society would define cannibalism as acceptable. For example, if one is stranded somewhere far from civilization with no food supply, *would* cannibalism be acceptable? Many people might say yes, with the proviso that the persons to be eaten are already dead and have not been killed in order to be used as food. As the social context differs, so too do the socially constructed definitions of the act as deviant or as normal (or at least necessary). In other words, deviance is not only culturally relative, it is also "situationally relative."

Since deviance means different things to different people in different circumstances, no sociological explanation of deviance will ever cover all of the possible ways in which some people will come to consider some form of behaviour as deviant. Especially when you remember—which students are sometimes apt to forget—that sociologists are people too. We form a very particular audience watching a limited set of actors engage in deviance in a very specific setting—sociological research. As sociologists have learned from long experience, we are as affected by our own personal biases and emotional responses as anyone else. Part of our task when studying deviance is to recognize that fact and what we can call "methodological relativity" to avoid these kinds of biases in understanding deviance. However, as we shall see in our concluding chapter, this task is made more difficult by changing intellectual and professional circumstances affecting sociologists. Sociologists have had to consider the possibility that there are limits to relativism; that some forms of behaviour such as murder and rape are unacceptable to us as human beings; and that as social scientists we have a responsibility to do what we can to help change the world for the better. But how do we decide on those limits and what actions do we take? Again, disagreement rages.

THE AMBIGUITY OF DEVIANCE

It is not only sociologists who have difficulty in defining deviance or deciding what to do about it. With the exception of the major crimes, little agreement about deviance exists in our society as a whole. In a survey conducted in 1965, J. L. Simmons asked 180 people what they considered deviant. They responded with a total of 252 *different* forms of behaviour they considered deviant. The answers ranged from homosexuals to atheists to divorcées (Thio, 1983: 3). This suggests that, apart from the major forms of deviance, little consensus exists about what is or is not deviant. It suggests something more. If there is little agreement about deviance, then chances are there is little consensus about norms or rules. Both norms and deviance are ambiguous in our society.

Clearly, in a situation of low consensus, there will also be sharp and often bitter disagreement over whether or not some form of behaviour ought to be considered deviant. The continuing public controversy over abortion and the dramatic confrontations over the operation of abortion clinics in a number of Canadian cities is one vivid example.

Further complicating the public's conception of deviance is the decisive role the media play both in determining what *will* be considered deviant and in fostering the common-sense image of the deviant. Newspapers, magazines, television and film not only reflect everyday stereotypes, they also manufacture and perpetuate them. In modern "information societies," the media are the repository of the "folk wisdom," everyday truisms, and clichés which make up a significant portion of ordinary knowledge about the world.

In addition, there is often a very fine line separating the "deviant" from the "normative." "Much behavior," Birenbaum and Lesieur (1982: 115) assert, "that should be called deviant achieves alternative definition." One reason for this is that defining behaviour as deviant has serious implications for those "caught" engaging in that deviance. Under such circumstances, people may well go out of their way to avoid defining behaviour as deviant as much as possible, to avoid either an ugly confrontation or the humiliation of being wrong.

Some acts, it is true, seem more clearly to fall within the province of deviance, i.e., as behaviour which is "wrong"—for example, crime. As noted above, most people agree that crime is wrong and criminals should be punished (Law Reform Commission of Canada, 1974). But there is a great deal of disagreement over *how* they should be punished, as the recurring debates over whether Canada should reinstate capital punishment illustrate. Even if the public does agree that crime is Ideviant, the experts may well disagree. Some criminologists, for example, insist that crime is essentially a political phenomenon and is not the same as social deviance at all.

Mental illness provides yet another example of fundamental disagreements. Most people agree that the term "mental illness" refers to people or behaviour which are in some way "abnormal." But they are unable to agree on what they mean by mental illness. Studies have shown that many people who later came to be diagnosed as mentally ill continued to live for many years at home with their families long after they had begun to exhibit behaviour the rest of us would consider peculiar, odd or strange. Yet their families or friends either refused to believe or simply failed to consider that their behaviour was a symptom of mental illness (Yarrow et al., 1955). In contrast, when we asked students for examples of people whom they consider mentally ill, they referred to people whose behaviour they considered troubling (someone using drugs, for example), extreme (an aunt who cleans her home thoroughly every day) or outlandish (someone who regularly spends as much as $100 on a pair of jeans). They rarely referred to behaviour which fits the classic mold of "mental illness." If we turn to the media, we get yet another image of mental illness. Now the "insane" are portrayed as what sociologists call "folk devils." They are the embodiment of evil, depravity and mindless violence. These media images are so exaggerated that people cannot relate what they see on television or in the movies to their own experiences.

Suppose Canadians agreed on what they mean by deviance. Would that solve the sociologists' problem? No. The question of whether the world was round or flat was not solved when everyone believed it to be flat any more than it is solved today *because* everyone believes it to be round. Scientific explanation is not based on opinion but on accepted methods and canons of evidence. Unanimity would make it easier for us to specify what we are looking for and would make it easier to go about finding it, but sociological concepts, even if they are grounded on everyday concepts, are separate and distinct constructs meeting different criteria (Schutz, 1961).

DEFINING DEVIANCE

It should not be surprising that there is so much disagreement over deviance. What may be surprising is that an area of study such as "deviance" can be identified at all and that a book such as this one can be written to cover "the sociology of deviance."

Still, we need some kind of starting point or benchmark if we are all to agree on and understand what we are talking about. One common solution found in many texts is to present several different definitions of deviance derived from different perspectives and illustrate just how and why they differ. Hagan (1991), for example, presents eight different definitions of deviance. This approach has its merits, but since we will be discussing different perspectives in some detail, there is little to be gained by presenting several different definitions of deviance in advance.

Moreover, the difficulties encountered in defining deviance do not disappear simply because we have many definitions instead of one. Because of the social, cultural and situational relativity of deviance, any given act can mean different things to different people. We could, quite literally, uncover an infinite number of definitions of deviance. Some theorists insist that this means it is not the sociologist who defines deviance. As Gottfredson and Hirschi (1990: 3) put this argument, such theorists insist that "the state, not the scientist, determines the nature or definition of crime." The state may try to, but the state, too, has its opposition, and both the state and the law reflect conflicting group interests. Still, a sociological definition of deviance does not need to match what either the state or ordinary people *mean* by deviance, only what the sociologist considers relevant when looking at the various phenomena of interest. A sociological definition is neither a statement of "truth" nor an objective description; it is a tool with which to examine what we consider to be crucial features of the phenomena under investigation (Weber, 1949).

In our courses on deviance we make use of what we hope is a definition of deviance broad enough to cover many of the issues raised by all of the major perspectives. We define deviance as *behaviour which is interpreted as violating norms, rules or laws seen as significant enough to enforce*. Keep in mind that this definition is not intended to be either "right" or "wrong," but to serve as a starting point for thinking about and asking questions about deviance. Indeed, this definition raises many questions. What are "norms, rules or laws"? What constitutes "violations" of these and how are such violations recognized? Who decides whether these behaviours will be defined as violations and why? When are such violations seen as "significant" enough to enforce them and who gets to enforce them? How are they enforced? Since sociologists make use of different sociological perspectives to study and explore these questions, they get answered very differently. As we shall later see, different perspectives highlight some questions and underplay or even ignore others.

Despite all of these differences, we would argue that in sociology the areas of common agreement are more significant than those of disagreement. The essential notion underlying the sociology of deviance was set forth by Durkheim a century ago: society creates deviance. This same notion has been the starting point for all of the perspectives on deviance we will be covering in this book: differential association, functionalism, anomie, labelling, critical criminology and ethnomethodology. There may be enormous differences in describing *how* society creates deviance or in accounting for *why* society creates deviance. But despite these differences the sociologists of deviance all look to social processes to explain deviance.

The survey of the major perspectives on deviance presented in this book will illustrate this point. First, however, it is important to point out that this simple claim, that society creates deviance, is *not* the conventional understanding of deviance found in our society. Instead, the dominant explanation of deviance held both by ordinary persons and by those who claim to be experts in the "treatment" of deviance is the "constitutional approach."

THE CONSTITUTIONAL PERSPECTIVE

A "constitutional" approach refers to any explanation of deviance which looks for the causes of deviance *within* the person engaged in deviant behaviour (Rosenberg, Stebbins and Turowetz, 1982). Such a cause may be genetic, physio-chemical, or refer to the personality of the deviant, but in any case will see the cause of the deviance as inherent in the constitution of the deviant himself or herself. Such an approach is the most popular way to conceive of and explain deviance, both at the common-sense level of ordinary, everyday accounts of deviance and in some of the most sophisticated current scientific research on deviance.

As a common-sense explanation, most people will assert that deviance is the outcome of the "kind of person" who engages in the deviant act ("What kind of person would do something like that?"). Most people take for granted that what they consider deviant acts are naturally and intrinsically wrong, and that no normal person could commit such an act. Thus homosexuals are considered "naturally effeminate"; murderers are "animals" or "cold-blooded killers"; child molesters are "sick"; while alcoholics "have no self-control." Acts which, to the rest of us, seem senseless are accounted for by us in a relatively easy and comfortable way. What kind of person would do something like that? No one who is like *me*.

Such common-sense conceptions of deviance are based on impression, established opinion and bias. Nevertheless, they are so much a part of our generalized, cultural conceptions of deviance that they appear even in the work of many sociologists, such as the social pathologists discussed below, who prided themselves on taking what they thought was an objective, strictly sociological approach.

There have been many "scientific" theories of deviance which take a constitutional approach as well. From the claim of the Italian physician Lombroso in the nineteenth century that one can identify the "born criminal" by his physiognomy or features; the claim made in the 1960s that the presence of an extra Y chromosome turned a man into a "born killer"; to the contemporary claim that many forms of mental illness are the consequence of a "chemical imbalance"; the "scientific" versions of the constitutional approach have proceeded by reducing deviance to biology (Gould, 1981).

In Chapter Two we will examine the constitutional approach in some detail, looking in particular at some of the more popular of the scientific versions of this approach. Our goal will not be to deny the reality of biological processes nor to argue that biology has no bearing on behaviour. Rather, it will be to show that whatever the cause of any behaviour, the decision that such behaviour will be defined and treated as *deviant* and the resulting social processes put into play are sociological, not biological, phenomena.

SOCIAL PATHOLOGY

It took a long time for sociologists to free themselves from the common-sense assumptions inherent in the constitutional approach. This was made particularly difficult because many sociologists shared with constitutional theorists an unbridled admiration for the biological sciences. During the nineteenth century, Charles Darwin's theory of evolution not only revolutionized biology, it fundamentally altered how people understood themselves and the world around them. Sociologists, like many other social scientists, saw the new biology founded on Darwin's insights as a model of what a science ought to be. More to the point, almost all sociologists in the late nineteenth and early twentieth centuries made use of an "organic" comparison, describing society as "like" a body in which each part works in harmony with and contributes to the whole.

One early research tradition on deviance from a sociological point of view was undertaken by social analysts in the United States who have come to be called the *social pathologists*. For the most part, these sociologists shared with the constitutional theorists the notion that those who engage in deviant acts are constitutionally or individually abnormal. Yet they claimed that not all societies are subjected to the same sort or degree of deviance. In contrast to the constitutional theorists, the social pathologists asserted that if deviance varies by the type of society, then one should look to society as the primary cause of deviance. As their use of the term "social pathology" suggests, these social analysts emphasized that modern society was in some way "sick." They assumed that it was this "sickness," the "breakdown" of society and of its traditional social order, that made possible the increase in all sorts of social ills, including deviance. Their goal was to uncover the source of this sickness in order to reform society and thereby cure it.

Social pathology remained a significant influence on sociologists' views on deviance until well into the 1930s. As described by C. Wright Mills (1967), most of the social pathologists came from similar backgrounds, had similar conceptions of sociology and shared the same goals of social reform. Most were from middle-class families, and their work reflected the views of the middle-class, Protestant, small-town establishment that epitomized the conventional nineteenth-century morality of the United States. They themselves were educated in the small college towns that typically housed the elite American universities, and went on to teach students much like themselves in similar academic communities. A large proportion of the social pathologists were, as well, either the children of Protestant ministers or had themselves studied for the ministry. Coser (1978) suggests that much of their enthusiasm for social reform was displaced "moral fervor." Certainly their sociology is infused with a moralistic approach to social problems. For them, deviance was abhorrent and unfamiliar, a puzzle to be accounted for and a problem to be solved.

Mills (1967) points out further that most of the social pathologists equated deviance with the city. For them, deviance was typically an urban problem resulting from the breakdown of traditional rural values that develops in an urban setting. Sheltered within the protected environs of the academic world, they lived neither in the rural communities they idealized nor in the big industrial cities. Unhampered by either research or familiarity, they were free both to fantasize about the simple purity of America's rural past and to exaggerate the evils of its urban present.

Why were the social pathologists so convinced that American society was breaking down? The rapid industrialization of the United States which began after the Civil War, and the subsequent mass immigration which began in the 1880s initiated a whole series of dramatic changes in American society. Within a short period of twenty years the United States went from being a primarily rural society to a major industrial and imperial power. Hundreds of thousands of immigrants arrived every year; poor, with few educational skills, unable to speak English, and with diverse cultural and religious backgrounds which could not comfortably be fitted into nineteenth-century America. They remained in the big cities, living in tenements close to factories and industrial centres. In a remarkably short time they began to transform those cities to meet their needs, house their institutions, and reflect their values. For many of these immigrants, the rapidly expanding industrial economy of the United States provided extraordinary opportunities for educational or economic improvement; but many others found themselves locked into a life of poverty or inhuman working conditions from which crime, alcohol or madness were the only escapes.

Without the analytical skills to recognize the real political, economic and social changes happening to their society, "concerned citizens" such as sociologists, philosophers, clergymen and newspaper editors pointed to the "social ills" that the immigrants had supposedly brought to America with them. This moralistic concern with the social problems of deviance and poverty was really a sign of their dissatisfaction with the changes occurring in American society. To the social pathologists, society seemed to be breaking down into a mass of individuated persons free of all conventional decency and restraint. The cry for reform was really a desire to return to an imaginary, idyllic, preindustrial past.

This is best illustrated by the sorts of social ills that were of concern to the social pathologists. As Clinard and Meier (1979: 63) note, "Their reform efforts dealt principally with such issues as poverty, child labor, divorce, ordinary crime, and assorted 'vices' such as drinking alcoholic beverages and prostitution." This focus upon the problems of the immigrant, urban poor illustrates the ideological convictions upon which the social pathology perspective was founded. Nevertheless, despite the evident shortcomings of their approach, the social pathologists were among the first to begin the process of pointing to social process rather than individual biology as the explanation for deviance.

CANADIAN PERSPECTIVES ON DEVIANCE

None of the perspectives discussed in this book originated in Canada, and the sociology of deviance in Canada continues to make use of perspectives derived largely from the United States and Britain. To date, Canadian sociologists have not developed their own distinctive approach to studying deviance.

There are a number of possible reasons for this. The sociological study of deviance in Canada is still relatively new. Research on prostitution and other forms of deviance began at McGill University in the 1920s, largely at the initiative of Carl Dawson, who had been trained at the University of Chicago (Shore, 1987). E. C. Hughes, himself a major figure in the Chicago School and a key influence on several of the early labelling theorists, also spent some time at McGill, as did another Chicago-trained sociologist, William Westley, who did research on police violence (1953) and on homosexuality in Montréal (Leznoff and Westley, 1956). But deviance has not had the same fascination for Canadian sociologists that it has held for Americans, and it is only in very recent years that major research and writing on deviance has developed in Canada.[1]

This difference in attitude towards deviance may in part be a consequence of the fact that Canada's economic and social development has been quite different from that of the United States. Canada's more gradual, smaller-scale immigration, industrialization and urbanization was less disruptive then the rapid and massive social changes that transformed American society so profoundly. Social change in Canada did not lead to the sort of massive culture shock experienced by middle-class Americans and expressed in the moral activism of the social pathologists. Canada did have its share of moral activism and moral fervor, but, perhaps because it was a society composed of both British

Protestants and French Catholics, it was more accepting of difference.[2] Even the moral activism which swept through Western Canada in the 1930s led more to political movements than to social reformist activism. One could argue as well that Canadian society does not value individualism to the same degree as does American society (Friedenberg, 1983) and that consequently deviance does not raise the same issues concerning the reconciliation of individual liberty and social order that so perplex American social scientists.

While Canadian sociologists have not developed their own perspectives, they have made significant contributions to the study of deviance, whatever their research tradition. Many Canadian sociologists are acknowledged as major voices in the sociological literature on deviance. Erving Goffman stands out both for his international stature as a sociologist and for his major contribution to the labelling perspective (see Chapter Six). There is nothing particularly *Canadian* about Goffman's work, however, either in theory or data. The same can be said of R. D. McKenzie, who was a major participant in the Chicago School, especially in developing the ecological model (see Chapter Five).[3] On the other hand, American sociologists such as E. C. Hughes (1958) and British sociologists such as Ian Taylor (1983) have done some of their most significant work while in Canada, have made extensive use of Canadian data, and had a significant influence on Canadian sociologists.

Is a distinctively Canadian perspective on deviance likely to develop? Tepperman (1977), for one, argues that it is. Since deviance is intimately tied to the social setting in which it arises, he suggests that a Canadian sociology of deviance would be addressed to specifically Canadian concerns. One place to look for it might well be in the dynamic francophone sociological community, many of whose members are currently blending American and European sociology (Cusson, 1983).

In reviewing the Canadian literature on deviance while preparing this text, it became apparent that one feature of a distinctively Canadian approach to deviance may already be developing. This is a greater sensitivity to the crucial role played by the state in defining and managing deviance (Caputo et al., 1989; Fleming, 1985; West, 1984). The state has been more significant in controlling and determining the development of Canada's economy and society than is true in either Britain or the United States (Panitch, 1977). One consequence of this, argues Friedenberg (1983) is that Canadians tend to be submissive towards the state and political authority, not only accepting the state's social welfare programs, but also its paternalism, arrogance and elitism. Friedenberg gives as examples the invocation of the War Measures Act in 1970; the tendency to legislate strikers back to work; the expropriation of private corporations;

and the brutal suppression of prison "riots" as the "darker side" of paternalism. Canadians accept that the state has a right to interfere in their personal lives to a much greater degree than is true of Americans, Friedenberg argues. Lipset (1991: 93) quotes Guy Rocher as saying that whereas in the United States "the courts have been perceived and used as a check on the power of the state ... in Canada, the courts have been ... perceived as an arm of the state."

Friedenberg may well be exaggerating the passivity of Canadians vis-à-vis the state. After all, it is Canada, not the United States, which has a social democratic political party in both federal and provincial legislatures, and Canadians have frequently engaged in social and political protest. If the Canadian literature on deviance is any indication, then the role of the state is being subjected to very detailed examination, indeed, and it is in Canada that significant reforms—such as the introduction of new legislation on sexual assault—have been successful (Boyle, 1991). As well, Lipset (1991) argues that while individualism has been growing in Canada, the role of the state has become more central in the United States.

Still, let us reiterate, none of the perspectives we will be discussing in this book are Canadian in origin. Nor do the debates that rage among the supporters of the different perspectives often make reference to either Canadian society or Canadian data. In examining the various perspectives on deviance in the following chapters, however, we have tried to make use of Canadian data and research findings.

AN INTEGRATED APPROACH

In this text we will examine the major sociological perspectives which have been used by sociologists to understand the phenomenon of deviance. For the most part, basic texts in the sociology of deviance have followed a standard format in which they are divided into two distinct and largely unrelated sections. The first section usually consists of a discussion of the major theoretical perspectives that have been used by sociologists to account for social deviance. These perspectives are presented in rough chronological order, typically beginning with functionalism and anomie, and moving through labelling theory to finish off with conflict or control theories.

The second section is empirical. Here the texts deal with some of those behaviours that are generally considered significant forms of deviance in our society. Usually such a section will present research on, and a general discussion of, such issues as alcoholism, drug use, homosexuality, crime, rape, mental illness and suicide. Little effort is made to link these two sections together or show how the discussion of sociological theories found in the first section is relevant to the understanding of specific forms of deviant behavior discussed in the second.

How did such a disjointed form of textbook organization come to be characteristic of the sociology of deviance? Teachers rightly insist on the presentation of the theoretical material because they seek to provide students with a solid conceptual framework for understanding deviance. Additionally, it is the contemporary theoretical ferment, controversy and creativity surrounding the study of deviance that has made this area of study so fascinating to the sociologist. But students often find this theoretical diversity confusing and the sequence of different perspectives a sign that sociologists "can't get their act together." Students, however, often enjoy the presentation of empirical research on different forms of deviance that they may find exotic, bizzare, wicked or somehow appealing. The contemporary organization of textbooks reflects this divergence and perpetuates it.

Even if sociologists have not yet succeeded in generating an integrated sociological approach to understanding deviance, we nevertheless believe that texts could be better organized and pedagogically more integrated. Our goal in this book has been to produce a text in which both theoretical and empirical materials are presented in an integrated manner. Over the years in which we have taught courses on deviance, we have evolved a course design in which discussion of a specific form of deviance—such as homosexuality, mental illness or alcoholism—is used as a focus around which the discussion of a particular theoretical perspective is organized. We have found this design more theoretically and pedagogically sound than the standard text format, and we hope that by utilizing such a design this book meets a real need of both teachers and students for an integrated approach to the sociology of deviance.

Is it likely that sociologists will overcome the many theoretical differences we chronicle in this text and develop a *theoretically* integrated perspective on deviance? This is neither likely nor necessarily desirable. In our last chapter we examine some of the social, historical and political factors that lead to the continuing emergence of new and competing perspectives on deviance. We show that new perspectives do not appear only because there is a new way of thinking about something, but also because there is something new to think about.

We also have an axe to grind. It seems to us that we are in an era of rampant "medicalization" of deviance (Conrad and Schneider, 1980) and the re-emergence into respectability of biological determinism. We have no wish to deny the very real discoveries about the biochemical and genetic bases of behaviour that are being made, but we feel that biological determinism inevitably leads to the denial of individual and social responsibility for crime and deviance, and to a resurgence of racism. Recent arguments that Blacks are more prone to sexual promiscuity, lawlessness and rape than are whites are an example (Ellis, 1989; Rushton, 1989). That is why we are devoting the next chapter to a relatively lengthy look at the constitutional approach to deviance, a topic most texts cover very sketchily. Sociologists have much to say to counter the arguments for biological determinism—indeed, for any kind of determinism—and here, too, there is a hope for an integrated approach, if not of theory, then of purpose.

NOTES

1. Texts and readers on deviance or criminology by Canadians, for example, are a very recent phenomenon. Some examples are Buckner (1971), Fleming and Visano (1983), Haas and Shaffir (1974), Hagan ([1977] 1991), Tepperman (1977), Boyd (1986), Ellis (1987), Linden (1987), Sacco (1988), Stebbins (1988), Jackson and Griffiths (1991).

2. This acceptance of difference is relative, of course. In the past, Canada has had a long history of racist and discriminatory laws and policies directed at the Chinese, South Asians and Blacks, such as discriminatory immigration policies (Bolaria and Li, 1985).

3. Other examples of Canadians whose work is frequently cited in international literature on deviance would include Clark and Lewis (1977), Ericson (1981; 1982), Letkemann (1973), Prus ([Prus and Sharper, 1979]; [Prus and Irini, 1980]), Reasons (1983; [Reasons and Rich, 1978]), Stebbins (1971), West (1984).

CHAPTER

2 The Constitutional Approach

The impact of the computer on society, particularly the personal computer, has been dramatic. A machine most people considered unfamiliar and somehow threatening fifteen years ago is being routinely used today by millions. Children, some as young as four years of age, are learning to use computers, and in some cases even to program them, in daycare centres, nurseries and elementary schools. The computer is able to engross and challenge its users, to respond instantly without threat, and to obey orders without question. All of this gives users a sense of intimacy with the personal computer and makes it seem that the machine is somehow an extension of themselves. It is for this reason the computer has for many people become what Sherry Turkle (1984) calls a "second self." And if we interpret how the computer works and responds in terms of our "self," then this has obvious implications for how we, in turn, view ourselves. As Turkle (1984:7) puts it:

> People are thinking of themselves in computational terms. A computer scientist says, "my next lecture is hardwired," meaning that he can deliver it without thinking, and he refuses to be interrupted during an excited dinner conversation, insisting that he needs "to clear his buffer."

The computer's extraordinary ability to change how people view themselves and how they view their interactions with the rest of the world has been remarkable, but it is not unique. For it is not really the computer that has this ability; it is we ourselves. Human beings have always understood ourselves and our place in nature through metaphor, by looking around for something that can serve as a model, as a stand-in, for us. In pre-modern societies people turned to nature, seeing in the pattern of relationships among animals a key to understanding the pattern of relationships among people. For this reason the myths and legends of pre-modern societies frequently emphasized the similarities and the differences between human beings and animals in explaining the world. In medieval Europe the metaphor was one of harmony, of an integrated hierarchy in which each person had his or her place and society was in perfect balance (Zijderveld, 1974). After the Protestant Reformation it was *differences* among people that were seen to need explanation, rather than harmony. Many came to believe that social differences could be attributed to innate moral differences: good people were successful, chosen by God to achieve their goals. Beggars, criminals, the poor or the lame were morally inferior, their lives of misery on earth a deserved foretaste of what was to come in Hell. After the Industrial Revolution, more secular views of society began to develop. For example, some saw in the workings of industrial machinery an image of the working of society. As science and technology developed further, the metaphors used became scientific ones, and society was explained as comparable to natural processes such as the ones uncovered by physicists. By the beginning of this century, attention began to focus, not only on social group differences, but on differences in individual personality. Sigmund Freud, for example, saw in the tales of the ancient Greeks a clue to understanding the hidden, unconscious workings of the mind.

The "computer revolution," then, has produced only the latest in a series of conceptual revolutions which have regularly transformed our image of ourselves during the last one hundred and fifty years. Karl Marx, Friedrich Nietzsche, Sigmund Freud, and Albert Einstein, each in his own way, altered our understanding of ourselves, of our society, and of the world in which we live. But it may well be that the the the most fundamental of all these conceptual revolutions was initiated by Charles Darwin and his theory of biological evolution.

In brief, Darwin demonstrated that animal species have evolved through a process of natural selection. As individual animals compete for survival and reproductive success, those that are the "fittest" succeed and survive to pass on their genes to the next generation. In this way weak individuals and undesirable genetic attributes are weeded out, while desirable attributes are passed on. Over time, as circumstances change, changing patterns of desirable attributes will alter the animal species itself, leading to the evolutionary development of new species. As a scientific explanation, the theory of evolution was a conceptual breakthrough. But it was much more than that, for among the animals for whose evolutionary development he sought to account, Darwin included human beings. It was Darwin's theory more than anything else that eroded the traditional religious view of humans as the products of divine creation and made possible the modern development of sciences such as medicine, biology and the social sciences. The ready acceptance of Darwin's theory by so many people so quickly shows that there was a willing audience ready to hear what he had to say, but Darwin was the first to say it in a way that made sense to most people.

Until Darwin's theory of evolution was popularized, the majority of people had thought of themselves as the crowning glory of divine creation. Now, the human being was demoted to being just another animal in an evolutionary scheme. To many this new science demeaned "Man,"[1] transformed the human from potential angel to a somewhat more capable ape. To others it was profoundly liberating. Biology became the new science of unlimited promise; it offered new solutions to age-old questions: What is the real nature of man and woman? How do we differ from other creatures? How do individuals differ from one another? What is our place in the cosmos? The answers, secular, scientific answers, changed forever our ways of thinking about ourselves.

Although Darwin used his theory to account for human evolution,[2] he did not apply his notion of survival of the fittest to describe specific differences among human groups. There was no shortage of persons willing to undertake this task, however. Darwin's theory provided the possibility of an alternative, secular and scientific explanation of social differences: that people are constitutionally, that is, biologically or physiologically, different. Some are better adapted to their environment, emerging successfully from the struggle to dominate. Others are less fit or are members of groups that are less evolved. Such an approach, the use of evolution to justify social differences and social inequalities, is called *Social Darwinism*. During the late nineteenth century, there was a proliferation of attempts to generate Social Darwinist theories of human behaviour and group differences. Some of these theories claimed to explain why some individuals rather than others are successful, particularly in business. In other theories groups were evaluated as differing in degree of evolutionary development and moral or cognitive worth.

BIOLOGICAL RECAPITULATION

One of the most important concepts in the development of biological or Social Darwinist explanations of social differences was that of "recapitulation." Recapitulation refers to the idea that "the tree of life might be read directly from the embryological development of higher forms" (Gould, 1981: 114). The claim is that the fetus, during its embryological development, passes through all of the previous evolutionary stages of its ancestors. For example, the human fetus was believed to pass through a stage in which it has a tail as it repeats or recapitulates the "monkey" stage of human ancestry. As Stephen Jay Gould (1981: 114) puts it, "an individual, in short, climbs its own family tree."

This theory provided a means for ranking human groups and races. It was assumed, for example, that less developed, that is, less evolved, races are like the children of more evolved races. White Europeans, the generators of these theories, put themselves at the top in terms of intellectual, moral and biological development. They then ranked all of the other races below themselves, placing Orientals just below Europeans, followed by American Indians, the "brown" races, African Blacks, and at the very bottom, Australians, assumed by them to be the most "primitive" of races.

Clearly, such an approach was well designed to justify white military, economic, political and cultural domination of the "inferior" non-whites in an era of imperialism and colonialism. It also served to justify class and sexual differences in Europe and North America. It was assumed, for example, that social class differences were based on differences in biological endowments, that class inequality was "natural." Social Darwinists assumed that those who are "successful" in business are biologically superior, more "fit," than those who must labour. The lower classes were considered less evolved, more childlike. Like children, they needed the firm direction of adults; the foreman, manager or boss. Women, too, were seen as morally and cognitively inferior—more savage and less civilized, more emotional and less rational, than males. As for children, they *were* savages. Gould (1981: 114) gives an illustration of the impact of this type of thinking: "Several school boards [in the nineteenth century] prescribed the *Song of Hiawatha* in early grades, reasoning that children, passing through the savage stage of their ancestral past, would identify with it."

None of these theories questioned the received order of the world. Quite the contrary, they were widely accepted because they they fit in with and justified that received order. There were close ties between ideological explanations of social inequality such as Social Darwinism and the competitive, individualistic capitalism of the late nineteenth century (B. Turner, 1988).

One prominent advocate of recapitulation was Dr. John Langdon Haydon Down, after whom Down's Syndrome is named. Down himself described this form of mental retardation as "mongolism." He explained retardation as a form of evolutionary "degeneracy" in which a European child is born locked into an earlier evolutionary form. As Gould (1981: 134) notes:

> Down argued that many congenital "idiots" [a quasi-technical term in his day, not just an epithet] exhibited anatomical features absent in their parents but present as a defining feature of lower races. He found idiots of the "Ethiopian variety—white negroes, although of European descent" ... others of the Malay type, and

"analogues of the people who with shortened foreheads, prominent cheeks, deep-set eyes, and slightly apish nose, originally inhabited the American continent."

Down is best remembered for this identification of the "mongoloid" form of mental retardation (what we today call Down's Syndrome), an identification he based on the supposed similarity between the characteristic shape of the eyes of the person with Down's Syndrome and the "slanted" eyes of the Oriental. He claimed as well that both the Oriental and persons with Down's Syndrome "excel at imitation" (Gould, 1981: 135).

Social Darwinists such as Down regarded themselves as scientists. They believed that the racist, sexist and elitist views they held were scientific facts. Many tried to prove these "facts" using what they supposed were scientific methods. One of the most popular of these methods in the nineteenth century was craniometry: the comparison of brain size among different groups by measuring the cranial volume of the skull. Indeed, craniometry preceded Darwin's theory of evolution by several decades. The early craniometrists assumed that the different races were different species which had been separately created by God, and looked for differences in cranial capacity as indications that the races are fundamentally different. After Darwin's theory of evolution was popularized, craniometrists assumed that the more evolved a race, the larger its brain. It was the large brain of human beings, they reasoned, that gave humans their intelligence, their culture and their "self-control" over their animal-like tendencies. The larger the brain, the more civilized a race would be; the smaller the brain, the more savage they would be.

Craniometrists would collect skulls from around the world and use a variety of means to measure their capacity, such as filling them with sand or with small lead shot and then pouring the contents into containers. Based on this research, they claimed that the Social Darwinist theory of racial difference was proven "correct." The original ranking of races developed by Samuel George Morton (1849) was consistently supported by the findings of craniometrists over the next forty years.

Few scientists take craniometry seriously today. Despite its seeming scientific objectivity, craniometry fell into disrepute for a number of reasons. One was that once the craniometrists had proven to their satisfaction that White Europeans were at the evolutionary and cultural pinnacle, disagreements broke out over *which* Europeans were superior to the others. French and German craniometrists became engaged in a debate in which each successfully demonstrated that *their* nation was superior to the other. This dispute began to make clear to some the subjective and biased nature of craniometry. Another factor that posed severe problems for the craniometrists was that many famous men of genius turned out to have had quite small brains, whereas many criminals had large brains (Gould, 1981). The most significant reason that craniometry fell into disfavour, however, was that it used a very broad brush to paint different "races" as morally, intellectually and culturally inferior. This served as an excellent justification for colonialism (inferior races are incapable of ruling themselves) and imperialism (superior races both deserve and have an obligation to rule), but it did not provide a practical method for determining or explaining *individual* differences, such as moral differences among Europeans themselves; that is, why some obey the law while others do not. In effect, it failed to provide a constitutional explanation of crime and deviance which would allow for prediction and control.

A constitutional approach to deviance is one that assumes that the source of deviant behaviour can be found within the individual; that it is innate; in modern terminology, that people are programmed to commit deviant acts. The explanation may focus on innate drives and instincts, on "body type," on a genetic predisposition or on psychological or physiological disorders. There have been a great many different theories throughout history. What they have in common is reference to constitutional type as an explanation of deviance.

It was in the late nineteenth century that attempts to develop scientific or so-called "positivist" theories of crime began to be common. Most of these attempts were strongly influenced by Social Darwinism and attempted to apply Darwin's work on natural selection through "survival of the fittest" to deviance. These early attempts were not particularly successful. *The* problem of deviance to the positivist criminologist consists in determining who is engaged in deviant or criminal behaviour or is likely to engage in such behaviour in the future. If individuals can be identified as deviant or potentially deviant, then they can be locked up, monitored or given some form of treatment designed to keep them from becoming deviant. The real promise of the constitutional approach lies in the ability to predict, and therefore to control, deviant behaviour. Identifying differences in groups' potential for deviance does not do the job. The first important step in the application of the positivist constitutional approach to the "scientific" study of crime was the search for indicators of individual tendency to criminality. This step was taken by an Italian physician, Cesare Lombroso.

LOMBROSO'S RESEARCH ON THE "BORN CRIMINAL"

Lombroso holds an odd place in the history of science. On the one hand he popularized notions of crime and of the criminal that we today not only consider false but potentially malicious and possibly dangerous.

Yet many of his ideas led as well to significant reforms of the criminal justice system which most criminologists consider to have been valuable. In addition, whatever the serious flaws in his approach, Lombroso popularized the notion of a scientific criminology and provided much of the impetus for the development of modern criminology. Above all, both Lombroso's positive and negative influences persist to this day. Lombroso popularized and systematized the theory of recapitulation, insisting that it was possible to identify the "born criminal" on the basis of visible, external, physical characteristics (quoted in Taylor et al., 1973: 41):

> the criminal [is] an atavistic being who reproduces in his person the ferocious instincts of primitive humanity and the inferior animals. Thus [are] explained anatomically the enormous jaws, high cheek bones, prominent superciliary arches, solitary lines in the palms, extreme size of the orbits, handle-shaped ears found in criminals, savages, and apes, insensibility to pain, extremely acute sight, tattooing, excessive idleness, love of orgies, and the irresponsible craving of evil for its own sake, the desire not only to extinguish life in the victim, but to mutilate the corpse, tear its flesh and drink its blood.

Criminals have these physical "stigmata" and deficient moral characteristics because they are "atavistic," that is, they are evolutionary throwbacks to the apelike ancestors of human beings. They might have been born to human parents, but morally they are apes. Lombroso claimed that he had developed an objective, scientific basis for determining who is the "born criminal," and he often appeared in court to testify as an expert witness on the anatomical evidence of the defendant's "criminality." Lombroso made very far-ranging claims for the link between outward appearance and inner morality: he even claimed to be able to predict which girls would become prostitutes, based on the anatomical structure of their feet (Gould, 1981: 129).

Lombroso's theory today seems to us to be, as Taylor, Walton and Young (1973) put it, "laughable." We certainly do not take his claim to scientific objectivity very seriously. For example, Lombroso said he could identify born criminals in court by their "sinister look." The idea that a tattoo is a physical "stigmata" indicating born criminality seems ridiculous. Yet Lombroso was taken very seriously during his lifetime and was considered the world's foremost authority on crime and criminals.

A look at Lombroso's assumptions and method helps to illustrate the pseudoscientific status of the positivist criminologists. Lombroso consistently confused his opinion with objective fact. As an example, Lombroso was convinced that epilepsy was a sign of criminality and that epileptics are prone to violent crime. His discovery that one famous murderer was an epileptic was taken by Lombroso to be sufficient proof of his views. When other researchers pointed out that much fewer than half of those in prison have the visible stigmata that Lombroso described, he did not give up on his theory. Instead he claimed that most of these criminals were "criminaloid" rather than atavistic (Thomas and Hepburn, 1983). The "criminaloid" is only a partial throwback, not enough to exhibit his ape nature externally; but internally, in terms of personality, mental processes, even superstitions, the "criminaloid" is still a primitive, savage, born criminal.

Lombroso also rejected the idea that social circumstances can lead most people to commit crimes. People do not steal because they are poor, Lombroso argued, rather both their crimes and their poverty are a consequence of "their extreme idleness and astonishing extravagance, which makes them run through huge sums with the greatest ease" (quoted in Thomas and Hepburn, 1983: 152).

Our contemporary distaste for Lombroso's ideas should not make us underestimate his achievements. By directing attention away from the crime to the criminal, Lombroso sought to change the nature of sentencing. He believed that the punishment should fit the criminal rather than the crime. Despite his claim that most criminals are criminals by nature, he insisted that some are merely normal people who, through passion or misjudgement, have made a mistake they are unlikely to repeat. Such characteristics of the modern criminal justice system as indeterminate sentencing and parole are in large part a consequence of Lombroso's work (Caputo and Linden, 1987).

Compared to the craniometry that preceded it, Lombroso's account of the "born criminal" seemed to be a major "scientific" advance. But in reality it was a crude, biased and awkward way to go about determining who is or is not likely to become a criminal. There is an important lesson to be learned here, for Lombroso's theory did not disappear because it was shown to be wrong or people came to find it ridiculous. Its detractors remained a minority during most of Lombroso's lifetime. Lombroso's method of identifying the "born criminal" fell into disuse because it failed to specify what distinct constitutional features, other than being born animal-like, give rise to deviance. Most criminologists did not question Lombroso's assumptions. Indeed, there were numerous later attempts to identify the criminal by "body-type," the best known of which is William Sheldon's (1949) description of the "mesomorph," a heavily muscled "body-type" with a supposed propensity to crime. Nevertheless, many criminologists felt that what they needed was a more objective and measurable way of determining an individual's propensity to criminality than external physical appearance. There were just too many people committing crimes whose "body-type" did not match that of the model, and too many whose bodies did but who did not engage in crime. The search was therefore on for some more individual indicator of propensity to become a criminal. Many criminolgists and psychologists believed they had found just that with the development of the intelligence test.

INTELLIGENCE TESTING AND THE ATTRIBUTION OF DEVIANCE

The craniometrists had believed that inferior races had smaller brains and were thus less intelligent than the more evolved Europeans. It was also the smaller brain which was responsible for the lack of self-control and which permitted savage or criminal behaviour. Craniometry was unable to account for individual differences, however. But if one could measure intelligence directly, it was thought, one could have an objective indicator of genetic inferiority and thus of propensity to crime.

The intelligence test was first developed in France by Alfred Binet in 1905. The use of such tests appealed to American psychologists, and the IQ (for "intelligence quotient") test was developed at Stanford University as a modification of Binet's test.

The individual most responsible for popularizing the test in North America was H. H. Goddard. Goddard was the director of research at an institute for the "feeble-minded." He was convinced that American society was morally and culturally endangered by increasing numbers of mental defectives, people for whom he devised the term "moron" (Gould, 1981: 159). Goddard believed that such morons were increasing in numbers because their lack of self-control led to sexual promiscuity. This meant that they were breeding at a faster rate than the general population. Goddard was also convinced that a high proportion of new immigrants coming to America were feeble-minded. It was Goddard who popularized the notion that low intelligence was a sign of criminal tendencies. He tested prison inmates and found that 70 percent were "feeble-minded" (Caputo and Linden, 1987). This seemed to him to be clear proof of a direct link between low intelligence and criminal activity.

The big advantages this sort of individual testing seemed to have over Lombroso's cataloguing of anatomical indicators of criminality were that it seemed more "objective" and scientific, and that it allowed authorities to act to prevent deviance. Based on his research, Goddard and many others called for the sterilization of morons in order to insure they did not reproduce. In one famous case, the United States Supreme Court upheld the right of the state to sterilize the feeble-minded with the decree that "Three generations of imbeciles are enough" (quoted in

Gould, 1981: 335). In Canada too, the retarded have in the past been routinely sterilized for their own and society's "good" (Jackson, 1991).

Goddard also initiated testing of new immigrants to the United States. Again, his testing showed the vast majority to be mentally deficient. Goddard seemed unaware that the test he was using was culturally biased and not suited for evaluating the mental ability of immigrants fresh off the boats. These people were disoriented by leaving their families and familiar worlds behind, were often weakened by their voyages, and were still attempting to come to terms with arrival in a new and alien culture. Unable to speak the language of the officials around them, they neither understood why they were being given these tests nor had the familiarity with American society needed to do well on them. Nevertheless, the American government sharply limited immigration in the 1920s, in large part on the basis of this "scientific" evidence.

Goddard's views on the feeble-minded had their supporters in Canada, too. The Canadian National Committee for Mental Hygiene linked the high rate of mental deficiency among children in British Columbia's industrial schools to the high rate of juvenile delinquency among them (Jackson, 1991: 183).

Questions about the validity of Goddard's IQ tests arose in the 1920s when the data on IQ tests given to two million American soldiers in 1917 were examined. It was found that, if these tests were valid, then half of the American male population was "feeble-minded"! It soon became obvious that the tests were so seriously biased as to be essentially worthless. Psychologists set new criteria for ranking intelligence and designed new, less blatantly biased, tests. Today little difference is found in the level of intelligence of those in prison compared with the general public (Caputo and Linden, 1987).

MODERN CONSTITUTIONAL THEORIES OF DEVIANCE

Although constitutional theories of deviance have been discredited again and again, they also seem to re-emerge again and again. Even craniometry is not dead. Reference to skull and brain size continues to be used today to justify theories of racial difference. A good case in point is the work of psychologist J. Phillipe Rushton of the University of Western Ontario. In a recent article (1989), Rushton claims that "Orientals" are more intelligent and have larger brain sizes than do "Whites," who in turn are more intelligent and have larger brain sizes than "Blacks." Rushton explains these differences by arguing that data on DNA sequencing indicate that Whites "emerged" from the "ancestral hominid line" more recently than Blacks, and that Orientals have "emerged" more recently still (Rushton, 1989: 2). Rushton then claims that "the later the emergence of an animal group in earth history, the larger its brain size, and the greater its culture" (Rushton, 1989: 12). Rushton's work makes almost no mention of the extraordinary variety of group and individual differences *within* each "race" (this is left to the last page) nor does he make note of the serious scientific challenges to craniometry and intelligence testing as objective measures of intellectual ability. As to what could be meant by an animal species' "culture," your guess is as good as ours.

Rushton goes farther. He suggests that there are significant racial differences in sexuality and sexual restraint, speed of maturation, personality and temperament, including aggressiveness, and social organization, including "law abidingness" (Rushton, 1989). Notice that since laws are created by society and are not inherited, it is hard to imagine how a genetic basis for "law abidingness" could possibly arise. Or is simply following norms, rules or laws to be taken as a sign of innate intelligence?

It does not take much to refute either Rushton's data or his logic; a comparison of the murder rate in the Phillipines (an "Oriental" nation) with that in France (a "White" nation) will suffice. As for "law abidingness," is Black opposition to apartheid laws in South Africa a genetic deficit or a consequence of the fact that those laws are racist, oppressive and cruel? In any case, how can one describe Blacks as more prone to crime than Whites when we look at such historical atrocities as the systematic murder of millions of people by White Nazi Germans during the Second World War?

In addition to the regular rebirth of old constitutional theories, there are always new ones being developed, which seem to offer some instant key to recognizing the deviant, then slowly fade away into obscurity. The best example in recent years is the XYY chromosome explanation of violent and aggressive behaviour among men. This theory was based on the discovery of a genetic "abnormality." Normally, females have two X chromosomes and males have one X and one Y. Since both males and females have X chromosomes but only males have the Y, one can argue that biological sex is "determined" at the chromosomal level by the presence or absence of the Y chromosome. From a common-sense point of view this would suggest that male "qualities" such as aggressiveness are a consequence of having the Y chromosome. When it was discovered that some men have an extra Y chromosome, it seemed reasonable to suppose that such men would have masculine qualities in exaggerated form. If one Y chromosome makes a man aggressive, then two must make a man "super" aggressive. The media grabbed onto this notion, and the claim that an extra Y chromosome provides a propensity to violent crime was widely disseminated. However, recent research shows no relationship between an extra Y chromosome and criminal violence (Hodgins, 1987). More importantly, it is estimated that about 96 percent of XYY males do not have any history of criminal violence (Gould, 1981). In fact, there is no clear evidence that an extra Y chromosome has *any* effect on behaviour (Hodgins, 1987).

While constitutional explanations of deviance continue to be the most popular with the public, such explanations are rarely used to account for crime among professionals nowadays. Criminologists today largely agree that most crime is a form of social behaviour and one must look to social processes to account for crime and to control it. No consistent and clear constitutional differences have been found to differentiate the criminal from the law-abiding citizen.

But many other forms of deviance continue to be explained constitutionally: alcoholism, mental illness and hyperactive children are three recent examples. Both in common-sense thinking and in scientific research, the constitutional approach remains the dominant mode of accounting for deviance.

Why, then, do sociologists persist in rejecting constitutional explanations of deviance? There are two basic reasons. One is that a constitutional explanation of deviance, whatever its form, scientific or common sense, is a view that subscribes to the thesis of biological determinism. As Stephen Jay Gould (1981: 20) has noted, biological determinism "holds that shared behavioral norms, and the social and economic differences between human groups—primarily races, classes and sexes—arise from inherited, inborn distinctions and that society, in this sense, is an accurate reflection of biology." They treat obvious *social* differences among people as *biological* differences.

Second, regardless of whether there is or is not a biological component to behaviour that is defined as deviant, reference to that component does not provide answers to the most crucial questions that sociologists ask about deviance. Take alcoholism as an example. A constitutional approach does not explain why alcoholism is considered deviant, why some who drink heavily come to be labelled as alcoholic while others are not, or what happens to people who are treated as alcoholics. Constitutional theories may explain some forms of *behaviour*, but they do not explain *deviance*.

Biological Determinism

Biological determinism seems to provide a simplified account of human behaviour: we do what we do because we are programmed to do so. Actually, it leads us into an explanatory quagmire in which we have to account for the infinite variety of human behaviour by an infinite number of pre-programmed codes dealing with the most trivial, the most contingent, the most happenstance of incidents. Lewis Thomas (1979) provides a recent example of this sort of reductionist account. He describes an episode in which he stopped to watch some beavers and otters at play in their glass-enclosed pens at the Tucson Zoo. He describes himself as "transfixed" by the vitality and "perfection" of their behaviour. But he then accounts for this sense of wonder on his part as follows (Thomas, 1979: 9):

> I am coded, somehow, for otters and beavers. I exhibit instinctive behavior in their presence, when they are displayed close at hand behind glass, simultaneously below water and at the surface. I have receptors for this display. Beavers and otters possess a "releaser" for me, in the terminology of ethology, and the releasing was my experience. What was released? Behavior. What behavior? Standing, swiveling flabbergasted, feeling exultation and a rush of friendship. I could not, as a result of this transaction, tell you anything more about beavers and otters than you already know. I learned nothing new about them. Only about me, and I also suspect about you, maybe about human beings at large: we are endowed with genes which code out our reaction to beavers and otters, maybe our reaction to each other as well. We are stamped with stereotyped, unalterable patterns of response, ready to be released. ... It is compulsory behavior.

We have quoted Thomas, a physician, at such length because this passage exhibits the consequences of biological determinism in such an unselfconscious way. Think of what an extraordinary burden Thomas places on genes in this passage! What a detailed load of codes they must carry. To be coded specifically for otters and beavers (and, by implication, have specific codes for all other living things). To be coded for seeing them behind *glass* when glass is such a recent human creation and putting beavers and otters behind glass is an even more recent design developed by zoo planners. To be coded to swivel from otters to beavers and back again when placing otters near beavers is such a conditional, historically specific decision on the part of those who planned the Tucson Zoo. What an enormous set of specific, detailed, behavioural responses Thomas assumed us to be coded with. What an enormous load of receptors. Think of the genetic inefficiency of such an approach, in which we carry around receptors for a display that may never happen. What if Thomas had never entered this particular zoo or had somehow missed this particular exhibit or had gone past when the otters and beavers had been feeding or sleeping rather than swimming and playing? The behaviour of swiveling, flabbergasted, sitting pre-packaged in some gene, would never have been released. How many receptors must we assume if we take into account all of the multitudes of experiences we never have but could have had?

It should also be clear that biological determinism, if correct, would mean the end of sociology. For if social behaviour is pre-programmed by biology then social processes by themselves explain nothing. Society itself is simply reduced to biological processes. Whatever their differences among themselves, most sociologists firmly reject such a reduction, along with any theory of the constitutional determination of social behaviour.

The Sociological Critique of Biological Determinism

Biological determinism provides neither a lean nor a simplified account. It assumes too much and produces a ponderous, overly complex model of human behaviour. The human body is an awesome mystery. Despite enormous progress in medicine, physiology, genetics, biochemistry, neurology and psychiatry there remains much to be discovered—perhaps more than has so far been uncovered. Given that no other object of study is as intimately tied into our own fate, it is not surprising that so much of the hopes, dreams and expectations of humanity hinges upon learning to understand and control our bodies.

Nevertheless, human beings are not merely biological machines. We are, in addition, the products and producers of culture and symbols. We live in a humanly constructed environment, one of families and friends, schools and banks, magazines and television, courts and prisons. We do not interact with one another only as biological organisms but as participants in social relationships, as parents and children, students and teachers, doctors and patients, thieves and police officers. Our world is a cultural world and we understand this world by interpreting the meanings and symbols that surround us. As later chapters in this book will make clear, it is society, not biology, that creates deviance.

In arguing against using constitutional theories to explain deviance, our goal will not be to deny the reality of biological processes nor to argue that biology has no bearing on behaviour. Rather, it will be to show that whatever the cause of any behaviour, the *definition* of that behaviour as *deviant* and the resulting social processes put into play are sociological and cultural, not biological, phenomena. For example, evidence is piling up that biochemical factors are significant in various forms of mental illness. There seems to be strong evidence that persons we consider mentally ill may have what is referred to as a "biochemical imbalance" such as an excess of chemical neurotransmitters in the brain. This may well be true, but what must be emphasized here is that in everyday life neither we nor psychiatrists make use of biochemical data in defining some individuals as mentally ill. We base our opinions on behaviour—observable, external behaviour which we *define* as abnormal. Only after someone has been defined as mentally ill do they come to be tested for biochemical composition. In order for us to argue that biochemistry "caused" the deviance we should have to argue that mental illness is some absolute condition. That everyone, everywhere, having that same biochemical state will be considered mentally ill. That is not the case, however, because behaviour that is taken to be an indicator of mental illness or of some sort of mental disorder is relative to a particular society. Someone who insists that they can talk to spirits or can fly when the moon is full would certainly be considered mentally ill by most people in our society, but might have been respected and feared as a powerful "medicine man" or shaman in another society (Eliade, 1971: 19). The very same behaviour that would lead us to define a violent person as a "psychopath" might have led to their being considered a great warrior in another society. Whatever the biochemical bases of the behaviour, it is people in the society who define that behaviour as normal or abnormal, desirable or repugnant, evil and insane or wonderful.

This does *not* mean that no behaviour is "really" deviant. It means that it is our responsibility as members of a society to decide what we shall treat as deviant, to decide what kind of world is a decent world to live in and how to achieve such a world. It is not our bodies or our genes that can make these decisions for us.

To make the case for a distinct and definite constitutional cause for mental illness, we would also have to argue that biochemistry is unaffected by social circumstances or by the myriad social encounters which make up an individual's life. Yet it is very clear that human biochemistry responds to social and biological circumstances as well as causing them. Hormone levels will alter radically, based on expectations or social circumstances. To give a simple yet obvious example, women (and men) can alter hormone levels by taking pills, such as birth control pills. Biochemistry also reflects the effects of social interaction. To give another everyday example, a pregnant woman has a dramatic level of biochemical "imbalance" if we use biochemically "normal," non-pregnant women as our standard. In this case biochemistry reflects rather than causes a biological state; it was not the biochemistry that caused the pregnancy. But that biological state, pregnancy, is itself a consequence of social behaviour. The biochemical changes undergone by a pregnant woman are the same whether that woman is already a married mother of two or a single, teenage girl, but the social consequences, including whether that pregnancy comes to be defined by some as an instance of deviance, may be dramatically different.

Let us take a test case to illustrate the sociological critique of constitutional explanations of deviance. Suppose that the biochemical imbalance theory of mental disorder is right in seeing physiological brain disorder as *caused* by an imbalance of neurotransmitters. Even in this strongest case, however, it is a long step from identifying the cause of some *physiological* state to identifying *behaviour* as being directly caused by that state. And it is an even greater step to explaining how such behaviour comes to be seen and treated as *deviant*. We can illustrate these points by using the example of alcohol use. Alcohol is a psychoactive drug (Goode, 1984) which, among its other effects, alters the individual's mental functioning by inducing a temporary state of "mental disorder" we call drunkenness. Drunkenness and the mental and behavioural changes associated with it provide a strong case for a constitutional approach because we know that the presence of alcohol in the bloodstream both precedes the "disorder" and causes it. This provides us with the opportunity to examine the connection between some physiological state and behaviour. In addition, since many forms of behaviour exhibited while drunk are considered deviant, we can examine the connection between the context within which some behaviour occurs and how the behaviour is or is not defined as deviant. Alcohol and drunkenness provide us with the strongest test case of the strengths and limitations of a constitutional theory of deviance.

Alcohol provides us with a valuable test of the constitutional approach for another reason. Relatively few people engage in violent crimes or suffer from mental illness, and as we have suggested, the issue of a constitutional *cause* for these forms of deviance continues to be debated. But most people in our society drink some beer, wine or other alcoholic beverages on occasion and it is reasonable to expect that most will have had at least one experience with being drunk. And almost everyone agrees that alcohol *is* the cause of drunkenness and its attendant behaviours. Thus our examples and descriptions are ones most readers will find familiar. Most people are already familiar with what is meant by being drunk or intoxicated. They are familiar with the physiological effects such as slurred speech, staggering, impaired reflexes and the variety of inappropriate or peculiar behaviours many people exhibit when drunk. In addition, drunkenness is readily recognizable in others; it can be smelled on their breath, seen in their walk, recognized in the ways in which they act out of character when they have had "too much to drink."

Assumptions about Alcohol

Whatever their personal degree of familiarity with alcohol, almost everyone agrees that it has certain well-defined and recognizable effects upon people. We have a well-developed set of assumptions about alcohol: how it works and on whom, what it does and when. We can point to people who can "really hold their liquor," we can predict with a smile how awful the drinker will feel the next morning. Moreover, this set of common-sense assumptions has been incorporated into the medical and psychiatric theories of alcohol use and alcoholism. Finally, almost everyone assumes a close constitutional link between alcohol and behaviour. Alcohol does have certain basic effects upon sensorimotor and other physiological performance. Goode (1984: 126) summarizes some of these effects:

> Alcohol's strictly physiological effects include cellular dehydration, gastric irritation, vasodilation [increase of blood flow through the capillaries], a lowering of body temperature [though the surface of the skin does become flushed, creating an illusion of greater body warmth], a nearly total oxidation [only about 10 percent of the alcohol one consumes is excreted from the body unchanged], no storage or accumulation in the body, some anesthesia, and a depression of many functions and activities of the organs of the body, especially the central nervous system. Alcohol ingestion also has the effect of disorganizing and deteriorating the ability of the brain to process and utilize information.

The depression of the central nervous system causes the slurred speech, staggering gait and slowed reflexes associated with alcohol use. It is this that makes the drunk driver significantly less competent to drive and more prone to having a traffic accident. The most extreme effect on the individual's mental functioning, of course, occurs in the form of hallucinations, but few people experience this. There are effects as well on other organs of the body. For example, the rapid consumption of alcohol may cause the pyloric valve between the stomach and the small intestine to spasm, resulting in vomiting (Mendelson and Mello, 1985: 167), a common consequence of becoming very drunk.

In addition to these physiological effects, alcohol is often credited with altering personality or style of interaction with others. Alcohol seems to change a person's mood, altering or exaggerating their feelings about themselves, about others or about the world. Alcohol at low doses seems to have a tranquillizing effect which reduces anxiety, tension and guilt. It is also claimed that alcohol promotes friendliness and reduces inhibitions, especially sexual inhibitions. Paradoxically, alcohol is also presumed to increase aggression and hostility, which we would expect to reduce conviviality. Professionals also note that alcohol seems to release self-destructive urges, seems to increase one's willingness to take risks, and that many criminals commit their crimes while drunk (Mendelson and Mello, 1985).

Despite the public's general agreement that alcohol has a wide variety of specific effects, sociologists question these common assumptions on three grounds:

- It is unclear that all of the behaviours usually associated with alcohol use are really caused by the alcohol. Sociologists distinguish the universal effects of alcohol—which consist mainly of biochemical and sensorimotor effects—from those that differ from culture to culture. The latter consist of those behaviours that involve interaction with others and are therefore referred to as "drunken comportment" (MacAndrew and Edgerton, 1969).

- Common assumptions about alcohol and its effects ignore the complex sets of symbolic and cultural meanings attached to alcohol and alcohol use. These meanings indicate significant contradictions in social attitudes towards alcohol and towards those who drink. It is the contradictory sets of meanings associated with alcohol in our society that lead many of us to define drinking as an essential part of a good time but to nevertheless consider alcohol as a significant cause of much of the crime and other forms of deviance in society.

- Sociologists thus look at the social significance of drinking practices and the social relationships to which alcohol use gives rise. For example, sociologists have noted that we use alcohol or drunkenness variously to condemn or excuse behaviour, depending on the social context within which the behaviour occurs, its frequency, and who it is that is engaging in the behaviour. For example, drinking at a party or in a bar is acceptable but drinking at work is taken to be a sign of being an alcoholic.

Drunken Comportment

You may have noticed that effects of alcohol in the discussion above fall into two categories. There are the sensorimotor or other physiological effects which are manifest in behaviour such as slurred speech, staggering, slowed reflexes or vomiting. Then there are forms of observable social behaviours such as conviviality, aggression or reduced sexual inhibition. These latter are referred to as "drunken comportment" (MacAndrew and Edgerton, 1969) because they refer to one's behaviour directed towards other people. Slowed reflexes will characterize the solitary drinker as much as the social drinker, but aggression requires the presence of other people.

By examining data collected from many different societies and cultures around the world, MacAndrew and Edgerton make obvious the interconnection between socially learned expectations and the physiological effects of alcohol. They found that drunken comportment varies considerably from community to community. Aggressive behaviour when drunk, common in Canadian society, is absent from most traditional or tribal societies. Some people, such as the Mixtecs of Mexico, insist that drinking alcohol cannot lead them to become aggressive. Where aggression is found, it is often a consequence of Europeans introducing the drinking of alcoholic beverages for non-ceremonial purposes or the breakdown of traditional social structures. While some cultures insist that alcohol alters mood, making people convivial and festive, in other societies alcohol has no apparent effect at all, other than the obvious sensorimotor effects. Neither alterations of mood nor reduced inhibitions nor aggression are seen in these societies.

As for sexual arousal or the reduction of sexual inhibitions, MacAndrew and Edgerton found a wide variety of behaviours. In some societies alcohol may promote sexuality; in others it has no apparent effect. More importantly, however much people in a particular society respond sexually to alcohol, few people transgress the "socially sanctioned limits" which regulate sexual relations in that society (MacAndrew and Edgerton, 1969: 85). People's behaviour may become very different when they have been drinking, but most behave in an *appropriately* different way. The same, of course, is true in our society. Many people may find that alcohol makes them more amorous, but few men exhibit an urge to make love to their mothers because they have been drinking. As Goode (1984: 131) sums it up, MacAndrew and Edgerton's data indicate that "there is ... a time, place, and an object selectivity both for violence and for sex under the influence: disinhibition takes place within limits set by the community."

Particularly significant in this regard is the absence of wide variability of behaviour within a particular community, among people who are drinking alcoholic beverages. In most cultures people are influenced by alcohol in very much the same way. The Yuruna of South America become withdrawn, the Ifaluk, Pacific islanders, become festive; the Camba of Bolivia remain puritanical; the Tarahmura of Mexico engage in mate swapping (MacAndrew and Edgerton, 1969).

Why, then, is there such an extraordinary variety of ways in which people in our society are affected by alcohol? The answer is that with so many different cultural, ethnic, and religious backgrounds to be found in Canada, our society has neither a set cultural definition of drunken comportment, nor a standard way in which everyone behaves when they are drunk. There has been little research done on alcohol use among different groups, but there are some indicators which suggest that there are low rates of alcoholism among Italians, Chinese and Jews, although all three groups find alcohol use acceptable (Smart and Ogborne, 1986). In effect, these groups approve of drinking but not of drunkenness. Hindus and Moslems, who disapprove of alcohol use, also have low rates of alcoholism. Alcohol use and drunkenness are more frequent among the Irish, Eastern Europeans, Germans and French (Smart and Ogborne, 1986) who seem to see drunkeness as part of having a "good time." We do have general cultural expectations, but these expectations themselves include a wide variety of behaviours as possible ways of being drunk (Fingarette, 1989: 64).

The evidence that drunken comportment consists largely of cultural expectations, that it is a consequence of learning the community's definition of appropriate and inappropriate forms of drunken behaviour, is very strong (Heath, 1987: 19). The question then arises, how are these forms of behaviour linked to the presence or absence of alcohol in the bloodstream? There is compelling evidence that the link consists of two components: sets of social expectations and also a physiological "trigger"—the sensation of being "high" or drunk—which tells us when to put those expectations into play. Evidence is also strong that these expectations can lead to the "appropriate" response even when the physiological "trigger" is absent. Let us take two examples on which research has been done, sexual desire and aggression, to illustrate this link. Alcohol does have an impact on sexual desire. In men, alcohol reduces the level of testosterone, a male hormone essential to sexual performance. This results in the production of other hormones designed to increase testosterone levels, which are interpreted by the brain as increased sexual desire. This leads to the well-known phenomenon that whereas sexual desire is increased by the absence of testosterone, performance is diminished.

But there is no simple and direct relationship between sexual desire and alcohol intake. Mendelson and Mello (1985) report on several research studies which indicate a very complex relationship in which expectations play a large part. In one experiment, men were shown erotic films and measured for physiological indices of sexual arousal. Half the men were told they would be given alcohol, the other half a non-alcoholic beverage. In reality, half of *each* group was given alcohol and the other half a non-alcoholic tonic. That means that some of the men who thought they were drinking alcohol had really been drinking tonic, while some who thought they were drinking tonic were really drinking alcohol. The pattern of sexual arousal reflected what the men thought they were drinking, not what they had really been drinking. Those men who were drinking tonic and those who were drinking alcohol but thought they were drinking tonic showed a similar sexual response. Those men who thought they were drinking alcohol but were really drinking tonic showed a similar sexual response to those who knew they were drinking alcohol (Mendelson and Mello, 1985: 188). Research on women showed similar results.

As for aggression, physiologically one would expect alcohol to decrease rather than increase aggression. Decreased testosterone levels is equated with decreased aggression (Mendelson and Mello, 1985: 186). Yet most of us take for granted that alcohol promotes aggression. In an experiment similar to that on sexual arousal, expectations were again found to be basic to the display of aggression. Aggression was measured by the administration of electric shocks to another person as part of a "learning" experiment. Those who thought they were drinking alcohol, whether or not they were, exhibited more aggression than those who thought they were drinking tonic (Mendelson and Mello, 1985: 188).

The point being made here is not that alcohol has no physiological effects. No one can reasonably make such a claim. But human physiology is intimately tied into sociality. As these examples show, hormones such as testosterone and blood chemistry facilitate sexual and aggressive behaviour, they do not determine such behaviour. Our bodies respond to social stimuli as well as to biochemical and sensorimotor stimuli. Rather than see a physiological state based on relatively low blood alcohol level as a cause of behaviour, we can see physiology as a *trigger*, an indicator which puts into play a complex combination of other physiological and social behaviours. At higher blood alcohol levels biochemistry may take over completely, but by then the individual will likely pass out and be in no condition to engage in any social behaviour. As one last illustration of this point, students in class have often mentioned situations in which they and others were drunk but during which some event occurred which instantly "sobered everyone up."

All of this emphasizes the importance of expectations in understanding alcohol and its effects. This suggests that we should examine the cultural and symbolic significance assigned to alcohol in our society out of which we build up those expectations. As we shall see, the social significance of alcohol we uncover thereby is even more complex than is its biochemical functioning.

THE SOCIAL AND CULTURAL SIGNIFICANCE OF ALCOHOL

Despite what we described earlier as a general agreement on alcohol's effects, there are deep-seated moral and cultural uncertainies in our attitudes towards alcohol and alcohol use (Pittman, 1967). Some of this ambiguity can be accounted for on the basis of the ethnic and religious differences among Canadians. Protestant sects, with their ascetic roots, generally disapprove of alcohol, particularly drinking to "excess," although this moral disapproval is not as pronounced in Canada as it is in the United States (Gusfield, 1963; Smart and Ogborne, 1986). For Catholics, wine itself is a part of the Mass, the most sacred ceremony of religious services. One result is that "sober Protestants" in the past typically associated Catholic ethnic groups with alcohol consumption: the Irish with whisky, Poles with vodka, Italians with wine, Germans with beer, and the French (from France) with champagne. As another example, people who themselves enjoy drinking beer or spirits will point to native people and refer to them as "drunken Indians."

In order to make sense of these moral and cultural ambiguities and their relationship to social deviance, we must differentiate the symbolic and social significance of alcohol from the specific sets of drinking practices characteristic of our society. We must further differentiate each of these from drunkenness as a temporary state with its attendant physiological and cultural components. Our society has distinct and different sets of cultural attitudes towards alcohol and drunkenness and displays distinctive patterns of drinking practices.

Alcohol as a Cultural Object

Let us begin with alcohol itself as a cultural object. Alcohol has a complex set of symbolic significances for many Canadians, including ceremonial, moral, religious and commercial significance. For some people, drinking alcoholic beverages is considered essential to having a good time, to others it marks special occasions such as birthdays, graduations or New Year's Eve. Different forms of alcohol, too, will have a different significance. Beer for many is an everyday drink, while wine is for entertaining and champagne is for celebrations. Alcohol as a physical substance remains the same in all these cases, but as a cultural object alcohol means different things to different people at different times and in different places.

We have just noted alcohol's religious significance: the wine used at Catholic Mass or in Jewish religious observance contrasted with the strong religious injunctions against alcohol among Moslems and some Protestant groups. In the United States, the strong negative attitudes towards alcohol derived from the Puritan tradition within Protestantism. The Puritans who first settled America were a sober, hard-working group of believers who banded together to create "God's kingdom" on earth. Anything that detracted from God's work—alcohol, but also the theatre, dancing or other forms of frivolous entertainment or leisure—was considered sin. The equation of alcohol with immorality remained a significant feature of American society long after the Puritan tradition faded away. It was this extra moral dimension attached to alcohol use in the United States which, in combination with other factors such as ethnic, economic and political conflict, made possible Prohibition in the 1920s (Gusfield, 1963).

In Canada the Puritan tradition was never a significant factor, but alcohol began to be seen as a social problem as the demands of rational, industrial capitalism required a sober, disciplined, self-controlled worker. Workers, too, began to see alcohol as a social problem, but for different reasons than did their employers. They joined the campaign against the "demon rum" in order to maintain their autonomy as craft workers (Palmer, 1976). Canada never went so far as to prohibit the manufacture and sale of alcoholic beverages, as the United States did, but provincial governments took control of the sale of alcohol through government liquor outlets. In addition, drinking alcohol came to be seen as a leisure activity suitable for after work or on the weekends

(Gusfield, 1984). Drinking at work came to be taken as a sign that the drinker was an alcoholic, while drinking in public during the day became the sign of the "wino." While few people nowadays see alcohol as a tool used by the devil to seduce weak souls and extend his evil dominion, many people remain vaguely uncomfortable about alcohol if it leads to what they consider inappropriate behaviour. We may no longer see drinking as evil but many still see it as leading to crime, traffic fatalities and alcoholism. One result of this is that the effects of alcohol on us may in fact be exaggerated in our society. Gusfield (1984) has written a detailed and fascinating account of the problem of alcohol in American society in which he argues that scientists, journalists, policy makers and concerned citizens have dramatized the link between drinking and driving accidents in order to transform a complex issue into a clear-cut matter of law and public order. As this example shows, even if alcohol as a substance is no longer treated as inherently deviant, certain forms of drinking practices continue to be treated in this way.

Drinking Practices

The complex set of meanings assigned to alcohol carries over to the public's perception of drinking practices. Drinking *per se* is not considered by most Canadians to be a deviant act. Indeed, some have suggested that in our society it is considered deviant not to drink. Most adult Canadians drink alcoholic beverages occasionally (63 percent of adult Canadians drink at least once a month [McKie, 1990: 91]), and Canada has one of the highest per capita rates of alcohol consumption in the world, ranking ninth out of twenty-two countries in alcohol consumption (Stebbins, 1988: 105). Drinking is treated as a social lubricant: it is believed to promote sociability and to allow people to have a "good time." The media, particularly television, help to promote this positive view of drinking. In addition, alcohol is an important commodity in Canadian society. As a commercial product, there are powerful vested interests concerned to promote the consumption of alcohol and to equate drinking with pleasure. Beer advertising largely funds sports broadcasts on radio and television, and most sports events are punctuated by ads showing attractive, happy, sociable people obviously having fun while they are drinking beer. Similar advertising is also directed at young people, and anyone viewing the all-music cable television shows will notice that most of the advertisements are for beer. At other times, stark public service messages, becoming increasingly dramatic and emotionally powerful, are warning "If you drink, don't drive." Unfortunately, it is difficult to take such a message seriously after seeing repeated commercials extolling alcohol as an essential part of any "fun" times, or in a society as dependent upon the automobiles as ours.[3]

One of the first sociological accounts of the social significance of drinking practices was developed by Robert F. Bales. Bales (1962) provided a functionalist account which examined how culturally specific drinking practices integrate the individual into his cultural milieu. Bales claims that alcohol fulfils a number of significant functions which integrate individuals: these functions are religious, ceremonial, hedonistic and utilitarian. He then illustrates his thesis with a study of drinking practices among the Irish.

Alcohol has historically played a particularly significant role in Irish society. In a nation characterized by a chronic shortage of food, alcohol served as a replacement for food. It is not only that the Irish could not afford to buy food; since few subsistence farmers in any society anywhere in the world can buy food. Rather, there simply was no food because of the overdependence of the farmers on potatoes as a crop. When the potatoes were not yet ready or, even worse, if there was a disease that killed off the crop, the people starved. The people became accustomed to going long periods of time without food, drinking alcoholic beverages instead for nourishment. In addition, says Bales, the Irish of the nineteenth century would rarely eat in public and seemed to be ashamed even to be seen eating at home. Since they rarely had much food, they could not share food with others and so would prefer not to eat at all if a visitor was present. Instead, since most people made their own whisky from potatoes, there was usually alcohol available which could be shared with others. Indeed, standing drinks for all friends and relatives was a valued form of hospitality.

Bales claims that alcohol also served as a socially defined "alternative" to sexual relations. Among the Irish, no man could marry until he had inherited his father's farm. Thus most men waited until their father either retired or died before they married; it was common for men not to marry until their thirties or even forties. Because of Ireland's extremely rigid sexual taboos, unmarried men stayed in the company of other men. Men thus developed a lifelong habit of spending evenings out drinking with the "boys." As Bales notes, this was encouraged; a man who did not drink was suspected of being out looking for trouble.

Bales also links alcohol with nationalist opposition to the English. The Irish were in the habit of distilling their own alcoholic beverages. The English government, for economic reasons, attempted to control the manufacture and sale of alcoholic spirits. Drinking home-made whisky, then, became an act of resistance to British occupation. Despite the efforts of the British government, the Irish peasants maintained their home distilleries and were proud of their ability to outwit, bribe or, if necessary on occasion, to kill government agents.

Although Bales mentions many other functions of drinking practices, one last one will be mentioned here: the perceived relationship between alcohol and aggression. Festive occasions such as fairs, pilgrimages, weddings and wakes were occasions for drinking. They were also occasions for fights and brawls. Bales notes that the brawls were loudly encouraged by the onlookers and were considered a form of recreation. That does not mean they were not taken seriously, and such fights led to serious injuries and even deaths. They were nevertheless seen as an important opportunity to display courage and strength.

As for his four functions, Bales suggests that alcohol had little religious significance in Ireland despite the role of wine in the Catholic Mass. Only the priest partakes of the wine during Mass and neither the priest nor the laity equated everyday drinking with the religious use of wine. Alcohol does have great ceremonial significance, however, as an indicator of solidarity with friends and kinsmen. It also has utilitarian functions in preparing for the fighting during brawls, by increasing courage and in its supposed medicinal properties. Bales discusses a number of other functions, all of which contribute to a model of alcohol as an integrative feature of Irish life.

One last feature of Bales' analysis is worth noting. Bales suggests that intoxication, drunkenness, is itself a goal of drinking; that in Ireland people would drink in order to get drunk. Intoxication fulfilled personal and psychological needs quite apart from any interpersonal or ceremonial functions it might perform. Sociologists tend to underestimate the significance of such motivations as getting drunk "for the hell of it," because we look to social behaviours and social interactions as our subject matter. We therefore assume that drunkenness, being an "internal" experience, is an individualistic act. But drunkenness, too, as we shall see, can be a form of social behaviour.

Drunkenness

Why do people get drunk? Drinking need not lead to drunkenness, and on many occasions and for many people it does not. It is usually assumed that people get drunk for individual reasons. To "drown their sorrows," to get in touch with their creative "muse," to forget the past or to prepare for the future. Or just because they enjoy the sensation of being intoxicated. There are doubtless many reasons why people intentionally or unintentionally get drunk, but from a sociological point of view it is not *why* people get drunk but what happens when people get drunk that is the starting point for research. In this respect, MacAndrew and Edgerton (1969) argue that the common-sense meanings assigned to alcohol use allow it to serve as "time out" from everyday normative expectations.

By "time out," MacAndrew and Edgerton refer to a situation in which we tend to excuse people whose behaviour violates the norms of what we normally consider acceptable behaviour. In our society, and in many others, drunkenness provides such a "time out." Because we assume that people who are drunk are not in full control of themselves, we accept drunkenness as a legitimate excuse for minor norm violations. This means that individuals can get away with behaviour when drunk which might get them into serious trouble if they were sober. They can flirt, fight, say foolish things, sing off key, recite poems, insult their friends, all without fear of embarrassment or retribution. There are limits, however. The deviance allowed must remain within the limits of acceptable behaviour in the society. It is considered all right to flirt when drunk, not to rape.

This raises several further questions. Why would a community provide its members with occasions during which they can engage in minor deviance? Do people become drunk in order to engage in such socially approved deviance? Finally, why is it alcohol use that provides the occasion for a "time out" in so many societies?

MacAndrew and Edgerton provide answers to all three questions. They suggest that all communities require some flexibility in order to allow their members the opportunity to try out forbidden or disapproved behaviour. By making such violations part of ceremonial occasions, their incidence is kept under control; by blaming the transgressions on alcohol, the moral authority of the community remains unchallenged. However much the transgression may have been a secret longing of the heart, blaming it on the alcohol makes sure that the transgressor can return to normal life with a minimum of fuss. It also deflects criticism and resentment of the community for blocking or inhibiting such longings. As for whether people knowingly get drunk in order to transgress, MacAndrew and Edgerton seem to suggest that they usually do not. In most societies, people's behaviour when drunk does not depart significantly from accepted norms; where it does, it seems to work as a "learned" response to alcohol and drinking. Once learned it will be carried out without requiring conscious thought, just as riding a bicycle, once learned, does not require the rider to think about what he or she is doing. Still, some people may plan to get drunk in order to do something they would not be willing to do sober, whether that be to kiss their best friend's girl or to rob a bank—not only in order to work up courage but as a mitigating circumstance in their own defence.

Why do so many people in so many different societies use alcohol for these purposes? MacAndrew and Edgerton give several reasons. One is that alcohol's effects are easily apparent to the drinker who "can 'look within' and determine whether or not ... he is 'under the influence'" (MacAndrew and Edgerton, 1969: 170). Since alcohol is easily produced, it requires little skill or investment of time to manufacture. Also, the sensorimotor effects of alcohol are easily visible to others; if you are going to be excused because you are drunk, then others have to know that you have been drinking. In this respect the fact that alcohol can be smelled on the breath gives it an advantage over other drugs, because its effects are obvious even to those who may not have seen the drinking that led to the intoxication. Finally, because the sensorimotor effects are so dramatic, it seems logical to assume that the sensorimotor "incompetence" produced by alcohol is matched by a "moral incompetence" (MacAndrew and Edgerton, 1969: 171).

Forms of Determinism and Sociological Explanation

One criticism of the approach used by MacAndrew and Edgerton is that they replace biological determinism by a cultural determinism, what some sociologists call an "oversocialized" view of the individual (Wrong, 1961). MacAndrew and Edgerton assign very little significance to the biochemical properties of alcohol in explaining human behaviour when drunk. Although they present extensive data on the cultural conditioning of drunken comportment, it is possible that research on small-scale societies overemphasizes conformity. Observers, after all, are looking for recognizable patterns in order to make sense of the foreign customs and unfamiliar behaviours they witness. Informants, too, tend to generalize and simplify in order to explain their customs to a stranger. And everyone might be on their "best" behaviour (however they define "best") in the presence of a foreign anthropologist who may be seen as representing colonial or state authorities. Certainly the data on modern industrial societies indicate no high degree of conformity; people become drunk in a wide variety of ways.

A one-sided sociological or cultural determinism is no more useful as an explanation of human behaviour than is biological determinism. Alcohol is a psychoactive drug. It has real effects on the behaviour of individuals. It is only because alcohol does have real sensorimotor and biochemical effects that it can work as a trigger for socially learned forms of drunken comportment. We see here a combination of biological and sociological processes which work together to produce behaviour. But note that the meaning of the behaviour, its definition as "appropriate" or "inappropriate," and whether it is considered to be within or to exceed the bounds of acceptable behaviour, is social in origin.

Determinism of any sort, biological or sociological, represents a failure of nerve, an unwillingness to face up to the complexity of human behaviour and to understand what it means to take responsibility for our own actions. To repeat the point illustrated by our lengthy discussion of alcohol and drunkenness, behaviour is neither intrinsically deviant nor moral. Nor, for that matter, is the individual. It is we as a community who decide who and what shall be considered moral by us and who and what we shall condemn. Our modern world is one of nuclear weapons, mass famines and wholesale pollution and destruction of the environment. If either our biology or our culture determines our fate, then there is nothing we can do to change either society or ourselves. Most sociologists reject such determinism. They believe both that we can control our own destiny and that in order to do so we must look to social processes to understand the fundamental features of the social world in which we live.

NOTES

1. It is only in the last few years that significant attempts have been made to avoid gender bias in the social sciences. Before that it was quite common to use the term "man" when referring to people in general. The works of classical social theorists such as Durkheim (see Chapter Three) are replete with references to "man." Rather than cover up the gender bias found in these writings by inserting the terms "woman" or "people," we feel it is more appropriate to let an author's words speak for themselves.

2. Darwin believed that human evolution was more affected by what he called "sexual selection" than by natural selection. He presented his arguments on human evolution in his book *The Descent of Man* (1871).

3. Although there has been a decline in both the amount of alcohol being consumed by Canadians and the number of "heavy drinkers" (McKie, 1990: 89).

CHAPTER

3 Émile Durkheim on Crime and Suicide

Throughout the nineteenth and early twentieth centuries, the explanation of deviance was dominated by pseudoscientific constitutional theories or theories of social pathology. These theories of deviance were both moralistic and mechanistic. They were moralistic because they simply took for granted that deviant behaviour is "wrong," "immoral," "evil," "wicked" or "depraved." As such, the questions they sought to answer were, "How could people possibly engage in such deplorable behaviour?" and "How can such pathology be prevented?" They were mechanistic because they searched for simple causal explanations which would account for *this* particular form of behaviour by *these* particular people. Most often the explanations would focus on the characteristics of the person: these people do those things because they are "born criminals" or because they are of inferior intelligence or because they are "subhuman." More sociologically inclined commentators would point to the disintegration or disorganization of society or the collapse of traditional values. Yet even those who did accept such explanations, such as the social pathologists, were inextricably caught up in a moralistic perspective which prevented them from looking at deviance objectively. Inevitably, the discussion of deviance became a description of the degeneration of modern society and a call for reforms which would eliminate all social ills.

Like the United States, Europe, too, had its social pathologists. One topic of particular interest to these "moral statisticians," as they were known, was suicide. The approach of Thomas Masaryk was typical. In his book on suicide published in 1881, the Czechoslovakian social scientist claimed that suicide has its cause in "the decline of religious faith, which is the direct result of the overthrow of the traditional order" (Giddens, 1971: xxxvii). For analysts such as Masaryk, the occurrence and rate of suicide was taken as an indicator of the state of a society's moral "health."

The first significant break with this sort of moralistic critique of modern society came in the work of the French sociologist Émile Durkheim (1858-1917). Durkheim's account of the functions of deviance generated what we today consider the real beginnings of a sociological approach to deviance. By arguing that deviance was a normal, inevitable, even necessary aspect of society, Durkheim simultaneously began the process of "de-moralizing" the analysis of deviant phenomena, and developing an approach that sees deviance as integrally tied into the very nature of society, rather than marginal to society or a sign of social breakdown.

Throughout Durkheim's academic career he was engaged in a twofold task: to establish sociology as a distinctive science and academic specialty of its own, and to fashion that science into one that fit his own particular image. When Durkheim began his academic studies in university, there were neither departments nor professors of sociology. Durkheim, like other early sociologists, received his formal academic training in another discipline; in Durkheim's case, it was in philosophy. Since Durkheim sought to establish sociology as a legitimate scientific and academic discipline, his work repeatedly emphasized the ways in which sociology differs from philosophy and from psychology. Durkheim was particularly concerned to separate sociology from psychology, which was already an established academic discipline laying claim to being a complete explanation of human behaviour.

Like the functionalists who came after him (see Chapter Four), Durkheim was basically concerned with accounting for social order, although his conception of order was one of "moral order" rather than of an institutional order. And, like the functionalists, Durkheim saw his sociology as being the key to unlocking the mysteries of society. But Durkheim shared with the European sociologists of his time a conviction that society is in a state of crisis and transition which brings about a wide variety of "pathological" phenomena and other social ills. He sought to use his knowledge of society and of its workings to remedy these social ills. The later functionalists, for the most part, insist that society repairs itself, much as an injured organism does.

To Durkheim, society is a moral order, but one which is external to the individual. Society is characterized by *order* to the degree that it regulates the actions, desires and thoughts of individuals by providing socially approved goals, norms and motives. In describing society as a *moral* order, Durkheim meant that society is integrated to the degree that individuals internalize these goals and motives. In this way they come to share common sentiments and norms, ways of thinking and feeling that Durkheim referred to as a "collective consciousness." This collective consciousness is *external* to the individual in that all of us are born into a society in which these values, norms and sentiments already exist. Once we learn and internalize the moral order, most of us will simply accept it as the natural state of affairs and will think, feel and act as society has taught us to. But it is important to remember that Durkheim emphasizes that these ways of thinking and feeling are not natural to us. They do not arise within us but are imposed on us from the outside.

Durkheim's sociology, then, asserted a form of social determinism: the individual is a product of society, determined by that society. From the moment of birth the individual is under the compelling influence of other people and the social institutions they represent. Individuals are then moulded, shaped, into particular kinds of social objects as they adopt the values, norms and beliefs of others around them. These two processes, the *regulation* of individual wants and actions by external constraints and the *integration* of individuals through their internalization of the norms and values of the collective consciousness, were central to Durkheim's understanding of how society works, and as we shall later see, to his theory of suicide.

We will not discuss here all of the merits or weaknesses of Durkheim's approach. But one problem is immediately apparent. In everyday life the people we meet and with whom we interact do not strike us as "socially determined." None of us are what the ethnomethodologists (see Chapter Eight) call "cultural dopes," robots who simply act out all the demands and expectations of society. If society shapes and moulds us, how is it that we experience each other as so different from one another? How is it that we clearly differ in interests, desires, goals or lifestyles? More importantly, how is it that some rebel, successfully resisting society's influence to break the norms, rules and laws of their society? If our behaviour is determined by society, how can there be deviance?

Durkheim was quite aware that dealing with this issue was essential to the credibility of his entire sociology, and his ingenious solution was consistent with his fundamental assumptions. It is society itself that both creates and fosters deviance. If there is freedom, it is society that grants it to its members; if there is crime, it is society that calls it forth.

In asserting that society creates deviance, Durkheim was not arguing that society somehow corrupts the individual or that a breakdown of social order leads to personal or social disorganization. Durkheim rejects the notion that deviance can be understood by looking at individual, personality or constitutional differences. At best, such differences can tell us something about *this* individual and his or her specific behaviour. It does not explain the way this behaviour is viewed by the collective consciousness nor the social circumstances in which it arises. In any case, since society is much more powerful than the individual, society could clamp down on those exhibiting undesirable differences and thereby eliminate deviance. But it does not.

Instead Durkheim argued that deviance is itself the outcome of social processes, that deviance is as determined by these social processes as is conformity. Durkheim thus broke with the moralistic attitude towards deviance typical of the social pathologists. For Durkheim morality does not reside in acts but in society. The morality of behaviour is socially determined—determined by society as a moral order—rather than being universal.

Durkheim's break with prevailing moralistic attitudes was evident in his depiction of crime as "normal." Crime is neither a sign of social disorganization nor an aberrant form of behaviour which can be eliminated. Instead (Durkheim, 1982: 101):

> Since there cannot be a society in which individuals do not diverge to some extent from the collective type, it is also inevitable that among these deviations some assume a criminal character. What confers upon them this character is not the intrinsic importance of the acts but the importance which the common consciousness ascribes to them

Crime is "normal" because it is inevitable that some form of behaviour will be characterized as deviant in every society. Even if all individuals ceased to engage in deviance and began to follow faithfully all of the norms, rules and laws of the society, "crime would not thereby disappear; it would merely change in form, for the very cause which made the well-springs of criminality to dry up would immediately open up new ones" (Durkheim, 1982: 99). No matter how conformist the members of a society become, some will still be viewed by others as deviant (Durkheim, 1982: 100):

> Imagine a community of saints in an exemplary and perfect monastery. In it crime as such will be unknown, but faults that appear venial to the ordinary person will arouse the same scandal as does normal crime in ordinary consciousness. If therefore that community has the power to judge and punish, it will term such acts criminal and deal with them as such.

This is a sociological argument. Crime is not inevitable because some are attracted to it, but because society will inevitably confer criminal status upon some form of behaviour. This, says Durkheim, is not a fact of social life to be regretted. Crime is "an integrative element in any healthy society" (Durkheim, 1982: 98). It contributes to that health. In more modern terms, crime is functional for society.

In what ways can crime be functional for society? An example might help to illustrate the point. Suppose you are eating a hot dog at the counter of a hot dog stand with a set of strangers. Since none of you know each other, chances are you will not interact, but remain silent as separate individuals eating by yourselves. Now suppose a transvestite walks by. The appearance of the transvestite would completely alter the pattern of interaction among the customers. They would nudge each other, mutter, begin to talk, laugh and generally commence to interact *as a group*, with a common set of interests and attitudes. The presence of the deviant, then, creates a group which defines itself in terms of "us" versus "him," "we normals" versus "that freak." Moreover, by expressing prevailing negative attitudes towards the deviance, the group reasserts and reinforces the group norms that see transvestism as deviant. Additionally, if one of the customers has often fantasized going about in women's clothes, the clear indications of hostility and contempt on the part of other customers towards the transvestite would serve as indicators that such behaviour is beyond the boundaries of acceptable social behaviour.

As we see, the presence of the deviant does the following:

- creates a group
- articulates the boundaries of group membership
- reaffirms and reasserts shared norms.

To the degree that deviance fulfils these functions, it can be seen as essential to the normal functioning of society.

There are a number of other functions as well. Suppose someone in the group assaults or openly mocks the transvestite. The others are likely to find this amusing and enjoy the spectacle of the deviant being punished. We *like* to see others punished if they violate the norms of society, suggested Durkheim, and the deviant provides us with an opportunity to do so. Think of it this way: Suppose you were driving and could not find a legal parking place near your destination. You might be strongly tempted to park in a place designated as a no-parking zone. But you do not, parking instead some distance away. Then, walking back, you notice that someone else *has* parked in the no-parking zone, and now has a parking ticket on the windshield. Few of us could resist a sense of satisfaction that we had done "right."

Finally, if society were so rigid, so inflexible that it allowed no deviance, there would also be no possibility for social change, for adapting to new circumstances or discovering new and possibly superior ways of thinking or acting. Such an inflexible society would be at the mercy of any historical change and would disappear when its mode of functioning was no longer adapted to its circumstances. Some degree of flexibility, of freedom, is necessary to keep society itself flexible. Such flexibility fosters deviance as well as creativity, but you cannot have one without the other.

Thus Durkheim rejected the moralistic criticism directed at the various forms of social "pathology" identified in society. Such criticism is misguided by the failure to recognize either the real cause of the deviance or the real problem it may pose for society. The real problems of modern society are not crime or prostitution or suicide. They are only the evidence of more serious underlying problems. Only by examining objective social facts can one uncover those real problems facing modern society. In particular, Durkheim was convinced that the most serious problem facing modern society lies in the nature of the relationship between society and the individual. Modern society often fails to *integrate* individuals into a system of institutional supports which allow the individual to feel a part of society. It also often fails to *regulate* the aspirations of the individual, creating unrealistic expectations as a consequence of dramatic technological changes. The result is deviance, and a study of a particular form of such deviance would illustrate the deeper, underlying social forces plaguing modern society.

Durkheim chose as his example suicide. No one, including Durkheim, argues that suicide is functional, and Durkheim believed that in a "perfect" society there would be no suicide. Nevertheless, suicide is still the outcome of social forces, and by identifying these forces Durkheim hoped to identify—and find a cure for—the real problems of modern society.

DURKHEIM'S THEORY OF SUICIDE

Durkheim's book, *Le Suicide*, served as a milestone in the development of sociology and continues today to be regarded as a classic by most sociologists. In this ambitious work Durkheim attempted much more than a study of suicide—he sought both to show that sociology has a distinct and definite subject matter of its own and to illustrate the method appropriate to analyse that subject matter. Although few sociologists today would still accept his explanation of suicide, it is Durkheim's success at achieving his broader goals that keeps his book on the list of required readings for aspiring sociologists.

In order to present Durkheim's analysis of suicide, we must first deal with the broader issues mentioned above, since both Durkheim's choice of topic and the method he utilized were designed to meet his broader goals. Durkheim used his analysis of suicide to show how sociology can be set apart from both philosophy and psychology and has a clearly defined subject matter of its own.

To the philosopher, suicide is a moral issue. The philosopher's questions are absolute ones: "Is suicide moral or immoral? Does one have the right to commit suicide, and if so under what conditions?" The philosopher takes the concept of suicide and examines this concept in order to determine the morality of suicide.

In contrast, Durkheim saw the sociologist's question as scientific, and put aside the issue of "ideal" morality. In any case morality, as we noted above, was for Durkheim a matter of social determination. Whether or not suicide ought to occur, people do kill themselves, and the sociologist examines that fact and seeks to understand how suicide "works" in our society. How and under what conditions does suicide occur?

To the psychologist, too, suicide is a fact, but the psychologist sees suicide as the act of an individual who is undergoing some type of mental or psychological distress. The psychologist attempts to uncover the "state of mind" that leads some individuals to commit suicide and to develop, if possible, preventative measures.

In contrast, Durkheim asserted that any statements made concerning the state of mind of individuals which led them to commit suicide are mere guesses. Only suicide victims may know why they committed suicide and they are no longer in a position to tell us. Whereas the act of suicide is a scientific fact and thus can be used as data, the assumptions of the psychologist concerning the state of mind of the suicide victim are not facts, Durkheim held, but mere suppositions.

How, then, are we to make sense of suicide if we can make no assumptions about the individual acts of suicide? Durkheim believed he had solved this problem by shifting attention away from suicide as an individual act to *suicide rates* which, as collective phenomena, are the outcome of collective social processes. Although we can know little for certain about individual acts of suicide, suicide rates show remarkably consistent patterns, which can be linked statistically with many social factors. For example, Durkheim showed that, while suicide rates tend to be consistent from year to year within a nation, there are dramatic differences in suicide rates between nations. Between 1866 and 1870 the suicide rate in Belgium was 30 per million but was 135 per million in neighbouring France. Unless we assume that there is some physical or mental difference between the Belgians and the French which leads the one to commit suicide more often than the other, we must look to the social factors that differ from Belgium to France to explain the difference in suicide rates. Durkheim found, as well, that Protestants have a higher suicide rate than do Catholics; that men have a higher rate than do women; that unmarried men have a higher rate than do married men (with widowers falling in between); that city-dwellers have a higher rate than do those who live in rural areas. None of these are individual differences but are differences of social status and social circumstances, and the dramatic differences in suicide rates found relative to social differences implies that they are the outcome of social processes. By emphasizing the individual and the factors that drove him or her to suicide, the focus on individual acts of suicide obscures the patterns to be found in collective acts.

In his theory of suicide, Durkheim identified four different types of suicide: egoistic, altruistic, anomic and fatalistic, which differ either in terms of the individual's degree of institutional *integration* into society or in the degree of normative *regulation* over individuals. To Durkheim, an appropriate degree of integration into society or of regulation over oneself provides a defence against the "suicidogenic currents" to be found in every society. Figure 3.1 illustrates the relationship between Durkheim's four types of suicide and his concept of integration and regulation.

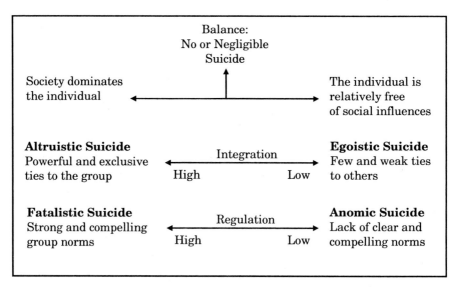

FIGURE 3.1   Durkheim's Theory of Suicide

Egoistic Suicide

In his simplest description, Durkheim defines egoism as "excessive individualism." This is a state in which the individual "depends only on himself and recognizes no other rules of conduct than what are founded on his private interests" (Durkheim, 1951: 209). In and of itself, egoism will not necessarily lead to suicide. Durkheim points out that both the child and the very old are egoistic, yet neither is likely to commit suicide. He also asserts that women, being "less social beings" than men, are more egoistic, yet are less likely to commit suicide. Egoism may weaken society's moral authority and thus free the individual to commit suicide, but what is it that drives the egoistic individual to desire death in the first place?

Durkheim points out that as a moral order, society imposes on individuals the desire to participate in it, to seek to achieve the goals it defines as worthy, and to effectively act out its expectations. "Social man," as Durkheim (Durkheim, 1951: 213) points out, "necessarily presupposes a society which he expresses and serves."[1] Properly socialized individuals do not identify with their own physical, selfish, individual goals, but have learned to yearn for those goals that meet society's needs.

Excessive individualism tears individuals away from the conditions that allow them to meet these needs (Durkheim, 1951: 213):

> If this dissolves, if we no longer feel it in existence and action ... whatever is social in us is deprived of all objective foundation. All that remains is ... a phantasmagoria vanishing at the least reflection; that is, nothing which can be a goal for our action.... Thus we are bereft of reasons for existence ... there is nothing more for our efforts to lay hold of, and we feel lost in emptiness. ...In such a state of confusion the least cause of discouragement may easily give birth to disparate resolutions. If life is not worth the trouble of being lived, everything becomes a pretext to rid ourselves of it.

It is the creation of a moral desire for social bonds coupled with the absence or shrinking of these bonds that is crucial.

Altruism

As Durkheim's discussion of crime illustrated, society is so much more powerful than the individual that society must limit its own power over the individual to prevent itself from becoming inflexible. Unless a society learns to moderate its control over its members, it runs the risk of doing harm to itself. So, too, for the individual. When social integration is too strong, Durkheim says, the result is a state that may result in altruistic suicide.

There have been societies in which suicide was considered a duty under certain circumstances. For example, the suicide of servants upon the death of a king or the suicide of a Hindu widow upon the death of her husband. Such forms of suicide are imposed upon the victims by the pressures of social expectations and the high regard with which such acts are viewed. In such societies (Durkheim, 1951: 221):

> Everyone leads the same life; everything is common to all, ideas, feelings, occupations. Also, because of the small size of the group it is close to everyone and loses no one from sight; consequently collective supervision is constant, extending to everything, and thus more readily

prevents divergences. The individual thus has no way to set up an environment of his own in the shelter of which he may develop his own nature and form a physiognomy that is his exclusively. To all intents and purposes indistinct from his companions, he is only an inseparable part of the whole without personal value.

In modern societies, Durkheim admits, such instances are comparatively rare, but Durkheim still points to what he claims are some instances of it. Durkheim asserts that the high suicide rate he found among soldiers can be considered a form of altruistic suicide. At first glance it seems that the military, with its strong traditions, extensive regulation of the soldiers' lives and high degree of integration should be free of suicidal tendencies. Durkheim suggests, however, that those very qualities, especially an excessive level of integration, make the individual soldier careless of his own life and likely to "throw it away" with only a little provocation.

A contemporary example which may also fit Durkheim's altruistic type of suicide would be the mass suicide of several followers of Rev. Jim Jones in Guyana in 1978. Here individuals were expected to subordinate themselves and their personalities to the leadership of Jones. Suicide was seen as the ultimate act of loyalty to Jones and to his "church."

Anomie

To Durkheim, the term *anomie* refers to a breakdown in the link between individuals and the moral order whereby those individuals are regulated by society. Durkheim, as noted above, argued that society constitutes a moral order which exerts a regulative force that "must play the same role for moral needs which the organism plays for physical needs" (Durkheim, 1951: 248). The complete absence of such a normative regulating force would mean the absence of moral order, and therefore the absence of society itself, which to Durkheim is impossible. However, there may be certain circumstances in which the individual is no longer being regulated by this force.

Like an organism, which has physical needs and desires, individuals have socially created needs and desires. From Durkheim's point of view the physical needs can never be satisfied. We can never attain what we want because our wants always outstrip our attainments (Durkheim, 1951: 247):

> Nothing appears in man's organic nor in his physiological constitution which sets a limit to such tendencies. ... Irrespective of any external regulatory force, our capacity for feeling is in itself an insatiable and bottomless abyss. But if nothing external can restrain this capacity ... [then] being unlimited, [desires] constantly and infinitely surpass the means at their command; they cannot be quenched. Inextinguishable thirst is constantly renewed torture.

Since society is an external regulatory force, it moderates those needs by replacing them with social needs. Since social needs are created by society, society can regulate and modify them.

This explains why poor people are more satisfied with their lot in life than are the wealthy. Poor people are placed in situations in which their social wants are sharply limited. The wealthy are in a position where more is possible; thus, they are more likely to be dissatisfied should they fail to attain their goals. It is the separation between the individual's wants and the socially available means of attaining those ends which creates anomie.

Anomie may occur because of a dramatic change in an individual's circumstances, changes with which the regulative force of society has not yet caught up, so to speak. Or it may reflect long-term change within the society itself, to which certain aspects of the moral order have not yet adjusted. Or it may reflect particular segments of society which are more at risk of social or moral dislocations, such as certain economic sectors. Durkheim suggested that the rapid pace of social change brought on by continuous industrial and technological change creates a state of "chronic" anomie in society. This constitutes a much more serious social problem than the social ills typically decried by social pathologists.

Fatalism

Durkheim's fourth and final type of suicide is mentioned only in a brief footnote. This form of suicide, the fatalistic, is the opposite of anomic suicide. As Durkheim puts it, fatalism is the consequence of excessive regulation, "of persons with futures pitilessly blocked and passions violently checked by oppressive discipline" (Durkheim, 1951: 276).

Durkheim refers to egoism, anomie and altruism as "suicidogenic currents," by which he means external social forces which put pressure on individuals and lead them to commit suicide. Ultimately, Durkheim still resorts to use of "psychopathic states" (Durkheim, 1951: 324) to explain why any given individual succumbs to the suicidogenic currents. Egoism leads to confusion and discouragement, altruism to a poorly developed sense of self, and anomie to depression and "mental torture." Although he rejected a psychological *explanation* of suicide, he insisted that there are psychological *consequences* to social processes.

Suicide Rates Today

Although Durkheim's theory is rarely used as an explanation of suicide today, his method and procedures are still used by many of those studying suicide. Both a recent comprehensive report of suicide in the province of Québec (Charron, 1981) and the report of the National Task Force on Suicide in Canada (1987) provide good examples. Charron's report defines suicide in almost the same terms as Durkheim did one hundred years ago, makes use of similar official suicide rates to examine suicide, and uses many of the same categories for comparison: gender, age, marital status, geographical region, income. Significantly, comparisons along linguistic lines replace the comparisons among religious groups considered relevant in Durkheim's time.

Charron's report provides a detailed portrait of suicide in Québec, compared to the rest of Canada. Comparing the suicide rates per 100 000 people for the years 1976-78, for example, we see that Western Canada has a higher suicide rate than does Eastern Canada. Saskatchewan had the highest rate at 17.50 per 100 000; followed by British Columbia (17.44) and Alberta (17.35).[2] Newfoundland had the lowest rate (2.97) with Ontario (14.15) and Québec (15.76) falling in between.

Men have a significantly higher suicide rate than do women; 20.68 for men, 7.28 for women. As for age, the highest suicide rate is between the ages of 50-54, a rate of 22.5. Here Québec is an exception. In Québec the group with the highest suicide rate is between the ages of 20-24 with a rate of 24.2.

Suicide among adolescents and young people is a significant problem in Québec. Fourteen percent of males dying between the ages of 15-19 die as a result of suicide; 26 percent of those between the ages of 20-29 die as a result of suicide. Overall, suicide is the eighth leading cause of death. For young people it is second only to accident as a cause of death. The problem is even more acute in the later data provided by the National Task Force on Suicide in Canada. In 1983, the suicide rate for males in Québec aged 15-19 reached 30 per 100 000. It declined to 21.7 in 1985.

It is clear that the pattern of suicide is very different from country to country. The point Durkheim made when looking at the same sort of data is that such profound statistical differences must reflect profound social differences in the causes of suicide.

But what kinds of differences?

Critiques of Durkheim and the Durkheimian Tradition

Suicide emerged as a problem for social scientists in the latter part of the nineteenth century because it was taken to be an index of the disintegration or disorganization of society. Durkheim reformulated this problem by looking for the connections between suicide and broad social processes. He also provided a method, the examination of official statistics in the form of suicide rates, to illustrate those connections. In examining Durkheim's work on suicide and its later reformulations by other sociologists, we must keep these two issues, Durkheim's theory and his method, separate.

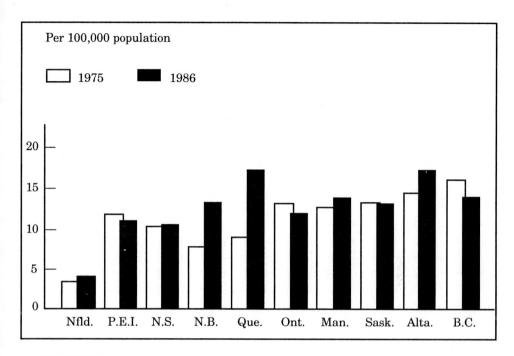

FIGURE 3.2   Suicide rate, by province, 1975 and 1986

SOURCE: R. Beneteau, 'Trends in Suicide.' *Canadian Social Trends*, ll, 1988, p. 24.

Although Durkheim claimed that his theory was derived from the study of suicide rates, it is generally accepted nowadays that Durkheim's theory, like his concept of anomie, came first and that suicide rates were used by Durkheim to illustrate his theory rather than serving as its source. In any case, suicide rates by themselves do not provide an explanation of suicide, nor do they validate any particular theory of suicide. The same rates could as well be explained as a consequence of anomie, or of frustration, of self-directed aggression, of status conflict or of any number of other theories that have been used to explain suicide.

For example, we could argue that the higher suicide rate in Western Canada is the consequence of "Western alienation," or of the dislocations caused first by the rapid economic growth of the 1970s and then by the economic slowdown of the 1980s. We could suggest that it is the outcome of a harsh, over-regulated life on the farms, or a consequence of the free-wheeling individualism of the Western lifestyle. We could argue that the suicide rate in Western Canada is higher because many have high expectations of "getting rich quick" which are rarely met, or that it reflects the poverty and hopelessness of the native people. The point is that in and of themselves the suicide rates neither prove nor disprove any of these explanations.

In general, we can say that Durkheim's theory has been rejected as an adequate account of suicide. Since Durkheim's study of suicide played such a seminal role in the development of sociology, it continues to be regarded as a classic work of sociological reasoning and explanation. Nevertheless, most sociologists realize that it is seriously flawed. A common criticism is that Durkheim fails to clearly differentiate integration from regulation and fails as well to make a convincing case that either integration or regulation is clearly linked to suicide (Pope, 1976). Because Durkheim's theoretical concepts, such as the "collective consciousness," "anomie," "suicidogenic currents," etc., are highly abstract, many complain that they are not really amenable to empirical research. In effect, they argue, because Durkheim does not provide a clear operational definition of these terms, he is free to fudge both his theory and his data to make sure that they fit one another. Many sociological critics of Durkheim's work, then, have attempted to operationalize his concepts and relate them to measurable features of everyday life.

One significant attempt to reformulate Durkheim's theory of suicide was undertaken by Henry and Short (1954). Combining Durkheim's theory with psychoanalytic theories of suicide and aggression, they begin by noting (Henry and Short, 1954: 15) that, "while suicide rises in depression and falls in prosperity, crimes of violence against persons rise in prosperity and fall during depression." This link between suicide and violence is explained by viewing both as consequences of frustration which lead to aggression. In the absence of "external restraint" this aggression may become self-oriented among high-status individuals (Henry and Short, 1954: 103): "When behavior is freed from external restraint, the self must bear the responsibility for frustration. Others cannot be blamed since others were not involved in the determination of behavior."

By *external restraint*, Henry and Short refer to the degree to which individuals are subjected to the demands and expectations of others. Since they consider low-status individuals to be more subjected to external restraint, they are seen as more likely to direct their aggression towards others in the form of homicide.

Taylor (1982: 29) notes that Henry and Short fail to provide data to demonstrate that homicide rates are higher than suicide rates among low-status persons. Certainly, the Canadian case does not fit Henry and Short's arguments. The group with the highest suicide rate in Canada is the Native people, a group that clearly fits into the "low-status" category as defined by Henry and Short. Suicide rates are also high among persons in custody, another low-status group (National Task Force on Suicide in Canada, 1987). All in all, a careful reading of Henry and Short's work indicates that they make an excessive number of assumptions and generate very questionable results.

Another well-known example of the attempt to operationalize Durkheim's work is provided by Gibbs and Martin (1964). They replace Durkheim's theoretical concept of social integration with what they claim is a more empirical concept, "status integration." When the various "statuses" occupied by individuals, such as the various roles they act out, become incompatible, the resulting role conflict generates "strain." If that strain becomes severe enough, suicide is the result. It is difficult, however, to see in what way this theory is more empirical than is Durkheim's own. How do we determine what degree of incompatibility is required to produce strain? Do not different people respond to role conflict or stress or strain in different ways? In any case, how do we know that the suicide victim was in fact subjected to status incompatibility, or if so, that this incompatibility led to strain which in turn led to suicide? Gibbs and Martin, like Henry and Short, begin by making a whole series of assumptions and then, *on the basis of these assumptions*, claim that the data support their interpretations.

It is questionable, however, how significant the social processes supposedly linked to suicide really are. Baechler (1979: 8) makes the point that suicide is an unusual event. By focusing on differences in suicide rate, we obscure the fact that very few people commit suicide. The suicide rate in Hungary is 44.9 per 100 000 while that in Greece is 2.9. This difference sounds impressive, and one could well insist that it must reflect profound differences between society in Hungary and in Greece. But if one looks instead at what Taylor calls the "non-suicide rate," one realizes that 99 955.1 per hundred thousand are *not* killing themselves in Hungary, versus 99 997.1 in Greece. A social force, "suicidogenic current" or social process which leaves so many people unaffected cannot be much of a force. As long as sociologists assume profound social differences to account for small statistical differences, sociological theories of suicide will fail to provide an adequate account of suicidal behaviour.

The Critique of Official Statistics

In *Suicide*, Durkheim makes the assumption that suicide rates have the advantage of being:
- objective facts about which there can be no doubt and which have been collected by officials according to scrupulous criteria;
- objective facts which require no recourse to assumptions or interpretations concerning the subjective "state of mind" of the victim.

In fact, Durkheim accepted or rejected the statistical data at will, depending on whether or not it supported his views and assumptions. While he placed great reliance on the suicide rate as a measure, he rejected statistical figures on "causes" of suicide because the figures were nothing more than "statistics of the opinions concerning such motives of officials, often of lower officials, in charge of this information service" (Durkheim, 1951:148). It was these very same officials, however, who made the determination that the death be classified as suicide and who generated the suicide rate in which Durkheim put such trust. Pope (1976) has argued that careful examination indicates that the data often do not support Durkheim's analysis and may sometimes directly contradict his assertions.

In his critique of Durkheim's methodological assumptions, Taylor (1982: 44) suggests that Durkheim's insistence upon the objectivity of suicide rates is justified only if one can correctly assume:

> (1) that the researcher's definition of suicide corresponds to that employed by the officials who compile the data (assumption of *validity*); (2) that this definition is applied efficiently and consistently (assumption of *reliability*); and (3) that the definition employed and the search procedures used are all the same in all the populations under consideration (assumption of *comparability*).

Most of the criticisms of reliance upon official statistics question the *reliability* of the data. Thus it is argued that official statistics are subject to many possibilities of tampering by friends, relatives or passersby prior to cases being reported to authorities; and to tampering by police, physicians, coroners or others in the course of investigation. Douglas (1967), for example, has argued that family members of a suicide victim may conceal information or otherwise attempt to avoid having a death categorized as suicide. The result would be, for example, that married men appear to be less likely to commit suicide, whereas it may simply be the case that many wives attempt to cover up their husbands' deaths as suicide. The wives' sense of guilt and helplessness, their embarrassment or their concerns about life insurance, etc., may lead them to tamper with the evidence.

Similarly, suicide rates would be higher in cities, where more individuals are likely to live alone or where their bodies are more likely to be found by strangers. In rural areas, it is family members who are most likely to find the victim and are therefore in a better position to conceal the true cause of death.

Unfortunately, while it has often been asserted that relatives will destroy evidence such as suicide notes, little empirical research has been done to verify this assertion. There is evidence, however, that coroners themselves avoid certifying a death as suicide.

> In a study of 350 Ontario coroners, the National Task Force on Suicide in Canada (1987) found that 33 percent were "reluctant" to certify a death as suicide. These coroners cited a number of reasons for their reluctance, such as the emotional effect on the family, problems that

could arise with life insurance claims, and the "stigmatization" of the victim. In addition, another 38 percent of the coroners stated that, "even in cases where suicide was probable, they would either certify the death as undetermined or would simply fail to denote the manner of death" (National Task Force on Suicide in Canada, 1987: 39).

Coroners also admitted that they were put under intense pressure by relatives of the deceased not to certify a death as suicide, and that they often went along in the face of such pressure (National Task Force on Suicide in Canada, 1987: 50). Ignoring for a moment all the other implications of this finding, one obvious consequence is that the suicide rate for single people—in whose case these considerations and qualms on the part of coroners are much less significant—will be higher than that for persons married with a family.

One can also argue, however, as to the *validity* of the data. Instances of death must be *interpreted* as suicides before they are recorded as suicides and then become part of the official statistics. Such interpretations may be the result of certain taken-for-granted assumptions about the connection between certain modes of death and suicide. For example, a death by hanging will almost always lead to an investigation of the possibility of suicide, whereas traffic fatalities are almost always considered accidents. Yet in and of itself, the mode of death is not considered sufficient for coroners to categorize some deaths as suicide. Taylor (1982: 84) suggests that British coroners look to:

• the state of mind prior to death

• the psychological and medical history

• evidence of recent problems

• the general life history

Canadian coroners and medical examiners, too, examine the medical and psychiatric records of the deceased, question relatives or friends, and in other ways attempt to determine the state of mind of the deceased. Only on the basis of such investigations do coroners feel comfortable about certifying a death as suicide. In his study of British coroners, Taylor found that relatives of the deceased giving evidence before coroners on the state of mind of the deceased typically "resisted" the possibility of suicide, and, in the absence of other evidence such as a suicide note or a history of mental disturbance, coroners will take their testimony very seriously.

Similarly one can question the *comparability* of the data, since differences in the procedures used by police, physicians or coroners in determining to their satisfaction whether or not some deaths can be considered suicide will generate differences in suicide rates. In Canada, two provinces, Alberta and Nova Scotia, make use of Medical Examiners, who are licensed physicians, to certify deaths as suicide; the other eight provinces make use of coroners. The designation of coroners, their qualifications, their jurisdiction, and their procedures vary from province to province, and sometimes from region to region within a province. Many coroners are themselves disturbed by this lack of standardization and point to this as a basis for avoiding the certification of a death as suicide (National Task Force on Suicide in Canada, 1987: 39).

Under the circumstances, it is difficult to compare suicide rates for one province with another. It is even more difficult to undertake cross-national comparisons. Taylor (1982: 91) gives the example of a 14-year-old British girl who had a relationship with a 30-year-old man. After being questioned by police and feeling herself harassed by her parents, she wrote a note to her parents, saying "I cannot go through with any more questions." She took an overdose of antidepressant tablets and died. The coroner refused to record the death as suicide, calling her note a "cry for help." The dramatically different adolescent suicide rates in Great Britain and Québec may simply reflect the unwillingness of British coroners to consider the death of an adolescent as suicide, something Québec coroners would seem more willing to do.

Some sociologists, such as Baechler and Taylor, take seriously the social psychologists' claim that suicidal behaviour is often a "call for help." They argue that only by going beyond suicide rates and taking into account all suicidal behaviours, including attempted suicide, can one adequately develop an understanding of the role suicide plays in society. Still, the sociological study of suicide today is locked into a causal approach. The question still being asked most often is, "Why do people commit suicide?" Durkheim went beyond the simplistic answers of his time to insist on a more complex, socially located causality. Yet his four types of suicide make use of psychological state as the immediate cause of suicide. The same is true for others such as Henry and Short, who look to frustration, or Gibbs and Martin, who look to strain. Even Baechler and Taylor, who reject the social factor approach, end up with typologies that set up categories of suicide grounded in different causes of suicide. Without going into details, it is obvious when reading the terms Baechler (1979: 444) uses to differentiate his eleven different types of suicide that these are causally differentiated: flight, grief, punishment, crime, revenge, blackmail, appeal, sacrifice, transfiguration, ordeal and game.

This raises a serious question. Are sociologists competent to explain why people engage in any particular form of behaviour? Is this really the task of sociology? In their recent report, the National Task Force on Suicide (1987: 58) concluded:

Suicide is an over-determined, multi-dimensional behaviour, the essence of which is still undefined. The more one learns, the more acute is the awareness of ignorance. Thus, although our probability statements become increasingly complex and sophisticated, we still cannot predict with certainty in any given situation which person will choose to end his life and which will choose to live.

Many sociologists, particularly labelling theorists, have argued that it is in answering questions of "how," not "why," that sociology can make a contribution. Sociologists would then leave the question of why people commit suicide to psychiatrists, social workers and others. Instead sociologists would focus on the following: How is suicide understood in our society? How do persons go about attempting suicide? How do their deaths come to be defined as suicide? How are treatment programs, remedial programs and certification procedures socially organized?

Suicide may have been the first area of deviance subjected to detailed analysis by sociologists, but its study remains locked into the terminology, style of approach and occupational motivations provided by Durkheim in the 1890s. It is time to show how very differently sociology deals with other forms of deviance in the 1990s.

NOTES

1. The works of classical social theorists such as Durkheim are replete with references to "man." Rather than cover up the gender bias found in these writings by inserting the terms "woman" or "people," we feel it more appropriate to let an author's words speak for themselves.
2. The suicide rate was highest of all in the Yukon and Northwest Territories at 40.45, but the actual number of cases was very low.

CHAPTER

4 Functionalism and Anomie

It took almost forty years before the influence of Émile Durkheim's work began to have a significant impact on the sociology of deviance in North America. Durkheim's work had an earlier influence on British anthropology, and anthropologists such as Radcliffe-Brown (1935) made use of Durkheim's sociology to fashion a new perspective, functionalism. By the time Durkheim's work was being introduced to North American scholars, in the 1930s, it was Durkheim's "functionalism" that was being emphasized by commentators and interpreters such as Talcott Parsons (1937) and Robert Merton (1968).

The chief distinguishing characteristic of functionalism is its adoption of a view of society as a homeostatic, self-regulating social system, essentially equivalent to a biological organism. The homeostatic model assumes that society takes the form of a rationally organized, hierarchically structured, and institutionally differentiated social system. The various components of this system are interdependent and functionally integrated in order to achieve systemic "needs."

When it came to deviance, the functionalists differed sharply among themselves in their approach. Many functionalists saw deviance as a sign of social instability or of the breakdown of social order. They tended to avoid both serious discussion of deviance and research on specific forms of deviant behaviour; they preferred instead to make general remarks on the dysfunctions of deviance for society as a whole. Yet for the true functionalist virtuosi, such as Kingsley Davis or Robert Merton, deviance served as an ironic example of how social order underlies and is supported by even the most seemingly bizarre, senseless or irrational of social phenomena. Davis's work on the functions of prostitution or Merton's on the latent functions of corrupt political "bosses" were no longer moralistic tracts seeking simple explanations and offering naive "solutions," but attempts to argue that, despite all public claims to the contrary, enough people benefited from these institutions to ensure their perpetuation. By examining how some forms of deviance benefit some people they, like Durkheim, believed they could show how society as a whole benefits from the persistence of deviance. The first of these virtuoso performances was Kingsley Davis's ([1937] 1980) analysis of prostitution.

KINGSLEY DAVIS

Davis begins by noting that prostitution can be found everywhere, despite being both morally condemned by most individuals and legally prohibited in most societies. This raises two questions: Why is prostitution universally condemned? How does it flourish despite legal prohibitions?

In asking his first question, why is prostitution condemned, Davis displays the new attitude characteristic of contemporary sociology. The morality or immorality of social behaviour is no longer taken for granted but is now problematic. In line with Durkheim's assertion that morality derives from society, not from the character of the act itself, the functionalist can ask, "Why?" when faced with any form of behaviour considered deviant. After all, Davis notes, prostitution is not a dramatic departure from the more conventional use of sex in social relationships. It is (Davis [1937] 1980: 11) "one end of a long sequence or gradation of essentially similar phenomena that stretches at the other end to such approved patterns as engagement and marriage."

Davis argues that the difference between prostitution and morally approved behaviour is based on different *functional relations* between society and sexual institutions. Society regulates sexual behaviour by regulating who can have sex with whom, when, under what circumstances and following what customs. Society must regulate sexual relations among people, since human biology does not. In order for sexuality to contribute to social order, rather than disrupt it, sexual relations must be regulated by society. The strength of these regulations will reflect the functional significance of sexual behaviour for society. Since reproduction is the most significant function for the survival of society, sexual behaviour that contributes to reproduction will be institutionalized and highly valued. Consequently, marriage, which is the the institution regulating socially approved reproduction, becomes the most "respectable" sexual institution.

Marriage, however, regulates and thus *limits* sexual behaviour. Individuals are motivated to accept this limitation through socialization and the internalization of the values and norms of "romantic love." Romantic love is an ideology, a set of values, norms, and ideas designed to make the individual *want* to accept the limitations inherent in marriage and raising a family.

In contrast, prostitution is a "contractual relation in which services are traded" (Davis [1937] 1980: 13). It contributes neither to reproduction nor to the other legitimate institutions concerned with reproduction. Instead it produces a sexual relationship that is "ephemeral" and that contradicts the ideology of romantic love. The moral condemnation of prostitution is a consequence of its equation of sex with money rather than with reproduction. The creation of legal prohibitions against prostitution is merely the expression of this common sense of moral condemnation.

Yet, Davis suggests, if prostitution is not functional for reproduction, it must have some other, secondary functions which allow it to survive despite legal prohibitions. The social pathologists had argued that the persistence of prostitution was a consequence of the poverty, moral indifference and inferior moral constitution of the lower-class women who came to be prostitutes. Davis argues against such moralistic and individualistic explanations. To a functionalist such as Davis, prostitution as a social institution *cannot* be explained by examining the individual prostitutes. They are merely providing a service to meet a demand. It is the nature and function of this *demand* that is crucial. Prostitution must be understood by reference to its customers rather than by reference to the prostitutes.

What, then, accounts for this demand, what are the "needs," the functional relations, upon which prostitution as a social relationship is based? Davis explains these functional relations as follows: Marriage, by regulating sexual conduct, regulates as well the "variety, amount, and nature of a person's satisfactions" (Davis [1937] 1980: 17). Prostitution, in contrast, provides sex easily and quickly, without the need to follow a complex set of rituals such as dating, courting, etc., and is also free of demands for emotional involvement on the part of those involved. It allows married men to have sex with a wide variety of women as often as they want and in whatever form of sexual activity desired. As Davis ([1937] 1980: 16) puts it, "the craving for variety, for perverse gratification, for mysterious and provocative surroundings, for intercourse free from entangling cares and civilized pretense, all play their part." Prostitution provides all of these in a manner that is relatively cheap, quick and impersonal. All that is needed is the cash. Since marriage inevitably limits sexuality, there will always be a demand on the part of some men for sex outside of marriage.

In addition, marriage is not a sexual solution available to everyone. As Davis ([1937] 1980: 17) puts it, "all men are not born handsome nor are all women beautiful." There are men, such as the disfigured or the handicapped, the mentally ill or the socially incompetent, for whom marriage may not be an option. There are men unable to strike up a normal relationship, or those travelling regularly who have no time to establish relationships, or those whose sexual interests are limited to forms that are not socially approved; for such men prostitution is the most convenient form of sexual relationship.

Davis suggests that prostitution will not be ended by strengthening the family, as the social pathologists had argued, because prostitution is functionally tied into a reciprocal relationship with the family as a social institution. The stronger the institution of the family, the more it regulates sexual conduct and the greater the demand for prostitution. Only when the family as an institution is weak does prostitution diminish; only if men and women are free to have sex whenever and with whomever they please will prostitution disappear. This latter cannot happen, Davis argues, because society *must* regulate sexual conduct. The unrestricted acting out of sexual desires poses a much greater threat to social order than the controlled release of sexual frustrations or interests through prostitution. It is in this sense that prostitution not only benefits society but is necessary for social order. It cannot be eliminated.

Davis's analysis of prostitution is weakened by his unquestioned equation of sexuality with reproduction. This equation displays his commitment to the conventional morality of his time. But even supposing that reproduction is the "primary" function of sex for *society*, how does that affect *individuals*? Throughout history, people have engaged in behaviour, often quite enthusiastically, that ultimately destroyed their society. That some form of behaviour will benefit society is no guarantee that it will be carried out. What are the actual mechanisms whereby individuals come to act out social needs? How do "functional relations" really work? To this the functionalists give no answer.

Note as well that Davis bases his analysis of prostitution almost exclusively on the sexual needs and desires—the *demands*—of men. Does marriage not limit women sexually as well? Yes it does, agrees Davis, and suggests that it is because of the inequality between men and women that men are more likely to have their sexual demands satisfied (Davis [1937] 1980: 21): "Men have authority and economic means in greater amount than women. They are, therefore, in a more favorable position to offer inducements, and this inequality characterizes not only prostitution but all relations in which sex is used for ulterior ends."

Significantly, this acknowledgement of economic and social inequality between men and women is found in a footnote, and the bulk of Davis's analysis focuses almost exclusively on the significance of males and the male demand for sexual gratification.

ROBERT K. MERTON AND THE THEORY OF ANOMIE

Although Davis identified what he described as the "secondary" functions of prostitution (as opposed to the primary function he assigned to reproduction), he failed to establish grounds for identifying when and which functions are primary, and others secondary. He also failed to specify the conditions under which such secondary functions arise. In any case, as noted before, the claim that reproduction is the primary function of sexual relations is a moral rather than a scientific claim.

One of Robert K. Merton's major contributions to functionalism is to insist on a more empirical approach to the use of functionalist analysis than that found in Davis's work. Merton argues that one should not begin by assuming indispensable social functions, which is what Davis does in the case of reproduction, but rather by looking to the "objective consequences" of behaviour such as prostitution. These objective consequences can be examined as functional relations without the biased claim that one or more of these consequences are primary, indispensable or secondary.

When you look at the objective consequences of behaviour, says Merton, you notice that some of these consequences are motivated or intended by the individuals involved, while others are neither intended nor necessarily recognized by them. So, for example, the social functions of prostitution discussed by Davis are largely or entirely unknown to those participating in prostitution. This distinction between motivation and function is the basis of Merton's distinction between what he calls "manifest" and "latent" functions. As Merton (1968: 105) explains:

> Manifest functions are those objective consequences contributing to the adjustment or adaptation of the system which are intended and recognized by participants in the system; ... Latent functions, correlatively, being those which are neither intended nor recognized.

As an example, Merton presents the case of the Hopi (American Indian) rain ceremony (Merton, 1968: 118-19):

> Hopi ceremonials designed to produce abundant rainfall may be labelled a superstitious practice of primitive folk. ... Were one to confine himself to the problem of whether a manifest (proposed) function occurs, it becomes a problem, not for the sociologist, but for the meteorologist. And to be sure, our meteorologists agree that the rain ceremonial does not produce rain. ... But ... ceremonials may fulfill the latent function of reinforcing the group identity by providing a periodic occasion on which the scattered members of a group assemble to engage in a common activity.

Merton's typology of manifest and latent functions assumes, in fact requires, a single system of normative consensus in order to work. It requires common agreement on goals and values if one is to be able to argue that specific, identifiable and objective functions are the consequence of any particular individual or institutional behaviour. This simply does not fit the facts of life in a modern, pluralistic society.

A key criticism of functionalism is its inability to deal with power. Today it would be a very naive sociologist indeed who failed to recognize the issue of power as central to understanding the social world. Yet the functionalists proved themselves incapable of dealing adequately with the issue of power, or even, for many of them, of recognizing it. Although Merton did claim that power has a vital role to play in society, Giddens (1977: 108) illustrates how the issue of power is missing in the distinction between manifest and latent functions; "Merton does not specify who has to intend and know what a function of an item is for it to be a manifest function."

When some know and others do not, we have a circumstance that can easily lead to differences in power. Knowing what is happening and preventing others from knowing implies control.

KAI ERIKSON

Durkheim and the functionalists asserted that deviance is both normal and necessary in the functioning of society. But what of the deviant? Is the deviant, too, normal and necessary?

This question is never addressed directly by most of the functionalists. While Davis, for example, makes it clear that the prostitute is not beautiful nor is her client handsome, whether they are "normal" is not discussed. Robert Merton's theory of anomie, which we shall be discussing shortly, does argue that the deviant is normal to the degree that his or her deviance is the outcome of structural conditions rather than personality characteristics. However, none of the functionalists gave this issue as much careful analysis as did Kai Erikson.

Society, says Erikson, creates the deviant in the same way and for the same reasons that it creates deviance. The deviant occupies a very specific and very necessary role in society, one that is given form by society itself and that cannot be enacted by anyone else.

In an article co-authored with Robert Dentler (1959), Erikson and his collaborator provide a clear and systematic summary of the functionalist view of deviance. Dentler and Erikson's core proposition is that social groups "induce" deviant behaviour in the same way that they induce other group qualities and roles such as leadership. By "induce," Dentler and Erikson (1959: 99) mean "a process by which the group channels and organizes the deviant possibilities contained in its membership." Why would groups do this? Dentler and Erikson assert that deviant behaviour helps to maintain "group equilibrium." By this they mean that society needs some people to achieve little in the way of social esteem and rewards, in order to balance those who receive too much. If all achieved equally, then the motivation to achieve would disappear, and if all receive equal rewards then rewards would lose their meaning.

Now, if deviance *too* is essential, then deviants must also be rewarded; only their rewards differ from the rewards allotted to those who conform. Dentler and Erikson give the example of schizophrenic "basic trainees" in the US army, whose clearly aberrant behaviour leads others to make special allowance for them. As Dentler and Erikson (1959: 105) put it, the schizophrenic becomes a kind of "mascot" of the group; the others do his work for him, protect him from authorities, and allow him "a wide license to deviate from both the performance and behaviour norms of the group." Rather than being rejected by the group, Dentler and Erikson argue that the deviant is sustained and maintained by the group, taking up a very special place and a very distinctive role within the group. In the most extreme variation on Durkheim's claim that deviance is "normal," Dentler and Erikson argue that in any group a special place—certain specific roles—are "reserved" for deviants. "Should the occupants of these roles be removed from the group," Dentler and Erikson (1959: 107) hypothesize, "the group ... would realign its members so that these roles would become occupied by other members." The deviant *as a person* is not necessarily different from any other member of the group, only the role being acted out is different. Even a saint, as Durkheim said, would be assigned the necessary role of deviant should it become vacant.

The role of the deviant is not only necessary, it is specific to the society in which it occurs. In his later study of deviance among the Puritans in seventeenth-century Massachusetts, Erikson (1965: 19-20) notes that:

> Every human community has its own special set of boundaries, its own unique identity, and so we may presume that every community also has its own characteristic styles of deviant behaviour. Societies which place a high premium on ownership of property, for example, are likely to experience a greater volume of theft than those which do not, while societies which emphasize political orthodoxy are apt to discover and punish more sedition than their less touchy neighbors.

Erikson takes his argument for the social construction of deviance several steps further still. He argues that every society has a specific "volume" of deviance, a set amount or quantity of deviance which remains constant over time. He argues as well that every society has its own "deployment patterns," that is, patterns "which regulate the flow of deviant persons to and from the boundaries of the group" (Erikson, 1965: 27). The deployment patterns insure that a sufficient number of persons are assigned deviant roles to maintain the appropriate volume of deviance.

This is a far cry from any constitutional account of deviance. If deviance is necessary, if it is essential to maintaining the group's balance and its boundaries, then deviant roles will be institutionalized in the society and people will be assigned to them just as people are assigned to any other institutional roles.

In order to test this extreme functionalist account of deviance, Erikson went back to Durkheim's example of a "community of saints."

What sort of behaviour would be defined as deviance among a society of saints? What specific functions would deviance fulfil in such a society? Finding a society of saints—at least of self-proclaimed saints—was no problem. The Puritans who sailed to Massachusetts in the 1630s were convinced that they were predestined by God for salvation, and thus that they were a community of saints. They sought to establish a community in Massachusetts, a "New Jerusalem," which would follow God's laws in every way and which would serve as an example to the rest of the world. By looking at this community and the forms of deviance by which it saw itself afflicted, Erikson (1965: 21) sought to show that "the deviant and the conformist ... are creatures of the same culture, inventions of the same imagination."

In his study of the Puritans, Erikson tries to show that the primary function of deviance among them was boundary maintenance. Because they had such a rigid insistence on absolute obedience to what they considered God's law, there was a multitude of insignificant deviances to which the Puritans responded implacably and with severity. But there also occurred three "crime waves" during the seventeenth century, which Erikson claims were instances of boundary maintenance. The last of these, the Salem "Witch Trials," is the most famous. A discussion of this case illustrates what Erikson means by boundary maintenance.

In 1692, in Salem Village, Massachusetts, two young girls began to exhibit strange and frightening behaviour (Erikson, 1965: 142):

> They would scream unaccountably, fall into grotesque convulsions, and sometimes scamper along on their hands and knees making noises like the barking of a dog. No sooner had word gone around about this extraordinary affliction than it began to spread like a contagious disease. All over the community young girls were groveling on the ground in a panic of fear and excitement.

The doctor who treated the girls felt helpless to deal with their behaviour and announced that in his opinion they had been bewitched. A group of Puritan ministers agreed with the doctor and pressed the girls to identify the witches who had done this to them. The girls identified three local women as witches: a Black slave belonging to the local minister, an "old crone" who smoked a pipe and begged from her neighbours in order to support her children, and a woman who had been involved in a local sex scandal some time before. All three of these women were marginal figures in the Puritan community, and the idea that they were witches was readily accepted by members of the community. In addition, Tituba, the Black slave, made a dramatic and lengthy confession during which she claimed that there was a conspiracy initiated by the Devil to destroy the Puritan community in Massachusetts, a conspiracy that included a great many other people.

Soon after, the girls affected by "witchcraft" claimed that they were able to identify other witches simply by being in their presence. They began to go about the village accusing more and more people of being part of the Devil's plot. It may be that the girls were caught up in the enthusiasm created by their story or that they enjoyed the fame and power given; whatever the case, they continued to identify people as witches for several months. After a time the girls began to name people from outside the community, people they had never met, as witches. In addition, while the first persons to be named had been marginal to the community, the girls soon began to accuse prominent and respected members of the community. Within a few months, twenty-two persons had been executed for witchcraft, one hundred and fifty put in prison, and over two hundred others accused but not yet arrested.

By the time the number of people accused reached such high figures, many community members began to wonder if the girls were really identifying witches. Might it not be that they were mentally disturbed or simply lying because they enjoyed the power they had achieved? As the social class and status of those being accused rose, more and more people began to question the whole affair. Finally, the persons being accused, including the wife of the governor, were considered by the community so unlikely to be members of a plot by the Devil that these latter accusations were simply dismissed. Soon the magistrates decided that all of the accusations were questionable and released all of the accused from prison. The hysteria, which had lasted a few months, was over.

But why did it begin in the first place? Erikson suggests that it was not the accusations of witchcraft that began the crime wave. Accusations of witchcraft—even confessions—had occurred before in the colony without producing a widespread hunt for witches. If anything, the Puritans of Massachusetts had often demonstrated a reluctance to take the idea of witchcraft seriously and usually considered such claims to be either lies or delusions. Then why were they taken so seriously in 1692?

Erikson argues that Massachusetts in 1692 was undergoing a dramatic set of social changes. It was no longer an exclusively Puritan community fired by a sense of mission to create a "New Jerusalem" ruled by God's law. It had become one of several British colonies in North America, administered like any other. The Puritans had lost their Royal Charter giving them special religious and political rights, they were no longer able to choose their own governor, and were no longer seen as the spiritual and moral leaders of the English Puritans. Their sense of mission, of being a select group doing God's work, began to disappear as they became successful farmers and merchants preoccupied with the ordinary concerns of commerce and everyday life. But if the Puritans of 1692 were no longer the Puritans of 1630, then who were they? Just as importantly, what were to be their goals and what was their mission?

The accusations of witchcraft seemed to provide answers to these questions and to reawaken the Puritans' sense of themselves as a special people. They must be special because the Devil had singled them out for his attention. However much it might seem that their community had failed, it was clear that the Devil did not think so. He had initiated this conspiracy to destroy the colony because of the threat it posed. Clearly, the Puritans were still the elect of God. Moreover it was now clear *why* the community had failed to achieve so many of its goals; it was because so many of its members were part of the secret conspiracy. They had done their best to destroy the community even while they had seemed to be loyal members of it. As for their sense of mission, the Puritans might no longer be taming a forest wilderness and battling heathen savages, but they were now in a spiritual wilderness surrounded by new enemies: demons, witches, and evil spirits. The witchcraft hysteria redefined the boundaries of the group, created a new "them" to counter against the community's sense of "us," and gave a feeling of purpose and unity to the group. Put in functionalist terms, since the traditional institutions of Puritan society were unable to fulfil their essential functions, deviance arose, both to re-establish those functions and—in Merton's terms—to fulfil new latent functions necessary to the group's new circumstances and for which no legitimate institutions yet existed.

There are two important points which need to be stressed. One is that we are dealing here with an example of socially constructed deviance. There were no witches and there was no plot by the Devil to destroy the colony. We are dealing with imputations of deviance—labels assigned to persons—which have no basis in behaviour. How such labelling works, the conditions that give rise to it, and the consequences that result from it, are the kinds of questions raised by the labelling perspective. Indeed, Erikson's study, despite its functionalist basis, is considered one of the important works in the development of the labelling perspective (see Chapter Six).

The second point relates back to Dentler and Erikson's original question: How are individuals induced to act out the deviant roles society expects of them? Take the example of Tituba, the black slave. She not only confessed to being a witch, but provided details of her activities and described an organized plot by the Devil far exceeding anything the magistrates had imagined when they began their proceedings. Did the woman believe she was a witch? Perhaps; perhaps not. Clearly she was outside the mainstream of Puritan society, a marginal figure on the boundary of that society. A person like this, Erikson tells us, constitutes a "resource," someone who can be called upon when deviance is needed. For her, too, the accusations provided an opportunity. This was her chance to lay public claim to special powers and special knowledge, to show that while seeming to be an insignificant slave, she was really an important player in the conspiracy, while other people, who seemed her superiors, were actually her subordinates. Tituba was rewarded for acting out her deviant role in a way that she never would have been rewarded had she insisted on her innocence. The community listened to her, believed in her powers, and treated her as a major player in a matter of communal life or death. Since the functions of deviance change with changes to the community's boundaries, such potential deviants are kept in reserve, as it were, to be assigned the appropriate deviant role when needed.

We noted earlier that functionalists seem unable to take account of the role of power in social life. Erikson's work on the Puritan crime waves is a significant exception. Erikson's interest is on precisely those moments when changing circumstances led the Puritan community to feel compelled to make extensive and dramatic use of power, in order to end what they saw as serious threats to their community. By creating deviance and promoting group conflict, they sought to re-establish consensus by redefining the moral boundaries of the group. Erikson's analysis is functionalist; it does interpret these events as oriented to group "needs" rather than individual actions, preferences or contingencies. But his functionalist account of the Puritan crime waves spelled out the exhaustion of the functionalist perspective. His study is clearly a transition from the functionalist emphasis on institutional needs to the labelling emphasis on social definition and societal reaction.

There remains a second tradition within the functionalist perspective, anomie theory, with which we have not yet dealt. Anomie theory, like the analysis of manifest and latent functions, developed in the work of Robert Merton.

ANOMIE THEORY

As we have seen, Robert Merton insisted on starting from the "objective consequences" of behaviour in order to analyze functional relationships. It was this insistence that was the basis for his distinction between manifest and latent functions. Despite this, Merton attempted to develop a structural account of deviance in his theory of anomie. Indeed, it is one of the criticisms of functionalist analysis that it inevitably drives its practitioners away from the empirical to the theoretical. Anomie theory was a structural explanation of deviance rather than an empirical account.

Merton's analysis of deviance goes further than the static functionalism of Kingsley Davis. Like Davis, Merton seeks the "structural sources" of deviant behaviour. But Merton is not satisfied to argue that the behaviour is present in order to meet a particular need. He seeks to identify how the behaviour develops, what circumstances give rise to the behaviour. If Davis identifies the *structural* sources of deviance, Merton looks for the structural *sources* of deviance.

Additionally, Merton is not satisfied to assume that there is a need for some form of deviance, that *someone* will engage in it. Such a view still assumes that if the behaviour is not pathological, the individual is. Instead, Merton suggests (1968: 186): "if we can locate groups peculiarly subject to such pressures, we can expect to find fairly high rates of deviance in these groups, not because the human beings comprising them are compounded of distinctive biological tendencies but because they are responding normally to the social situation in which they find themselves."

Merton is not really interested in the individuals, although, as we shall see, he makes some assumptions about those individuals. He wishes to identify "how the social and cultural structure generates pressure for deviant behaviour upon people variously located in that structure" (1968: 176). Merton is interested in the motives that give rise to deviance without being interested in the individuals being motivated.

Finally, Merton rejects a simple equation of deviance with socially disapproved behaviour. He points out that "*some* deviations may also be regarded as a *new* pattern of behaviour, possibly emerging among subgroups at odds with *those* institutional patterns supported by groups other than themselves and the law" (1968: 176) (emphasis added). This, as Merton points out, requires reference to power, for new behaviour comes to be defined as deviant by some group with the power to enforce its definitions.

Like most other functionalists, Merton looked to Durkheim both as a source of methodology and as a source of inspiration. In Durkheim's account of anomie, Merton believed he had found the key to unlocking the mystery of deviance.

The Concept of Anomie

While Durkheim saw anomie as a threat to the very fabric of the society, Merton was concerned to show how anomie functions latently to support and reconfirm the normative order of the society. Normative order, Merton suggests, can be analytically separated into two distinct orders. The first is a cultural and social-structural order. This order sets forth the culturally accepted goals of a society that call forth or motivate social behaviour. Then there is the second order, composed of institutional means made available to and approved by the social structure for achieving these goals. In Merton's usage of the term, anomie now refers not to the absence of normative regulation, but to a lack of fit between the two normative orders. It is not that these norms are absent, but that in specific situations one or the other sets of norms is unavailable or impractical.

Adaptations to Anomie

Merton (1968: 190) suggests that American society is one in which there is a "great emphasis upon certain success-goals ... without equivalent emphasis upon institutional means." When such a situation develops, there is a tendency for institutional means to lose emotional significance. Success itself, however it is attained, is the goal. Merton's example is the desire for monetary success.

In Merton's model, anomie leads to particular modes of *adaptation*, as Figure 4.1 indicates. The disjunction between cultural goals and institutional means generates several different forms of individual adaptation to anomie. Merton asserts that these adaptations are not based on personality characteristics but are forms of social behaviour.

Modes of adaptation	*Cultural goals*	*Institutionalized means*
I. Conformity	+	+
II. Innovation	+	-
III. Ritualism	-	+
IV. Retreatism	-	-
V. Rebellion	±	±

FIGURE 4.1   Merton's Theory of Adaptations to Anomie
SOURCE: Merton (1938).

Conformity

In keeping with functionalist assumptions, Merton does not feel that conformity requires any special explanation. Most people conform because they have internalized society's goals and values and accepted the means considered appropriate to achieve those goals. As Merton presents this basic functionalist assumption (1968: 195):

> It is only because behavior is typically oriented toward the basic values of a society that we may speak of a human aggregate as comprising a society. Unless there is a deposit of values shared by interacting individuals, there exist social relations, if the disorderly interactions may be so called, but no society.

Conformity, then, needs no special explanation and poses no particular problem for society. But deviance does.

Innovation

Innovation is described by Merton as an adaptation to anomie brought on when the individual has internalized the cultural goals but has not internalized the institutional norms concerning "ways and means" for the attainment of these goals. In its simplest form, innovation can be understood as crime, the use of illegitimate means to attain cultural goals. Innovation may occur because many social norms are neither clear nor decisive. As Merton notes, it is often left up to the courts to determine whether or not some practice violates the laws and norms. For example, there is conflict among the values relating to success and those of abiding by the law. In American society, Merton argues, success goals win. Moreover, in a capitalist, business-oriented society, the many pressures placed upon individuals to obtain success often make other norms appear trivial or irrelevant. The "Robber Barons" who grabbed corporate power and wealth in the United States towards the end of the nineteenth century knew that they had to lie, cheat and steal in order to succeed.

Nevertheless, while Merton argues that American society differs from other societies in that the cultural values of wealth, success and ambition are widely diffused among all social classes, he asserts that innovation—crime—is the form of adaptation most likely to be found in the lower class. While all classes may share the same goals, Merton sees the lower class as lacking access to the approved institutional means necessary to achieve these goals. The resulting combination of cultural goals and a social structure that limits access produces "an intense pressure for deviance."

Merton insists that it is the combination of these cultural and structural factors that produces deviance. By itself, a rigid social structure which limits access to opportunities does not generate deviance. It is such a structure combined with cultural goals that suggest that everyone—regardless of social location—ought to strive to achieve these goals, which is crucial. Under these conditions, those who have been imperfectly socialized to accept the legitimate institutional means will turn to crime.

For this reason, Merton does not see innovation as posing any threat to social order. Criminals may pose a specific threat to other particular individuals, but they neither challenge the goals of society nor seek to transform society. On the contrary, their adaptation reinforces the cultural goals. The criminal serves as a sign of success, an indication that anyone can make it—legally or illegally—in American society. By their conspicuous display of wealth and power, criminals effectively advertise the values of American society among the lower strata.

Ritualism

Ritualism refers to the "compulsive" adherence to institutional norms despite the "scaling-down" of one's expectations of personal success. Whereas the lower-class individual is likely to adapt to anomie by turning to crime, the lower-middle-class individual will adapt by becoming a ritualist. As a consequence of strong socialization for conformity, the lower-middle-class individual is unable to flout the rules and develop alternative institutional means.

Merton argues that this type of adaptation is a consequence of the high status placed on achievement. Anxiety about status and the ability to achieve produces fear. Unable to strive for success, the ritualists "seek a private escape from the dangers and frustrations which seem to them inherent in the competition for major cultural goals" Merton (1968: 205). They lower their aspirations to the point where the following of rules itself becomes their goal. In their redefined understanding of the relationship between goals and norms, strict adherence to the norms is itself taken to be a sign of success.

This is not conformity, although it gives the appearance of such. These individuals have given up striving and have developed individualistic rather than social criteria for success. Nevertheless, such people pose no threat to social order. They do their jobs, carry out their orders, and challenge neither the goals of society nor the approved means designated to achieve these goals.

Retreatism

Some people, Merton suggests, are socialized to place a high value on both cultural goals and institutional practices. When they find themselves in a state of anomie, their failure to achieve these goals, coupled with their failure to make effective use of institutional practices, generates internal conflict, frustration, and a sense of defeat. The individual "drops out" of this dilemma by looking for some means of escape from the conflict. As Merton (1968: 209) puts it, retreatism is:

> a privatized rather than a collective mode of adaptation. Although people exhibiting this deviant behavior may gravitate toward centers where they come in contact with other deviants and although they may come to share in the subculture of these deviant groups, their adaptations are largely private and isolated rather than unified under a new cultural code.

Typical forms of retreatist deviant behaviour would be drug addiction, alcoholism and mental illness, all of which are considered by Merton an escape from the reality of failure, frustration and defeat. Once drug users become addicted, for example, they are "asocialized." They are "in society but not of it" (Merton, 1968: 207). From Merton's

(1968: 207) point of view such people can be effectively dismissed from sociological interest: "Not sharing the common frame of values, they can be included as members of society (in distinction from the population) only in a fictional sense."

Merton suggests that of all forms of adaptation to anomie, retreatism is the least common because it is the most reviled. Retreatism does not contribute to the ongoing functioning of society as does ritualism, nor does it enhance the valued goals of society as does innovation. Still, if these escapees from society are of no individual benefit to society, retreatism as a mode of adaptation contributes to the stability of society. It provides a contrast to inspire others to maintain their commitments to social values. The wandering, foul-smelling "bum" dressed in filthy clothes who spends his time picking through public trash cans is a visual reminder of what we may become if we give up on society. Society and its system of values are ultimately bolstered by the homeless alcoholic, the desperate addict and the hopeless mentally ill.

Rebellion

Rebellion is an adaptation to a situation in which the "institutional system" has itself come to be seen as a barrier to success rather than as its means. As a consequence, the rebellious individual seeks to modify the social structure by changing both the cultural goals of society and the institutional means defined as appropriate. As such, Merton (1968: 210) suggests that it is the adaptation of intellectuals. It is intellectuals who tend to develop new "myths" around which to develop alternative visions of society and which serve as a "charter for action."

By asserting that deviance is a consequence of a structural disjunction between goals and means, Merton argues that there is a strain towards anomie in American society. All of the resulting forms of deviance are described as "adaptations." The choice of term is apt, because Merton saw them as functioning latently to support rather than to threaten social order and stability. Significantly, only rebellion—which is limited largely to the isolated world of the intellectuals—is considered by Merton to pose any sort of threat to the social order, and then only if the intellectuals succeed in mobilizing others who are similarly resentful and rebellious. In this respect, Merton's theory of anomie is typically functionalist and can be seen as an integral part of a functionalist model of the causes, workings and effect of deviance in society. Figure 4.2 presents such a model, which shows how Merton's theory of anomie can be integrated with the functionalist accounts of deviance presented by Kingsley Davis, Kai Erikson, and Merton himself. In all cases other than rebellion, social equilibrium is maintained, either in terms of systems of goals and values or in terms of systems of action and performance.

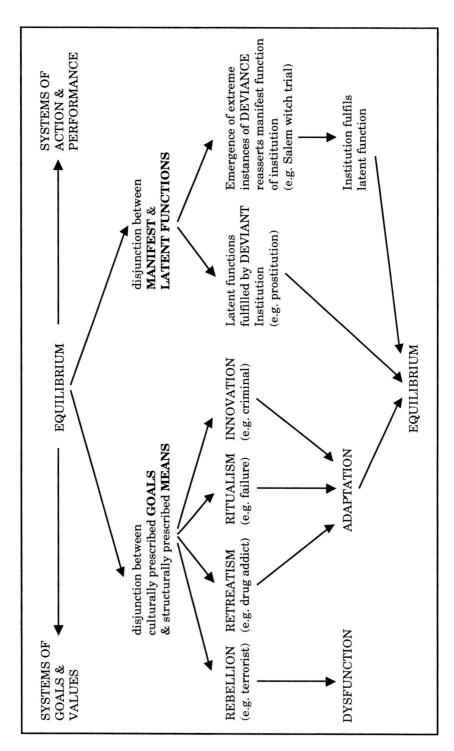

FIGURE 4.2 **The Functional Model of Deviance**

Critiques of Anomie Theory

Criticisms of Merton's anomie theory and of his approach to deviance have tended to fall into one of three categories: remedial critiques, theoretical critiques, and empirical critiques. Remedial critics have accepted Merton's basic assumptions and approach, but have sought to remedy what are seen as specific defects in his theory. Most of the remedial critiques can typically be seen as extensions of Merton's basic approach. Theoretical critiques point to flaws either in the assumptions made by Merton, in the logic of his argument or in the level of explanation he uses. Many theoretical critiques tend to be blanket dismissals both of Merton's theory of anomie and of functionalism in general. Empirical critiques essentially argue that the people Merton seeks to describe with his theory, and the particular forms of deviance for which he tries to account, have none or few of the motivational, behavioural or social characteristics that he attributes to them. Most empirical critiques describe deviant subcultures whose members differ markedly from what would be expected, given Merton's assumptions. (Examples of all three types of critiques can be found in Clinard [1964].) In order to provide continuity to the discussion of the strengths and weaknesses in Merton's theory of anomie, we will focus on the research on drug use and drug addiction, which Merton categorizes as retreatist deviance.

Remedial Critiques

One area of research in which significant use has been made of Merton's theory of anomie is the study of juvenile delinquency. In dealing with delinquency, researchers have tried to extend Merton's theory by combining it with Sutherland's notion of differential association and with Merton's own work on the "reference group." We will consider this research in detail in the next chapter.

Another significant remedial critique can be found in the work of Cloward and Ohlin (1960), who argue that anomie theory should take neither deviance *nor conformity* for granted. Cloward and Ohlin suggest there are differentials in the availability of illegitimate means just as there are differentials in the availability of legitimate means. Not everyone has the courage, skills or luck to make a good criminal. In addition, access to illegitimate means may be controlled, as is the case with juvenile gangs or organized crime. Some individuals are simply rejected by those who control the access to illegitimate means. Retreatism would then be a consequence of a "double failure," failure to make effective use of legitimate means *and* failure to make effective use of illegitimate means. Cloward and Ohlin (1960: 182) claim as evidence that "most drug addicts have a history of delinquent activity prior to becoming addicted."

Cloward and Ohlin present a view of delinquent life as being very much like the corporate "rat race." Delinquents compete for membership in gangs by striving to acquire status through violence. In this competition for status some will fail. These failures—double failures—may turn to drugs if they "are incapable of revising their aspirations downward to correspond to reality" Cloward and Ohlin (1960: 184). Drug use, however, only mires these lower-class boys further into a life of failure. They lose even more status with their peers as they come to be identified as addicts.

Alexander and Hadaway (1982) provide a more positive view of addiction as a form of deviant adaptation. They see addiction as an adaptation—often temporary—to a situation of stress. Rather than being an escape from reality, such an adaptation puts the individual on "hold," so to speak, allowing the individual to cope with his or her circumstances until those circumstances change. Rather than the addict becoming a life-long slave to the drug, addiction is understood in the context within which it occurs. Boyd (1988) gives as support for this approach the fact that many of the American soldiers in Vietnam during the late sixties and early seventies were regular users of heroin, but that most of them ceased using heroin when they returned to the United States.

Boyd (1988: 169) himself has extended Merton's typology by considering a broader range of deviant types involved in drug use apart from the retreatist:

> The "trafficker" is typically an innovator, working for the cultural values of wealth and prosperity through illegitimate means. The illegal drug distributor may also be a rebel, seeking to change the prohibitive strategy of substance criminalization by sheer defiance. The illegal drug user may be a ritualist, a retreatist or a rebel. There is even a sense in which some illegal drug users can be seen as conformists, supporting both the goals of the dominant society and the means used to achieve those goals. The marijuana user, particularly, may not consider his or her consumption to be deviant in light of the current size of this drug's market.

What is particularly significant about this example is that Boyd illustrates that Merton's typology is not rigidly related to specific structural conditions and patterns of socialization but refers to social identities—identities presented to others or imposed by others—in terms of which we make sense of people's actions. But if we are free to make use of terms such as "rebel," "ritualist" or "innovator" in such a variety of ways, that indicates that we are not dependent upon the assumptions made in Merton's theory to uncover social types engaged in deviance.

Theoretical Issues

Essentially a functionalist account of deviance, Merton's theory has shared the fate of other functionalist accounts. It has been criticized for ignoring power, for assuming consensus on values rather than demonstrating such consensus, and for being conservative in its implications if not in its intent. There have, however, been a number of criticisms specifically directed at Merton's description of deviance and anomie.

Merton asserts that anomie results from a disjunction between cultural goals and institutionalized means of achieving those goals. This structural condition leads to individual modes of adaptation such as retreatism. While conformity needs no special explanation, the other modes of adaptation are explained as a consequence of patterns of socialization in which individuals learn to value cultural goals, institutionalized means, or both.

Does Merton's theory achieve its stated goal? Does it really provide us with an account of the structural sources of deviance? Ultimately, Merton's argument comes down to attributing differences in deviance to differences in *socialization*. And socialization comes down to a process whereby personality is socially constructed. Merton thus *does not* identify the structural sources of deviance but provides an account of the different socially constructed personalities engaged in deviance. Moreover, if deviance is an adaptation to anomie, then either all societies have anomie because all societies have deviance, or else other societies have fundamentally different types of deviance from our own. What, then, are the structural sources of anomie in distinction from the structural sources tied to other types of deviance? Unless he is asserting that other societies have no deviance, which he is not, Merton has merely identified some structural contingencies affecting specific forms of deviance in a particular society, the United States.

One of Merton's fundamental assumptions is that cultural goals motivate individual behaviour. Merton does not consider the possibility that these goals may mean different things to different people, nor that cultural goals may be mediated through social groups rather than directly motivating individual behaviour. For example, obtaining money to use as a sign of success is taken by Merton to be an important goal in American society. Supposedly the drug addict has given up on such goals. But the drug addict in fact has an urgent and pressing need for money: in order to buy drugs. Addicts place great importance on money and engage in a wide variety of acts in order to obtain money. Many of these acts—drug dealing, prostitution, robbery and begging are examples—are acts in which most of us would be unwilling to engage, even though Merton supposes we, too, *are* oriented to money. The meaning of the goal and its motivation are different, but the addicts have not given up on either goals or means.

Cultural goals must always be interpreted in the context within which individuals find themselves. That context almost always includes other people. Most drug addicts first became drug users by participating in social activities with others; seeing others use drugs, being curious about drugs or being offered drugs. They may then become part of a community—a subculture—centred on drug use. Dealers, fellow users, police officers, social workers and many others will either be part of this community or will impinge upon it in various ways. Cultural goals are always mediated by social groups. It is access to these groups and the mode of participation within groups that, as we shall see in Chapter Six, motivate individuals. Deviance is most often a group activity, and many sociologists such as the labelling theorists argue that the appropriate level of explanation for understanding such activity is the level of individuals interacting as a group.

In any case, to speak of clear-cut cultural goals and norms implies that there is a broad consensus concerning those goals or norms and the legitimacy or illegitimacy of any particular form of deviance. If, however, we find that there is no consensus on deviance, on whether drug use is or is not a problem, for example, then there is even less likelihood of finding consensus on supposed broad cultural goals, values and norms. Looking for such consensus requires empirical research, and it is to the contribution of such research that we now turn.

Empirical Critiques

Why consider the empirical validity of Merton's theory if it has so many theoretical flaws? The reason is that a theory may be poorly thought out, be based on invalid assumptions, operate at a level of explanation other than the one intended, and yet provide valuable insights for empirical research. There are many examples of this in sociology, where controversy over different definitions of social behaviour may rage, and yet each of these definitions often provides an important clue to an adequate sociological understanding of these behaviours. The converse may also be true, a theory may be well thought out, logically integrated, but simply fail to account for the relevant data. Or, a theory may account for the data exceptionally well, but if the data are invalid or unreliable, so too is the theory.

How does Merton's theory fare as the source of empirical accounts of deviance? The most fruitful area of research influenced by Merton's theory of anomie was that of juvenile delinquency. However, as we shall show in the next chapter, Merton's theory was substantially altered to make it fit the case of delinquency, and so the research on delinquency does not provide a real test of the empirical validity of Merton's approach.

Another test can be found in the literature on drug use and drug addiction. Merton argued that specific forms of deviance constitute specific adaptations to anomie. Drug addiction is a retreatist adaptation—an escape from reality—brought on by the failure to make effective use of institutional means in order to achieve cultural goals. Cloward and Ohlin (1960) further extended this theory by arguing that retreatism is really a consequence of a "double failure," an inability to make effective use of both legitimate and illegitimate means in order to achieve these goals.

Lindesmith and Gagnon (1964: 163) argue that "the theory of anomie implies a positive statistical association between addiction rates and levels of anomie." In order to provide such a statistical association, however, we need (1) dependable addiction rates that are valid, reliable, and allow comparisons to be made among groups; and (2) an operational measure of anomie that allows one to determine different levels of anomie.

There are problems with drug-addiction rates and the portrait of the typical addict that they provide us. Since drug use involves addicts in activities punishable by law, they often do their best to keep their use and addiction secret. Some have the resources necessary to succeed at secrecy; others do not. Those who have such resources as money, power, privacy or easy access to drugs are less likely to get caught and appear in the statistical account of drug addicts. Those who lack such resources are more likely to get caught and to enter into the statistics on drug use. Drug-addiction rates do not provide us with a picture of the addict, but rather of those addicts who get caught.

As for determining the level of anomie, how do we measure anomie? There are a number of anomie scales that have been developed (Srole, 1956; Dean, 1961), but these attempt to measure *attitudes*, whereas Merton tells us that anomie is a *structural condition*. How then do we measure structural conditions? Merton (1964) admits that this is a daunting challenge and one not yet successfully met by the various empirical studies of "anomie."

An alternative approach would be to compare Merton's typology of retreatism with empirical research that *has* been done on drug use and drug addiction. How well does Merton's theory fare when compared with empirical descriptions of deviance? Merton's theory is found at fault in three areas: in his assumption of broad social consensus on norms, and by extension on drugs; in his assertion that drug use is "asocialized" behaviour; and in his depiction of the drug user as a "failure."

DRUGS AND DRUG USE IN CANADIAN SOCIETY

What do we mean when we refer to "consensus" and where do we locate consensus relative to drug use? The concept of consensus implies the existence of a consistent set of integrated values, goals and norms—what is often called a normative order—into which individuals are socialized and concerning the legitimacy of which there is broad social agreement. In his discussion of anomie, Merton assumes such a normative order at a very high level of generality, that is, in terms of the "cultural" signifi- cance of success. But consensus about "success" does not necessarily imply consensus about specific social behaviour, and different groups will define success differently. An academic may define success quite differently from a businessperson, a politician quite differently from a social worker. Success means different things to different people. In the same way, the concepts of success and of failure tell us very little about drug use and where drug use fits into the normative order. Could it be that a heroin addict has his or her own definition of success? In any case, regardless of whether there may be consensus in terms of broad cultural goals, once we examine a specific instance of behaviour or a specific social process such as drug use, we must determine whether there is equivalent consensus relative to this specific social process. Thus, even if we assume normative consensus at the cultural level, we must find out whether consensus at that level is translated into consen- sus at the level of specific social processes. Then, if we find no consen- sus at this level, that in turn suggests there might well not be consensus at the cultural level either. If there is no consensus, we should expect far more variety in values, goals or norms, and many of the differences which appear to Merton to be different adaptations to the same normative order are in fact oriented to alternative sets of val- ues, goals and norms.

Since drug use and drug addiction are complex social, political, physiological and psychological phenomena, we should not be surprised that we find little consensus about drugs in Canadian society. Drug use *per se*, like alcohol use, is not considered deviant in our society. Almost all of us use drugs which are legally available for a wide variety of spe- cific medical purposes: as antibiotics, decongestants, vitamin supple- ments, antihistamines and analgesics. They are used to control cholesterol, to reduce anxiety and to lower temperature when we have the flu. In addition to this legitimate use of drugs, of course, many people also make use of proscribed drugs such as marijuana, while many others abuse prescription drugs such as Valium or Demerol.

Why are some drugs prohibited or restricted while others are not? Even more than was the case with alcohol (which may itself be consid- ered a drug) the social definition of drug use and the conditions under which such use will be defined as deviant must be understood in an en- vironment that is flooded by contradictory and confusing messages. Any parent taking a six-year-old to a "drug store" can readily attest to this cultural confusion. The extensive media campaigns against "drugs" have given the word an evil connotation, which is contradicted by the pharmacist cheerfully filling out for their parents a doctor's prescription for a "drug."

As an example of the ambivalent view of drug use in Canadian society, we can take the case of anabolic steroid use among athletes, to build up strength and speed healing from injury. The case of Canadian runner Ben Johnson, who was stripped of his Olympic gold medal in 1988 when he tested positively for steroid use, is a case in point. Many Canadians felt that even if Johnson had taken steroids, he was doing what all the other athletes were doing as well. If *all* the athletes use steroids, then his win is still legitimate and he still deserves the gold medal. Johnson's only fault, they claimed, was not in using the steroids but in getting caught. Others view Johnson as the innocent victim of the "system." His coach and his physician had advised him to use the drug, and it is part of the training process that athletes learn to obey the instructions and authority of coach and doctor. The conflicting emotions, claims and opinions raised by this affair well illustrate the conflicts surrounding the use of drugs in general.

The example of anabolic steroids raises another issue. Is the illicit use of drugs such as steroids to be considered in the same category as the illicit use of narcotics such as heroin? Clearly steroids are not the sorts of drugs that come to mind when we think of drug abuse. In what way, then, are steroids and heroin both "illicit" drugs? Many discussions on drug use are in fact prefaced by a preliminary consideration of the question: What is a drug? (Boyd, 1988; Goode 1973, 1984 are good examples.) The very fact that this question is so often asked indicates a general "cultural" confusion about how we determine what a drug is, the distinction between drug use and drug abuse, and why some drugs are prohibited when others are not. This absence of consensus about drugs, moreover, strongly suggests that there is an absence of consensus as well on the values and norms related to drug use; a strong indication of the inadequacy of Merton's retreatist account.

Drugs are defined by the Health Protection Branch of the Department of National Health and Welfare (1988: 13) as "any substance used in the diagnosis, treatment, mitigation or prevention of a disease, disorder or abnormal state, and in restoring, correcting or modifying organic functions, in man or animals." This definition emphasizes the medical use of drugs, as one would expect, given its source. In contrast, many ordinary people take the term "drug" to refer to substances that distort reality, enslave the weak-willed, and impair and degrade the user. For our purposes, a drug is categorized as such in terms of the beliefs and practices by which people in our society define them, deal with them, and seek either to prohibit or encourage their use. Thus, while Boyd includes alcohol, caffeine and tobacco in his discussion of drugs, most people do not consider such substances to be drugs, and they are neither legally prohibited nor is their use necessarily considered deviant. Opium, morphine, heroin, amphetamines, barbiturates, marijuana, LSD and cocaine *are* restricted and their use is considered deviant by significant segments of the population. It is these sorts of substances people think of when they think of illicit drugs, and so it is these we will consider in our discussion.

Why are the drugs listed above legally prohibited? It is not because they are more dangerous than others or more addicting. Heroin kills; so too do many other drugs legally available over the counter or through doctor's prescription at a pharmacy. Heroin is addicting; so too is Valium, one of the most commonly prescribed drugs in the world.[1] Any drug is dangerous if abused, ranging from heroin to beer to vitamin tablets, so strictly medical factors are not responsible for the choice of which drug is to be defined as deviant and which is not. Nor are drugs made illegal on the basis of their "effects." Some have argued that, because of the legacy of the Puritan and other Protestant traditions in the United States, the recreational use of drugs is seen as immoral and is therefore restricted (Inciardi, 1986). There may be some truth to this if we are considering the United States, but it certainly does not explain why the use of some drugs has been made illegal in Canada or in France, India or Saudi Arabia. In any case, all drugs have effects, some legally available drugs having essentially the same effects as drugs whose distribution is restricted. So, for example, alcohol and the barbiturates have almost the same effects, but alcohol is freely available while barbiturates are not. Additionally, different individuals will experience different effects from the same drug. The issue for sociologists, as Erich Goode (1984) has emphasized, is how these effects are socially interpreted and how much attention is paid to them.

Finally, drugs are not differentiated into licit and illicit drugs on the basis of their likelihood of leading the user to become an addict. Recent studies claim that the nicotine found in tobacco is more addicting than is heroin. Yet, while cigarettes made with tobacco are legal, those made with marijuana, which is not addicting, are illegal.

Why then *are* some drugs legal and others not? If the issue is really is *legality*, then we should not look at the drug but at the *law*. Certain drugs are illegal because the state defines them as such, and enforces that definition with penalties for their use.

Drug Use, Morality, and the State

Of course the statement just made, that drugs are illegal because the state defines them as such, begs the question; but at least it directs our attention away from pharmacological issues towards the actions of the state and the ability of the state to control "morality." The question then becomes, Why does the state define and treat some drugs as "illicit"?

If we assume that the state merely reflects public opinion and popular morality, then we could suppose that drug laws simply reflect public attitudes. This does not appear to be the case, however, at least not in the case of narcotics legislation. Green (1986: 24) argues that, "Contrary to what might be expected, it was changes in the criminal law that brought about [the] transformation of public attitudes, and not the converse proposition."

Functionalism failed to theorize the state effectively. For most functionalists the state was a set of institutions designed to coordinate and regulate the effective operations of the social system (Parsons, 1951). In this respect, the state serves to *integrate* the social system institutionally by controlling and coordinating the use of force. Quite apart from the many theoretical weaknesses in such a view of the state, we can simply point to the fact that the law, which is a product of the state, does not serve to integrate society but to create differentiated categories such as "burglars," "prostitutes," "drug dealers" and so on. Functionalists are left with no choice but to argue that such people pose a real or potential threat to social order, in order to account for social control and the law.

Labelling theory and critical theory are the major alternatives to functionalism in explaining *moral enterprise* or the process of criminalizing some previously legal form of behaviour. Drug use clearly qualifies here; prior to 1908 Canada had no laws prohibiting the use of narcotics.

The concept of the moral entrepreneur was developed by Howard Becker (1963) in explaining the origin of drug legislation in the United States, specifically the *Marihuana Tax Act* of 1937. The moral entrepreneur, according to Becker, is someone who initiates the creation or enforcement of rules or laws. Such a person (Becker, 1963: 148):

> operates with an absolute ethic; what he sees is totally evil with no qualification. Any means is justified to do away with it. The crusader is fervent and righteous, often self-righteous ... [believing] that their [sic] mission is a holy one ... [and] if [people] do what is right it will be good for them.

In the case of the *Marihuana Tax Act* such a moral entrepreneur was H. J. Anslinger, the Commissioner of the Federal Bureau of Narcotics. In the case of Canada's drug legislation it would be William Lyon Mackenzie King (Cook, 1969; Green, 1986).

Mackenzie King was sent to Vancouver in 1907 to investigate an anti-Oriental riot. During his investigation, King was made aware of the "problems" that widespread opium use created in the Chinese community. King began a campaign—a moral crusade—to have opium manufacture and sales prohibited. Largely at Mackenzie King's urging, the federal government passed two acts, one in 1908 and another in 1911, which initiated the legal prohibitions on the recreational use of narcotics in Canada (Green, 1986).

King's attitude towards opium (at least judging by his public utterances) was typical of the moral entrepreneur. Opium smoking was "a bondage worse than slavery" (quoted in Green, 1986: 26). "To be indifferent to the growth of such an evil in Canada," King said, "would be inconsistent with those principles of morality which ought to govern the conduct of a Christian nation" (quoted in Green, 1986: 27).

King's motives and role in initiating the anti-opium campaign have been a matter of debate. Green (1986) argues that King's attitude was that of a moral entrepreneur and leaves it at that. Cook (1969) relates the legislation to the strong, racist, anti-Chinese sentiment in British Columbia. Because of their low status, the Chinese did not have the political or economic clout to withstand this racist pressure. Green agrees that the legislation was really directed at the Chinese, but argues that once enacted, the drug legislation took on a moral resonance unintended by its framers, and by 1929 a series of amendments had given Canada essentially the drug laws that are currently in force. In other words, the legislation began as an act directed against the Chinese but eventually became the expression of a set of moral attitudes.

Comack (1985) argues that the assumption that Canada's drug laws were primarily anti-Chinese in origin or the outcome of Mackenzie King's moral enterprise are simplistic and ahistorical. Anti-Chinese sentiment long predated 1908, and there had already been several earlier attempts to prohibit opium. Additionally, many members of the Chinese community encouraged King in his actions against opium. It was not a simple case of Whites versus Orientals. As for Mackenzie King's moral passion, Comack suggests that his concern over drug use was secondary to his own career interests and that he viewed Canada's international leadership in restricting drug use less as a moral issue than as a matter of improving Canada's status in the world. Comack argues that it was class conflict rather than racism that was the key to the legislation. The Chinese were a cheap and reliable labour force for BC capitalists, but undermined "the position of skilled labour" (Comack, 1985: 75). As industrial unions began to form in the 1890s, opposition to cheap Chinese labour became better organized. This produced a potentially explosive situation of class conflict among three groups: the capitalist employers, the unskilled Chinese labourers and the unionized workers. At the same time there was a split *among* workers, some of whom were joining socialist unions (which, Comack claims, were *not* anti-Oriental) while others joined "conservative," racist unions. Mackenzie King's drug legislation, Comack suggests, directed attention *away* from class issues and towards racist and moral issues, thereby defusing the situation of potential conflict. Also, by reinforcing the racism of conservative unions, it weakened the position of the socialist unions.

Conversely, Boyd (1988) suggests that anti-Oriental sentiments *were* increasing in British Columbia in the early years of the century and that Mackenzie King's mission to Vancouver was primarily intended to prevent any damage to Canada's relationships with China and Japan. Boyd also notes that it was *primarily* Chinese clergymen and merchants who convinced King that opium should be restricted. The 1908 legislation was neither racist nor moralistic, and "there was no public interest in this legislative initiative" (Boyd, 1988: 162). On the other hand, both Boyd and Green point to the moral enterprise of the RCMP and Edmonton judge Emily Murphy during the 1920s as crucial in redefining narcotic use as a moral evil. Murphy was the author of a popular, racist book, *The Black Candle* (1922), which "suggested that cocaine use might lead white women to sleep with black men" (Boyd, 1986: 163), and that narcotics were being used in an international conspiracy by "foreigners" to bring "about the downfall of the white race" (quoted in Green, 1986: 32). As for the RCMP, as a "new" police force (amalgamated in 1919), the moral opposition towards drug use provided the force with an opportunity to obtain public recognition and approval relatively easily.

These disagreements about the "real" origin of narcotics legislation in Canada are not a sign of inadequacy on the part of these sociologists and criminologists, but of just how complex the issues involved really are. Politics, foreign affairs, pressure from the American government, racism, labour strife, class conflict, moral fervour, organizational needs, public relations; all of these and many more elements are present in the story. None provide a complete explanation. For example, the role of morality and moral entrepreneurs would be far more convincing if there were a clear and unambiguous set of moral attitudes and public opinion in Canada towards "drugs" and if the law were clear and precise in the criteria for differentiating licit from illicit drugs and drug use. But that is not the case.

Morality and Ambiguity

An example may illustrate the essential ambiguities involved in understanding drug use and addiction. No other drug is so linked in the public imagination with crime and addiction as is heroin. To the public heroin is a powerful and mysterious substance, a drug that can lead the addict to any depravity, yet simultaneously so seductive that merely trying it once is enough to get a person hooked. To the public, the heroin user is invariably an addict, trapped by a desperate need for the drug, out of touch with reality, and willing to commit any crime in order to obtain it.

There is, of course, some truth to this image. But there is much that is only partly true and much that may be true for some heroin users but false for others. Experts cannot agree on such basic questions as what the effects of heroin are on the user and why users become addicts. Some argue that heroin use produces an ecstatic euphoria (Inciardi, 1986: 61): "I felt like I died and went to heaven. My whole body was like one giant fucking incredible orgasm."

Inciardi suggests that the desire to re-experience this ecstatic "high" leads to repeated use and eventual physiological addiction.

In contrast, Goode suggests that tolerance to heroin builds up rapidly and that the euphoria of the high soon diminishes. "Gradually," Goode (1984: 112) notes, "the user derives less and less pleasure from the drug and takes it mainly to keep himself from becoming sick." It is the fear of withdrawal and the pain that results that keep the user hooked and lead to an obsessive reorganization of life activities around the search for a fix (Lindesmith, 1965).

Again, Inciardi disagrees. He describes the "fear of withdrawal" explanation as simplistic; as a case of sociologists falling for the addict's con. According to Inciardi (64), "withdrawal is no different, and no more severe, than the chills, cramps, and muscle pains that are associated with a good dose of the flu."

Neither Goode nor Inciardi sees drug use in Merton's terms as an "escape from the requirements of society" (1968). The idea that drug use provides an escape from reality presupposes that individuals know the effect of the drug before taking it. They then seek out that effect by seeking out the drug. Clearly such a view is neither logical nor empirically true. Those using a drug for the first time usually have little or no idea of what to expect. Often, they are curious to find out just what the effects of the drug are. Other times, they are unconcerned with the effects but merely seek to be a part of the crowd, to go along with everyone else.

Still another controversy rages over whether heroin use is dangerous. Yes, says Goode, but only *because* it is illegal. Narcotics are not toxic, they result in no known disease or disorder. "All of the diseases of addicts result from the way they live, not directly from the drug they take," claims Goode (1973: 42). So, for example, heroin addicts who overdose and die do so because of the variability in the doses of heroin available from different dealers. Only about 3 percent of the typical packet of street "heroin" is really heroin, the rest is composed of a variety of adulterants. Overdose occurs when the addict purchases a packet that contains substantially more heroin. If heroin were legally available, both its dose and its purity would be standardized and it would be much safer for users. Similarly the spread of hepatitis, and more recently AIDS, among heroin users occurs because the addicts share syringes. The high cost of illicit heroin leaves no money to spend on such niceties as individual needles. Again, if heroin were legalized it would be available at substantially lower cost, and the distribution of clean syringes among addicts would be easily done.

It is clear that Canadians, like Americans, do not know what to do about illicit drug use. There are many valid and reasonable arguments that can be presented in favour of de-criminalizing such use. There are also many valid and reasonable arguments that can be made in favour of making a more intense effort to enforce the laws. Since there is no real agreement, policy on drug use will likely remain the same.

Becoming a Drug User: An Escape From Reality?

Only one of Merton's forms of adaptation, rebellion, is seen as developing an alternative set of values, goals and means. While innovators develop new means and ritualists transform means into goals, the retreatist gives up on all goals and means and escapes to the private realities of alcoholism, drug addiction and mental illness.

The first serious criticisms of this view of "retreatism" were developed by Alfred Lindesmith and Howard Becker. In his work on opium addiction, Lindesmith (1947) argued that addiction was not a form of escape but an organized way of life centred on the addict's attempt to avoid the pains of withdrawal. Lindesmith provided an interactionist account of addiction in order to separate and clarify a number of issues that are confounded in the literature on drug use. In this case, the assumption is that regular use is simultaneously an indication of *and* a cause of addiction. Lindesmith argues that addiction is not caused by regular use of the drug, but results from the consequences of trying to give it up. In effect, Lindesmith argues that it is the experience of withdrawal and the fear of repeating that experience that causes the users to define themselves as addicts and to organize their lives around the acquisition and use of the drug.

Howard Becker's (1963) research on marijuana use among jazz musicians was a more direct criticism of Merton. Becker showed that marijuana use among those he studied was not an escape from reality or from social obligations but a form of active participation in a particular social world, the subculture of the jazz musicians. Becker's discussion is presented in detail in Chapter Six.

One of the motives often expressed by drug users, especially during the 1960s and '70s, was not that of escaping from reality but finding some alternative or more authentic "reality" (Timothy Leary, quoted in Zijderveld, 1971: 109):

> My first psychedelic experience was triggered by 400 milligrams of mescaline sulfate. It did indeed induce a flight, but instead of fleeing

from reality, I flew more deeply into it. I had never before seen, touched, tasted, heard, smelled and felt so profound a personal unity and involvement with the concrete material world ... . My exponentially heightened awareness saw through the static, one-dimensional, ego-constructed, false front which is the consciousness-constructed reality of the everyday world. This was no evasive flight from but a deep probe into reality.

Clearly, Leary's reality is not Merton's, but that merely points out another flaw in the "escape from reality" explanation: reality is not some absolute, intrinsic form of experience. The reality that most of us share is socially constructed; different groups can have quite literally different realities. What is a fact of nature or a matter of course for one is a pathetic delusion for another. Unlike philosophers or physicists, sociologists are not concerned with any ultimate reality but with what is generally taken to be real in a society by most of the people most of the time. What *is* at issue is that what Merton called an escape from reality implies a consensual view and experience of the world that does not exist. Empirically and experientially, the world of the heroin addict is not the world of the philosopher or the physicist.

Who Are The Drug Users?

Who are the illicit drug users; which of them become addicts? Are they the "failures" of Merton's account or do they have a quite different set of social characteristics? In answering these questions it is important to stress that deviant drug use, either in the form of illicit drug use or licit drug abuse is so widespread throughout our society that there is really no "typical" drug user. How do we determine the prevalence of illicit drug use and drug abuse in Canadian society? Boyd (1988: 166) suggests that marijuana is the "key variable" in determining the pattern of illicit drug use in Canada. Not only is marijuana the most popular of these drugs, its sale or possession accounts for the lion's share of narcotics convictions. It has been variously estimated, for example, that somewhere between two and four million adult Canadians smoke marijuana at least once in the course of a year (Boyd, 1988; Stebbins, 1988). How many others make use of heroin, cocaine or other illegal drugs, or abuse restricted or controlled drugs is hard to estimate. Clearly, we are dealing with a very large number of people who make up a substantial portion of the Canadian adult population. Is it really likely that all of these are "failures" by some objective measure or standard? In addition, both those who use drugs and the drugs they use change over time. Neither attitudes towards specific drugs nor legislation on drugs remains constant. As these change, patterns of use change as well, but more slowly. People using opium prior to 1908 were doing so legally. The drug had come to be seen by them as an essential part of their lives. These addicts were unlikely to stop using the drug just because it was now illegal. With time, however, opium use did just about disappear. But cocaine use, which had also become rare by the 1950s, is now widespread. Fads and fashions abound among drug users as among any other groups. The use of opium and cocaine was fairly widespread in the nineteenth century. The use of LSD, which was the drug of choice among some segments of the population in the mid-1960s, is rather rare now.

Even if drug use does not necessarily indicate "failure," what of drug addiction? Are the heroin addict, the cocaine addict or the Demerol addict "failures?" Lindesmith and Gagnon (1964) have pointed out that some estimate that 50 percent of all crimes are committed by drug addicts seeking money to support their addictions. Obtaining a drug such as heroin is expensive and involves the typical "street" addict in a life of continuous crime. Crime is work, often hard work which requires a great deal of time, a high level of commitment, and a high degree of risk. If they were failures before, Lindesmith and Gagnon suggest, they cannot remain addicts unless they become successful as criminals. Why, then, do we have an image of the addict as a disorganized, enfeebled, weak-willed failure? Partly because our image of the addict is based on those who get caught, and those who get caught are, by definition, failures. It is the failures at deviance who enter into our statistics on deviance, and by relying on such data based on such a sample, it is understandable how one could come up with a view of the addict as a failure or a "double failure." But this is to judge addicts by standards other than their own.

Just as importantly, the street addict is but one of several different types of addicts, many of whom can be described as "failures" only by using highly personalized criteria for success. One well-known example is the high incidence of drug addiction among physicians (Winick, 1964). Occupationally, physicians have high status and are among the highest paid professionals in Canadian society. In terms of the conventional views of "success" used by Merton, they certainly qualify as among the most successful. Yet they have a high rate of alcoholism and drug addiction, particularly to Demerol (Akers, 1985). Why is this so, and if anomie is not the reason, then what is?

Well, anomie *could* be the reason even if we assume that there are several competing sets of values, goals and norms in our society, what we can call normative sets. The physicians' success in attaining one set of goals, such as financial success, may preclude them from attaining success at another set, such as selfless devotion to humanity. There would then be a disjunction among normative sets rather than within a common normative order. This explanation provides an unnecessarily complex account, however, and is a good example of stretching a stubborn theory until it seems to fit the facts. Despite the best efforts of those who do such stretching, however, theories tend to break long before they can spread out to fit in all uncomfortable facts.

An alternative is to make use of Becker's notion of "access" discussed in Chapter Six. The physician is in a unique position to obtain easily and cheaply, and then to safely use, drugs. Physicians have legal access to a wide variety of drugs, they are easily supplied with samples by pharmaceutical-company representatives, and they can write prescriptions—of which, depending on the drug, they need keep no record and for which they need account to no one. Morphine and heroin are available in hospitals for use with terminally ill patients. For a physician who wants to try a drug, access is rarely a problem, and with their pharmacological training they know what to expect and how to control their intake.

We have seen, then, that Merton's theory does not successfully account for drug use and drug addiction. Drug addicts are not asocialized failures seeking to escape from reality. They *cannot* be, because the set of activities necessary to maintain illicit drug use force the addict to become an active participant in organized social activities. Merton's theory does not reflect the empirical reality of drug use. It reflects his values, his opinions, his assumptions and his biases. Understanding deviance requires that we understand behaviour in its social context, not from our own points of view.

The functionalists made a number of significant advances in the sociological understanding of deviance. By highlighting the ironic dependence of deviance upon conformity, and vice versa, they contributed to freeing sociology from its moralism and from taking for granted the pathology of the deviant. Following Durkheim's example, they tried to look beyond the obvious in order to account for deviance. They tried to uncover the structural conditions that give rise to deviance, that turn ordinary persons towards deviant acts. That they failed in much of what they sought to do is no real criticism; it must be understood in the context of when they were doing their work, what assumptions they were making, and what materials they had to work with. If the functionalists achieved much less than they hoped, they achieved much more than they are usually credited with.

NOTES

1. In 1975, for example, there were 61 million prescriptions written by doctors for Valium in the United States alone (Hills, 1980).

CHAPTER

5 Chicago Sociology, Differential Association And Delinquent Subcultures

SOCIAL DISORGANIZATION THEORY AND THE RISE OF CHICAGO SOCIOLOGY

In Chapter One we noted the prevalence of the social pathology perspective as an explanation of deviance in the United States and Canada at the turn of the century. This perspective had a strong affinity with the moralistic, small-town, middle-class background of the sociologists of that era. The first major change in this pattern within American sociology occurred in the sociology department at the University of Chicago. Here, too, the sociologists came from the same sort of small-town, middle-class background as elsewhere. But Chicago was not a small college town. Instead, Chicago, with its rapid growth, largely immigrant population and high crime rate seemed the very paradigm of the bustling urban metropolis whose problems were besetting America. The sociologists at the University of Chicago went beyond the ideological moralizing of the social pathologists to develop what has come to be called the *social disorganization* approach. Canadian sociologists trained at the University of Chicago later carried this perspective into Canadian sociology (Shore, 1987).

Founded in 1892, the University of Chicago was the first important university in the United States to be located within a major city. The sociologists at the University of Chicago, as reform-minded as the social pathologists, were unable to retain their distance from the deviance they claimed to analyse. As they became acquainted with the city and began to learn its ins and outs, they became fascinated by its ethnic, cultural, occupational, class and "normative" diversity. To these sociologists, the city became a kind of "laboratory"(Coser, 1978: 312) for the study of a whole range of social groups and social behaviours.

One early indication of a new approach to the study of deviance can be found in the work of W. I. Thomas. In his study of Polish immigrants to the United States and their adjustment to the new land, Thomas was struck by the fact that many of the immigrants who became "deviant" in the new world had been well-behaved, integrated members of their own society in Poland. Here a constitutional explanation was of no value, for the *same* person was deviant in one setting but not in another.

In his determination to uncover the source of this mystery, Thomas showed yet another significant difference from the social pathologists, who remained, for the most part, within the confines of the academic world. Thomas travelled several times to Poland, to see for himself what life had been like for the immigrants prior to arrival in America and to get background information about his subjects. He also began to collaborate with a Polish sociologist, Florian Znaniecki, whose participation did much to free the subsequent research of its American parochialism. Their publication, *The Polish Peasant in Europe and America* (1918), was the first systematic presentation of the social disorganization model to be adopted by the sociologists at the University of Chicago.

Thomas and Znaniecki (Thomas, 1966: 4) define social disorganization as "a decrease of the influence of existing social rules of behavior upon individual members of the group." Since it is the group and not the individuals who determine the level of social disorganization, they claimed, (Thomas, 1966: 5) "it is impossible to conclude from social as to individual organization or disorganization, or vice versa. In other words, social organization is not coextensive with individual morality, nor does social disorganization correspond to individual demoralization." Put even more simply, one cannot explain either social organization or disorganization on the basis of individual characteristics such as character, temperament, personality or constitution.

At first glance, Thomas's approach seems to agree with that of the social pathologists: traditional rural communities were free of the sort and quantity of deviance we are seeing now as a consequence of the breakdown of society. Thomas, however does not claim that rural society was held together by traditional values but by the effective group "repression" of individual "wishes" (Thomas, 1967). Such repression worked because it was enforced by significant groups, everyone was used to it, and everyone was more or less equally repressed. As for deviance in urban society, his description of this breakdown as "individualization" and "disorganization" rather than pathology shows his rejection of the simple-minded equation of anything different with deviance.

The point is made most forcefully in *The Unadjusted Girl*, originally published in 1923. Here, Thomas emphasizes that people do not come to engage in deviant acts because traditional values have broken down, but because of the plurality of values in modern society. People with different backgrounds, different education, different "universes of discourse" (Thomas, 1967: 78), are unable to agree on values. The result is that individuals, having no clear guidelines on how to behave, are able to act on their individual desires and "wishes" without reference to the needs of the group.

More importantly, Thomas does not simply dismiss social disorganization as a "social ill" and see changes to America's rural traditions as "bad." Thomas emphasizes that change leads as well to *social reorganization*. Because he actually went out and got to know these new immigrants, because he was aware of how they engaged in reconstructing their lives and creating new institutions, Thomas asserted that social disorganization is invariably complemented by social reorganization. Rather than breaking down, American society is being rebuilt into a fundamentally new society. To Thomas, the reform of deviance will not come about through "moral or religious preaching" but by creating "an organization and division of labour based on occupational interest [instead of the] demands of economic productivity" (Thomas, 1967: 257).

The other major figure in the development of the Chicago School of sociology was Robert E. Park. Even more than Thomas, Park was not a typical American sociologist of the era. He had been a journalist in several large cities, including New York, before studying philosophy and sociology in Germany. As a consequence of his cosmopolitan and journalistic background, Park saw sociology as an active research enterprise in which the sociologist goes out to study "what is actually going on rather than what, on the surface of things, merely seems to be going on" (Park, 1950: ix). Like Thomas, Park insisted that first-hand research must be the basis for sociological analysis, and, with the whole city of Chicago available to them, Park saw to it that there was no lack of opportunities for research on the part of his students.

Park saw the sociologist as a sort of "super-reporter." He was far less interested in answering questions related to "why" than to questions of "what" and "how." He was less concerned to know why young boys engaged in delinquent acts or women became prostitutes than in describing the life of a delinquent or of a prostitute. The result was that ethnographic field research emerged as the favoured research method at the University of Chicago. Such ethnography generates detailed descriptions of the ways of life of some group of people, gained by participating with them (to some more limited degree) in that life, by asking them questions, and by observing their actions. Park had little interest in developing theoretical generalizations based on this research. His students were to go out and record the details of life in Chicago, not engage in speculation about what it signified.

The Ecological Model

Despite this atheoretical orientation, or perhaps because of it, Park became an enthusiastic adherent of the "ecological model," a theoretical model of social organization developed at the University of Chicago by R. D. McKenzie and Ernest W. Burgess as an account of social change. The ecological model attempted to account for an apparent "fact" of American society taken for granted by all the early sociologists: the dramatic differences between the big urban centres and the small rural communities. The social pathologists had assumed that immigration *per se* had been largely responsible, i.e., that life in the big cities was a result of immigration and reflected a breakdown in traditional American morals and values. But as W. I. Thomas had shown, the life the immigrants forged for themselves in the United States was as different from the culture and values found in their "homelands" as it was from those of conventional Americans. The ecological model developed when this difference came to be explained as an "adaptation" to the city itself.

The Chicago ecologists continued the pattern, characteristic of the social pathologists and the functionalists, of borrowing biological metaphors to account for social phenomena. While the Chicago ecologists rejected the comparison to an organism, they looked to the social and institutional environment to explain social change much as the biologists looked to the natural environment to explain evolutionary change. The ecologists assumed that the structural environment of an urban region was divided into "natural areas" or "zones" characterizing a particular spatial distribution of people, type of residence, economic activity and degree of social disorganization. As shown in Figure 5.1, when applied to Chicago, this model assumes the existence of five zones which form a series of concentric circles. The innermost area, Zone I, is the core area of centralized economic activity and services, often referred to as a "central business district." Newly arrived immigrants, prostitutes, transients and other "criminal" elements are found in Zone II, the zone of transition or "interstitial" zone. These are pockets of social "disorganization" wedged between the central business district and the next ring of working-class houses and factories. In the interstitial areas the most recent immigrants find cheap, overcrowded housing. It is here also that the social failures, the misfits and the least successful remnants of earlier immigrant groups reside. Newly arrived immigrants lack authority over their offspring because they cannot provide

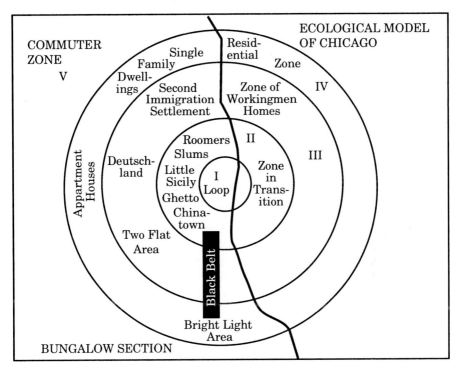

FIGURE 5.1 **The Ecological Model, adapted from R.E. Park and E. W. Burgess (1925),** *The City.* **Chicago: University of Chicago Press.**

useful knowledge to their children. These new immigrants work at the lowest-paid jobs, and both parents as well as other adults in the family work, so that the younger children are left to their own devices.

The third zone contains the homes of the established working class and those first- or second-generation immigrants who have succeeded in escaping from the slums. As they further improve their socio-economic status, people continue to move further away from the inner city and its crime towards the residential, single-family homes of the middle-class or the suburban, commuter zone of the wealthy.

This model was supposed to account for the changing social characteristics, particularly ethnic characteristics, of criminals and other deviants. It had been noticed that, as time passed, the ethnic characteristics of the "criminal elements" underwent regular change. For example, organized crime in Chicago at the turn of the century had been dominated by Irish criminals. By the 1920s, most of the Irish had become respectable middle-class citizens, and it was members of the newly arrived Italian immigrant groups, such as the underworld "kingpin" Al Capone, who seemed to have become the new leaders of the criminal elements.

The ecological model explained this sequence of changes by tying deviance to location rather than person. The new immigrants, likely law-abiding, respectable members of their original society, arrive impoverished in the new land. Because of this poverty, they are forced to live in Zone II, the area in which criminal activity flourishes. Some of these new arrivals quickly fill the criminal vacancies made available to them, just as others fill the more legitimate; in a condition of social disorganization, no strong norms or values prevent them from doing so. As they progress economically they move away from these neighbourhoods and *are removed from the location of crime and criminal activities.* Now they aspire to the respectability of their new neighbours and come to take on the norms and values of their adopted home. They begin the process of becoming conventional Americans. In the meantime, a new wave of immigrants has arrived to take their place in the criminal life of the city. In effect, the personal disorganization of the immigrants, fostered by the social disorganization of the city, is essential to their reorganization as Americans.

The ecological approach to the study of juvenile delinquency is typical of the ecological approach. Shaw and McKay (1931) used police arrest and court records to show that rates of juvenile delinquency were different in different areas of Chicago, and that these differences were stable over three decades despite the succession of different immigrant groups who had moved through the different areas as they assimilated and moved up the status ladder. Rates of juvenile delinquency were lowest in upper- and middle-class residential areas, higher in working-class areas, and highest in the inner-city "zones of transition" where the most recent immigrants found cheap housing and lived side by side with misfits, social failures and outcasts deposited by earlier immigrant groups.

Shaw and McKay explained their findings by arguing that "in the areas of low rates of delinquents there is more or less uniformity, consistency, and universality of conventional values and attitudes with respect to child care, conformity to law, and related matters; whereas in the high-rate areas systems of competing and conflicting moral values have developed." In effect, this was a combination of ecological factors with W. I. Thomas's social disorganization theory of competing standards.

Another early Chicago sociologist presented a more elaborate analysis of the development of youth gangs, still using the ecological approach. Frederick Thrasher was concerned with explaining the origins and evolution of youth gangs rather than developing a general theory of criminality. His work, *The Gang*, published in 1927, was a detailed ethnography, based on contacts with and observations of 1313 youth gangs in Chicago. Like Sutherland, he explained the development of urban youth gangs as, initially, the result of the ecological characteristics of the areas in which they flourish, i.e., the interstitial zones. Thrasher then argued that immigrant youngsters are at first merely inquisitive and adventurous, and that they do not differ from anyone else of the same age. However, the crowded inner-city streets offer many enticements to mischief, vandalism and petty theft. As well, the interstitial zones are not ethnically homogeneous, so that several youth gangs in the area will compete for space, resources and reputation. In the course of roaming the streets they find "many attractive and exciting opportunities for fun and adventure" (Bordua, 1961: 122), mischievous and illegal acts which will arouse responses from adults. As parents, teachers, merchants, police and clergymen denounce and try to reform the errant youth, some individuals and gangs gain a reputation for mischief and mayhem. These individuals and groups begin to coalesce and the play-group nature of the earlier gangs begins to harden into more serious delinquent activity, with an escalation of violent conflicts between them. In turn, these tougher gangs arouse harsher responses from the authorities, and the gangs evolve further, more organized patterns of actions, values and illegal techniques for self support and survival. These processes lead to a further "winnowing out" of gang members until only the most hardened remain, moving towards adulthood as self-identified criminals.

Thrasher's theory of the development of youth gangs was a complex one. It consisted of three major elements: i) the ecological characteristics of interstitial zones, which provide rich opportunities and attractions for acts of theft, mischief and vandalism; ii) the evolution of neighbourhood gangs of children from play groups to criminal gangs; and iii) the importance of authority figures and agents of social control in "pushing" this evolution towards a criminal outcome. Later subcultural writers have tended to lose this sense of complexity and instead emphasize one particular aspect over the others in their explanations of youth gang subcultures.

Thrasher's interpretation combined several levels of analysis: the social ecology of cities; the migration dynamics of multicultural settlement and pluralistic assimilation; a theory of childhood growth; and a theory of career contingencies related to the interaction between the play group and agents of social control. In place of this multidimensional theory, later research tended to focus on a narrower range of phenomena such as status deprivation (Cohen, 1955), access to illegitimate opportunities (Cloward and Ohlin, 1960), and a stable lower-class culture (Miller, 1958). In addition, the failure to treat Thrasher's work as the foundation for interpreting youth gang delinquency missed an opportunity to understand youth gangs in a more historically sensitive way.

How well did the ecological model mesh with the ethnographic strategy of Park and his students? In truth, they hardly meshed at all. The ecological model took no account of the individuals caught up in a life of deviance. It never considered their motivation for engaging in deviant behaviour or what this behaviour meant to them. The ethnographic method, for its part, was a research strategy which provided no explanation of any kind for the deviance it described, other than vague references to social disorganization. Ethnographic reports paid lip service to the ecological model, not by making use of ecological explanations, but by providing maps and other demographic data to locate the deviance spatially. Then they would move on to straight description.

The ecological model in the form promoted by Park, Burgess and McKenzie asserted a sort of structural determinism which reflected neither the historical reality of social change in North America, nor the more profound social processes underlying the superficial changes upon which they focused. And superficial these were. Like the social pathologists, the sort of crime and deviance the Chicago School sought to explain was the obvious deviance of the poor. They simply ignored the presence of crime or other forms of deviance elsewhere in society, and did not consider what the implications for their theory would be if they found that many of the clients of the Zone II prostitutes were men from Zone III or IV.

Yet the work of the Chicago School was very important in the development of sociology, particularly the sociology of deviance. While they were unable to generate an adequate theory of deviance, their ethnographic research provided a wealth of material which described deviance as it was "really going on." This material and the ethnographic tradition itself were important in the later development of the sociology of deviance. In addition, the Chicago School made major strides in freeing sociology from the moralistic and constitutional assumptions of the nineteenth century, in order to hold a more positive and open view towards social change. Rather than view their approach as a failure, we should see it as a first draft which was to be rewritten by many others in different forms.

DIFFERENTIAL ASSOCIATION

Although social disorganization theory attempted to account for deviance by pointing towards social processes, it had no coherent theory to account for the deviants themselves. Both Thomas and Park saw deviants as individualistic, able to act out their impulses once the constraining force of society is diminished. What they were unable to explain is why many other people in exactly the same circumstances do not become deviant, or why different people engage in different deviant acts. Even if, as Thomas claimed, there is no necessary link between *social* disorganization and *personal* disorganization, nevertheless he describes the "unadjusted girl" as "demoralized" as a consequence of social disorganization. Similarly, Park's ecological determinism assumes a one-sided, structural cause for deviance. In this respect, the view both held of deviance was not comprehensive.

A major step towards developing a more systematic view of deviance, i.e., one in which both structural and individual factors are considered, was the differential association theory of Edwin H. Sutherland. Sutherland was among the first to develop an approach to deviance that took into account a particularly significant finding on the part of many of the researchers at the Chicago School: deviants are not socially isolated and individuated persons bereft of norms, values or social institutions. Instead, deviants are usually members of groups—subcultures, in effect—which have their own norms and values, and often have their own forms of social organization. This had been shown in one of the first ethnographic studies published at the University of Chicago, the study of *The Hobo* by Nels Anderson (1923), yet the implications of findings of this sort were typically ignored by the Chicago School, which saw such social organization as, at best, an adaptation to social disorganization. A temporary way-station, as it were, on the road to Americanization, passed through by many immigrant and marginal groups.

In contrast, Sutherland tried to uncover the processes by which people actually came to be involved in deviant activities. His theory was an attempt to develop a comprehensive explanation of criminal behaviour, rather than to explain youth and youth gang delinquency alone. He argued that criminal behaviour is learned through interaction which exposes individuals to varying degrees of conformity and criminality. Sutherland developed this theory to explain how patterns of criminal activity (as recorded by police reports and arrests) fitted the ecological model of the city and the evolution of immigrant experience in America. Arrest rates and reports of crime seemed to be highest in the zones of transition and remained so whichever group of immigrants began their settlement there. Each new group had to look for new ways to survive in the host society. Most people learned conventional ways of earning a living and keeping their families together; a few could do neither. The latter were forced or were attracted to unconventional or illegal means of survival. In this they learned new lifeways from existing criminal groups. For Sutherland, then, criminal subcultures existed prior to the immigrant groups crowding into inner city areas. The ultimate origin of such subcultures was of historical interest perhaps, but was not an issue for sociological investigation.

Sutherland argued that the social structure of zones of transition provided many opportunities for extensive interaction with ongoing criminal subcultures, from youth gangs engaged in sporadic petty theft, to adult criminal groups engaged in extortion, burglary and gambling rackets. He argued that extensive interaction with ongoing criminal groups will lead to internalization of the values, attitudes, motivations and techniques of criminal subcultures. This "differential association" is the key process whereby those more exposed to and in close contact with criminal groups will become increasingly involved in and increasingly committed to criminal activity and a "life of crime."

In all social milieux there are a variety of values, role models, accepted inclinations, commitments, techniques and resources. Social regions will differ in the content and the balance between conformity and criminality. Individuals will differ too, in the exposure they will experience to these forces.

Thus for Sutherland (Sutherland and Cressey, 1955: 74), "when persons become criminals, they do so because of contacts with criminal behaviour patterns and also because of isolation from anti-criminal patterns." Higher rates of juvenile delinquency occur in inner-city areas because this is a region of cultural conflict, where there exists a multicultural potpourri of new immigrants, not yet fully conforming or assimilated to the host society, and alternative, deviant subcultures which flourish in the interstitial zones because of the weakness of local agencies of social control. In these regions of the city, then, many subcultures compete for the allegiance of youth.

Sutherland's insistence that deviant behaviour is learned, that it is learned from others, and that this learning includes the learning of subcultural norms, deviant techniques, motives for deviance and attitudes towards conventional society, set the stage for the later development of subcultural theories. As Bordua (1961: 120) remarked:

> the group nature of delinquency ... [is] a process whereby the individual becomes associated with a group which devotes some or all of its time to planning, committing, or celebrating delinquencies and which has elaborated a set of lifeways—a subculture—which encourages and justifies [such] behaviour.

Ultimately, this recognition of the significance of the many subcultures found in any society led to a repudiation of moral or normative consensus as a characteristic of American society. The result was a new concern with understanding what the deviant behaviour means to the individuals involved, and a new, more pluralistic view of society.

However, differential association theory raises more questions than it provides answers. Sutherland's theory is ambiguous on several important points. It is not clear whether association operates directly in moulding values and behaviour, or operates indirectly, alone, or in conjunction with other factors, and what the factors might be. Do you associate with deviants because you share their values? Do you associate because your family is partly or wholly connected with and/or supportive of the subculture? Are you attracted by deviant role models, or by the skills, the rewards or the excitements and risks of deviance? Is differential association a special social process, limited to the reproduction of deviant or stigmatized activities, or is it a general socialization process applicable to all role learning? Are differential association processes different in different areas of deviance? Despite its being a widely accepted explanation, there is surprisingly little investigation of these issues. Suffice it to say here that later use of differential association theory by subcultural theorists does not do much to clarify the ways youths are drawn into gangs, and what happens to them as they continue to associate with various types of gangs.

SUBCULTURAL THEORIES

By the 1950s, neither the dominant functionalist approach of Davis or Merton nor the ecological-social disorganization approach of the Chicago School seemed able to deal effectively with the changes occurring in post-World War II society or with the new forms of deviance that were emerging. During this era the phenomenon of big-city adolescent gangs was identified as a social problem in many industrialized societies. These gangs were identified by distinctive patterns of dress, popular musical taste and disapproved behaviour such as "vandalism" and "rowdyism." The recognition of this social problem was reflected in the rise of new words or the adaptation of existing words to label delinquent youth gangs and their unconventionality; words such as "teddy boy" in the UK, "bodgies" and "widgies" in Australia, *stilyagi* in the USSR, *halbstarke* in Germany, *blousons noires* in France, and *mambo* in Japan. These labels denoted groups of youth who, at best, were rowdy, insolent and outrageously dressed and, at worst, were predisposed to crime and violence. In the United States it was the latter aspect that attracted the attention of both the mass media and social researchers. Here the stereotypical youth gangs were the "fighting gangs" of New York, romanticized in the musical *West Side Story*.

A romantic view of youthful deviance is more the exception than the rule, however. Indeed, British sociologist Stanley Cohen (1972) has argued that youth have more often been cast in the role of "folk devils." A "folk devil" is an ideological construct, the common-sense embodiment of all that is wrong in society, the carrier of all evil, immorality and social disorder. The Hell's Angels motorcycle gang was assigned such an ideological role by the American public, and especially the media, during the late 1960s, as were the "Mods" and the "Rockers" in Britain

(Cohen, 1972). In this sense the rebelliousness and cultural distinctiveness of youth is taken as a sign of a fundamental challenge to social order and to established institutions.

This reaction to youthful behaviour reflected large-scale social, economic and political changes in all industrial societies after the Second World War (Taylor, 1982). Postwar reconstruction led to a long period of economic growth and prosperity, which involved extensive urbanization and the rise of mass consumption on an unprecedented scale. The postwar "baby boom" forced governments and private agencies to extend educational and social welfare agencies (Tanner, 1988). In addition, the increasing technical complexity of industry and the rise of ever larger government and business bureaucracies required a more educated labour force. Longer periods of compulsory schooling prolonged the dependent status of adolescents, and emphasized the importance of educational performance as a foundation for successful adult careers. In this context large numbers of children and youth had to be coped with by families, schools, social welfare and social control agencies, and labour markets. However, these various institutions were themselves changing. Urbanization led to the growth of suburbs and highway development, which swallowed or broke up smaller neighbourhoods and replaced them with uniform row-house tracts or high-rises. Social work and social control agencies moved from repressive and custodial styles of operation to a more liberal, therapeutic and reforming style. Schools became larger and more bureaucratic and took in a more heterogeneous group of students. Labour markets shifted away from informal, interpersonal recruitment practices to recruitment based on formal educational and training qualifications (Wilensky and Lebeaux, 1958).

Many journalists, social work professionals and social scientists pointed to these changes as contributing to the emergence of a distinct "youth culture," visible to adults by distinctive clothing and other items of material consumption. These observers also claimed to discover in the younger generation a set of values which, in various ways, were at odds with those of adult society (Coleman, 1961). In both Europe and North America, these new youth groups were associated with various deprivations associated with working-class life. In the United States, sociological explanations for the emergence and characteristics of youth subculture focused on clearly delinquent and violent behaviour. In Europe they focused more on "style deviance," that is, the forms of consumption specific to youth gangs such as their peculiar clothes, raucous music and affection for motorcycles.

As sociologists tried to come to grips with the new "subcultures" that had emerged, they combined elements taken from Merton's anomie theory, Thrasher's research on gangs and Sutherland's notion of differential association. The resulting mixture had numerous theoretical weaknesses, but the real significance of subcultural theories lies less in the details of their analyses, many of which are dated today, than in their change of focus. As Downes and Rock (1988: 137) note, these theories moved away from a view of deviant subcultures as posing a social problem towards seeing them as a way in which individuals had found a "solution ... to the dilemmas that they faced."

ANOMIE THEORY AND YOUTH GANGS

As we saw in Chapter Four, Robert Merton developed a functionalist theory of deviance which focused on the anomic pressures imposed on certain class and ethnic groups. Anomie theory assumes a coherent and dominant set of values and norms, centring on the the goal of individual economic success, which is uniformly internalized by all groups in society. However, the conditions for successfully living up to these values and conforming to norms are not uniformly distributed. This discrepancy produces various strains and pressures leading to deviant behaviour. Various kinds of adaptations to anomie were possible, Merton argued, to bring goals and means in line. For example, an individual could attempt to use criminal means to obtain economic success, i.e., "innovation," or could "drop out" and become a "retreatist" drug addict.

Combining Merton's analysis of anomie with Sutherland's emphasis on differential association, Albert K. Cohen (1955) and other sociologists developed a subcultural interpretation of juvenile delinquency and youth gangs. There were significant differences between Merton and Sutherland in their perspectives on deviance, particularly in their perceptions of the structural sources of deviance identified (unequal distribution of institutional means among social classes for Merton, ecological zones for Sutherland) and the assumptions they made about the role of culture (normative consensus for Merton, culture conflict for Sutherland). Similarly, while Merton tried to identify the social groups that are more likely to experience anomie, he saw deviance as an individual adaptation to anomie; Sutherland emphasized the social organization of deviant groups and the identification and learning required for individuals to become part of the group. Yet, despite these differences, it is quite possible to combine Merton's notions of normative consensus and anomie with Sutherland's notion of ecological distribution and differential association.

In its simplest form, such a combination would run as follows: While all Americans share broad common values and goals directed towards success, some individuals are disadvantaged by having less access to the legitimate means needed to achieve success and are therefore less likely to be successful. If these individuals live in areas where there are groups—such as delinquent gangs—making use of alternative, non-legitimate means of achieving success, disadvantaged individuals will seek access to these groups. They will then be taught the knowledge, skills and values necessary to participate in these groups.

Albert K. Cohen

Cohen's theory of subculture was more sophisticated than this, however. While Cohen accepted the idea of broad consensus of primary cultural values and goals, he recognized the existence of subcultures as groups whose values or goals differ in important respects from those of the mainstream society. In other words, the subcultures of lower-class groups already differ from those of the mainstream culture, making socialization to conformity less likely. In addition, a marked feature of Cohen's interpretation is his view that youth gang delinquency is not a rational act but an emotional one. That is, the subcultural response to the failure of living up to middle-class values fulfils basic emotional needs such as protecting or enhancing self-esteem. Delinquent subculture, then, is a "reaction formation," a cathartic response to the shame and guilt experienced at school.

Cohen viewed social classes primarily as "a set of more or less vertically layered cultural settings." He argued that socialization in lower- and working-class families resulted in a lack of preparation in the educational and interpersonal skills required to function in white-collar, technical and professional jobs characteristically held by middle- and upper-class people. Although lower-class and working-class people share the central values promoting individual striving for economic success, these are more weakly held and overshadowed by other features of blue-collar and lower-class subcultures, such as a short-term, "enjoy-it-now" attitude towards consumption and leisure which de-emphasizes thrift and postponement of gratification for long-term gains; strong loyalties to immediate family and friends, but less concern for abstract principles of morality; a relatively deprived childhood where there is a lack of the stimulating toys, games and books used by middle- and upper-class families to train their children early in the values of orderly behaviour, neatness, punctuality and so on. Finally, the lower- and working-classes use more physical aggression in bringing up their children, and tend to value physical aggression, at least in male offspring, as a problem-solving technique, whereas other classes use reasoning and positive reinforcement based on moral principles of behaviour control. Cohen takes the "value strain" or anomic condition of these youths for granted and explores the largely psychological mechanisms that turn this value strain into a subculture-sustaining deviance.

Crucial to this process, argued Cohen, is the education system. Lower- and working-class youth encounter a school system that is run by middle-class teachers operating through the dominant value system. Working-class boys often fail to adjust their behaviour and attitudes, and are judged as lacking the essential characteristics required for academic and career success. Since working-class pupils do not measure up to middle-class expectations, they arouse disapproval, rejection and punishment, which undermines their self-esteem. These experiences are a variant of anomie in that these youths are exposed simultaneously to the values and criteria associated with approved models of social mobility, and to their own lack of preparation for the pursuit of such mobility.

This anomie (in this case, the lack of fit between the subculture and the dominant culture) and status frustration arouse what Cohen terms a "reaction formation." This means that the self-perception of working-class youth is "under attack" as they are measured by middle-class standards of performance at school. This results in intense feelings of shame and guilt. The psychological response to these feelings takes the form of an elaborate defence against the dominant value system. This defence consists of a set of alternative values and norms to rationalize, account for or justify a lack of conventional success. In the course of becoming labelled "discipline problems" or academic "underachievers," several previously isolated boys come together, discover their common predicament and, using subcultural resources, develop an alternate social milieu in the form of a gang. Mutual discovery and increased interaction within lower-class youth establishes a deviant organization which recruits similarly rejected youth. Sustained involvement in gangs reinforces the deviant identity of their membership and the emotional solidarity of the gang and its cultural system. In the longer term, gang involvement may lead to deviant careers and contacts with criminal subcultures.

While Cohen followed Thrasher to a degree in arguing that different classes hold different values and norms, he diverged considerably in his portrait of the gang as shaped by the emotional reaction of lower- and working-class youth to their school experiences. It is the deeply emotional responses to their inadequacies at school that account for the irrational, malicious and non-utilitarian nature of gang delinquency—vandalism, gang fights, theft of unusable objects.

Cohen's work was extensively criticized on both theoretical and empirical grounds. His approach was a functionalist one in which social stability depends upon the internalization of norms and values which generate identical motives, identities and behaviour patterns (Wrong, 1961; Kitsuse and Dietrick, 1964). Despite his recognition of subcultural differences, Cohen in fact underplays the ideas of differential association, which might explain differences among individuals and subgroups. He also loses Thrasher's insight that the sense of being outsiders, of sharing a common fate, is the result of a complex process of interaction between gangs as they are developing, and the responses of various adults who label, catch, stigmatize and punish delinquent youths (Bordua, 1961).

Another criticism of Cohen's functionalist approach is his failure to recognize that there exist several distinct subcultures even among lower- and working-class youth in large cities (Wilensky and Lebeaux, 1958; Rosenberg and Silverstein, 1969).

In response to this criticism, Cohen and Short (1958) distinguished four types of deviant subculture: parent-male, conflict-oriented, drug addict, and semi-professional theft. In addition, these writers identify a subculture produced by short-lived adolescent rebellion among middle-class youths. The parent-male type is considered the most common, and one that forms the foundation or core of the other lower-class deviant subcultures. Parent-male subculture is associated with the early phase of gang development and is characterized by non-utilitarian, malicious activities and negativistic attitudes and hedonistic values. The organization of these types of gangs is volatile and unstable. Conflict-oriented subcultures evolve out of the parent-male type, to form a larger group focused on defence of turf and reputation. Drug-addict subcultures and semi-professional theft gangs are each quite distinct subcultures. Again, the origins of these subcultures and the reasons why inner-city youths are drawn to one rather than another are not analysed. The possible relationships between these gang types, or the possibility that some people go through different types in the course of a career in deviance, are also unexplored issues.

Cloward and Ohlin

An alternative interpretation of delinquency as a response to anomie was developed by Cloward and Ohlin (1960), who saw delinquent acts as more deliberate and rational. For these writers, as for Cohen, delinquent subcultures invert conventional values and norms by viewing certain kinds of deviant acts as essential requirements for group participation and membership. The result is a subculture promoting frequent and diverse delinquent acts; which is stable and resistant to change; and which involves a binding system of rules and behaviour models. Cloward and Ohlin follow Cohen in arguing that delinquent subcultures originate in the disparity between what lower-class youth are led to want and what is actually available. Limitations on legitimate avenues of access to official goals produce intense frustration and exploration of unconventional alternatives. However, Cloward and Ohlin argue that Merton and Cohen erroneously assume that illegitimate alternatives for the pursuit of success are fully available in lower-class and working-class communities. On the contrary, Cloward and Ohlin argue that different types of illegal opportunities are available in different communities, and the types of juvenile gangs that evolve will depend on differences in illegal as well as legal opportunities structures. Thus, conflict and criminal gangs will emerge where criminal and violent means to economic success are accepted and practised. Retreatist gangs, primarily organized to fulfil needs related to drug addiction, will develop in those communities where there are neither legitimate nor illegitimate means for success. Criminal gangs emerge in stable lower-class neighbourhoods where organized crime is deeply rooted and can provide role models and apprenticeships for local youths. Conflict gangs grow out of "disorganized" neighbourhoods such as new residential areas or transitional zones with high concentrations of new immigrants, high mobility, transiency and instability, and with few cohesive, culturally integrated authority figures.

Cloward and Ohlin observed that there had been a decline in the stability and social organization of the American lower class because of the decline in local community political power, new housing developments, and a flight from the inner cities. However, this interesting suggestion is not developed to show how patterns of youth delinquency may be changing.

Walter B. Miller

Another type of subcultural explanation also rejected Cohen's irrational-emotional interpretation of youth gang delinquency. Walter B. Miller (1958) argued that a distinct lower-class subculture had evolved over the course of America's industrialization and assimilation of immigrants from Europe. He argued that in the larger American cities there has developed a consolidated community of workers in the least skilled and less well-paid jobs such as longshoremen, truck drivers, warehouse workers, gas station attendants and the like. Their wives are also workers in menial jobs such as waitresses, textile workers, shop clerks and machine operators in light industries. These people were descendants of very diverse ethnic groups who had not been particularly successful in climbing the ladder of success. The long-term result was a lower-class whose culture incorporated specific norms and values which could generate gang delinquency.

For Miller, lower-class subculture is organized through five major focal concerns or principles for evaluating social situations and the behaviour of others. Individuals are evaluated and evaluate themselves by the degree to which they get into or skillfully negotiate around trouble. These focal concerns are:

- *Toughness*: the physical strength and skills, bravery and traditional male role ideals.

- *Smartness*: the ability to manipulate people and things to maximum personal advantage with a minimum of visible, conventional effort.

- *Excitement*: the focus on the contrast between routine, especially work drudgery, and risky non-conventional pursuits, which may have high costs but will have high rewards in case of success.

- *Fate*: the perception that one's life is determined by forces over which one has no control.

- *Autonomy*: the amount and type of control one has over others, or the degree and type of control others hold over you. The last concern is an ambivalent one, for lower-class males may overtly reject domination while less overtly equating coercion with care.

For example, gambling is prominent in the lower class and is an activity that expresses many dimensions of these cultural concerns—fate, toughness, smartness, excitement and, if successful, the possibility of autonomy. Such norms and values provide satisfaction and reputation in response to activities that would be viewed as at least marginally disreputable if not outrightly deviant by middle- and upper-class individuals.

THE CRITIQUE OF ANOMIE THEORY

Like all varieties of functionalist thought, subcultural interpretations of youth gang delinquency have been predominantly theoretical discussions. Sociologists looked to Merton's structural functional model of anomie either as a theoretical foundation to be modified and applied to a postwar social problem or, as in Miller's case, as an approach to be criticized in favour of an alternative functionalist explanation of lower-class subculture. Differential association theory was adopted and modified as a way to incorporate cultural differences into a model based on the assumption of normative consensus.

Yet the majority of lower-class people are conformists, and the distress they may experience in the face of barriers to social mobility does not produce a uniformly deviant response across the disadvantaged population. Deviance remains the exception rather than the rule. Cohen, Cloward and Ohlin, and Miller all recognize this problem and try to develop a model that includes some "factor" in the subculture of lower-class groups that predisposes individuals towards delinquency;

conditions that lead to a psychological reaction formation for Cohen, a turning towards illegitimate means for Cloward and Ohlin, and the emergence of a subculture that promotes deviance for Miller. Nevertheless, these sociologists find themselves in a dilemma. Because functionalism overemphasizes conformity, the need to argue that delinquency is simultaneously conformity to broad cultural goals and to subcultural norms requires constant modification and adjustment of the underlying functionalist paradigm. To account for the conformity as well as non-conformity (which is "really" a kind of conformity), and for different types of non-conformity, these sociologists turn to some variant of differential association theory.

Empirical research on youth gangs has not been supportive of the theoretical debates (Miller, 1974). Such research has questioned the assumption that delinquent gangs show high levels of organizational coherence and specialization in types of deviant behaviour such as conflict, criminal, and retreatist or addictive (Short and Strodtbeck, 1965). Gang organization has been found to be very loose, lacking clear rules and roles about appropriate behaviour in the gang milieu. Acts of deviance are also quite diffuse, episodic and unrationalized (Yablonsky, 1959). They appear to be largely a spontaneous response to immediate events in the environment rather than arising from fixed psychological formations or subcultural principles (Miller, 1974).

More generally, subcultural theory has been criticized for limiting its focus to violent or clearly delinquent youth gangs operating in metropolitan areas (Miller, 1974). This focus has had several consequences for the development of a theory of delinquent subcultures. First, sociologists of gang deviance tend to reflect the concerns of official agencies of social control and the mass media publicity associated with "moral panics" (Taylor, 1982). That is, subcultural theorizing has looked at youth gang phenomena that are already identified as social problems by the media and other societal agencies. This is reflected even in the sociological theories and concepts used to interpret gang delinquency. Thus the Chicago School in the 1920s emphasized immigration and economic competition between different ethnic groups as a major source of "social disorganization." Merton's essay on anomie emphasized the unequal distribution of opportunities, surely a reflection of the prominent features of the Great Depression. Cohen wrote during a period of concern about the changes in the postwar American family and character structure. Miller and Cloward and Ohlin wrote during the "rediscovery" of poverty in the late 1950s. Rather than working on problems and puzzles arising from inherited sociological analysis, sociologists of youth gang delinquency take their cues to defining problems and topics from social conventions themselves. Consequently, a focus on clearly deviant, big-city youth gangs omits analysis of middle-class and upper-class juvenile delinquency;

ignores female involvement in delinquent activities and groups; and overlooks juvenile delinquency in smaller towns, suburbs and rural areas. Further, by allowing "concerned citizens" and official agencies to define what is to be explained, sociologists may lose sight of the real strengths of accumulated sociological research, and also suffer from lack of historical understanding. That this is a failing of subcultural research on youth gangs and delinquency is suggested by Bordua (1961). He argues that Thrasher's work combined a massive body of data with "grounded theory" of considerable richness and sophistication. Subsequent developments in the field of subcultural theory developed without consistent grounding in ethnographic information, and also simplified the theoretical interpretation of youth gang phenomena.

The Decline of Subcultural Theories

Given the problems with subcultural theories, some sociologists have suggested alternative approaches for the analysis of "careers" in delinquency. Some return to Thrasher's view and argue that youth gangs only develop in a criminal direction because of the reactions of various social control agencies. That is, a clear sense of being outside of or in opposition to "straight society" or dominant values only emerges after gang members are caught, labelled and punished (see Chapter Six). This labelling cycle may have to be repeated several times before a firm deviant identity is produced.

In the 1960s, labelling theorists and ethnomethodologists began to question the reliance on official statistics as a guide to delinquency. Chambliss (1973) argued that delinquency is not a lower-class phenomenon at all; rather, it is lower-class boys who are most likely to get caught, stigmatized, and thereby locked into a career in deviance. Middle-class boys may engage in the same sorts of deviant behaviour, but they have more resources available to avoid getting caught, and, if they are caught, they are better at playing the game of contrition and regret to avoid being labelled as deviant (Piliavin and Briar, 1964). The recognition that delinquency may be more a consequence of differential labelling than of differential association was a key component in the development of the labelling perspective (Cicourel, 1968; Kitsuse and Cicourel, 1963).

Perhaps the most serious blow to the plausibility of subcultural theories on delinquency was landed by David Matza (1964). Matza effectively challenged the functionalist assumption of normative consensus within subcultural groups. His work marks a significant shift away from assumptions of distinct competing cultures into which individuals are simply socialized or to which they are directed by psychological mechanisms such as reaction formation. He also suggests that the development of a deviant identity is itself a more complex process than the model of social control as a labelling cycle suggests. Matza argues that conventional culture and society provide a range of subtle supports for deviance, while subcultures loosen or neutralize the moral hold of key elements of the parent culture. The mental combinations of these supports and neutralizers are diverse and complex, and emerge in very specific situations as useful resolutions of choices and dilemmas. Consequently, juvenile delinquency is not marked by a coherent, alternate value system, but results from a "drift" from the moral hold of generally accepted conventions, towards half-thought-out justifications and excuses for nonconformity.

This notion of "drift" helps overcome the serious weakness of subcultural theories noted earlier: so much emphasis is placed on showing the cultural and psychological supports for deviance that it becomes hard to explain why most lower-class boys do *not* become delinquents. The notion of "drift," in contrast, suggests that no special explanation of delinquency is needed at all; a boy becomes delinquent because of the particular circumstances and contingencies of his life. As Matza (1969) put it later, deviance is "natural"—as natural as conformity—and needs no special explanation.

While Matza's critique exposed the weaknesses of the subcultural approach, his alternative, that deviance is "natural," provides no answer at all to the crucial questions related to the nature of deviance and conformity. Matza's work illustrates the conceptual exhaustion of the subcultural perspective as it reached a dead end.

This dead end was not only conceptual but empirical. How could anomie theory, based on assumptions about the importance of personal and monetary success, explain the "Freedom Riders" who travelled at great personal risk to the southern United States to agitate for Black civil rights? How could differential association theory explain the convergence of tens of thousands of youthful anti-Vietnam-War protesters in Washington, DC? How could theories that assumed lower-class delinquency explain the participation of middle-class youth in countercultural movements that lauded hallucinogenic drug use, petty crimes such as shoplifting, and sexual "freedom"?

In the subcultural flowering of the 1960s, the concept of a dominant or mainstream culture, or of any sort of normative consensus, lost plausibility. Explaining subculture began to seem redundant, like explaining why some people like to jog, perform in amateur theatricals, collect stamps or eat tofu. Arguing that jogging is popular because of structural conditions, for example, would seem like theoretical overkill. The result, ironically, of this widespread explosion of cultural alternatives—a consequence of structural changes in American society—was a turn towards more individualistic explanations, the social psychological accounts of "emergent" identity found in the labelling perspective (Matza, 1969). This topic is taken up in Chapter Six.

Subculture as Style: British Perspectives on Youth Deviance

While subcultural theories went into sharp decline in the United States in the 1960s, they became the dominant approach to understanding youth deviance in Britain. This approach began, interestingly enough, in the study of education and the development of a research tradition on the relationship between education and class differences derived from the work of Basil Bernstein (1971; 1975) and the French sociologist Pierre Bourdieu (1977; Bourdieu and Passeron, 1977). The new subcultural theory views various cultural elements and traits displayed in the education process as symbolic manifestations of class relationships. Such cultural elements are, for example, what Bernstein calls "linguistic codes" or what Bourdieu describes as "cultural capital."

A linguistic code is a style of speech that reflects social structure. So, for example, Bernstein claims that the working-class child in Britain makes use of a "restricted" code of speech in which a few words stand for a great many objects and concepts. This makes the working-class child more dependent upon non-verbal cues and on sharing a set of common experiences with the listener than is true for the middle-class child. Working-class pupils therefore have literally less to say to a teacher than do middle-class students. As a consequence, they lack the linguistic resources to do as well in school. In effect, rather than mastering language, the working-class child is subordinate to it; a linguistic subordination that reflects and perpetuates the economic, political and social subordination of working-class life.

Cultural capital is a broader concept. It refers to sets of knowledge and interpersonal skills needed to do well in school, to interact comfortably with management in a work setting, and to act out a "comfortable," middle-class lifestyle. Examples would be (Tepperman and Rosenberg, 1991:55):

> knowing how to speak well and interestingly, what topics to discuss, how to order and eat graciously, what beverages to drink, how to dress stylishly but tastefully, how to play a variety of games and sports that others may want to play [e.g., tennis, sailing, bridge, chess, polo].

It also includes knowing enough about books, art and other elements of high culture to participate in "cultured" conversation. Such cultural capital is unavailable to working-class children because their parents neither possess it nor have the resources to obtain it, while middle-class children are often brought up to at least display the trappings of such knowledge and skills. This not only gives the middle-class child an advantage in school, it makes him or her more comfortable—more at home—in the cognitive and conceptual universe of the classroom.

Initially the study of education emphasized the *disadvantages* of working-class youths because it took the educationally successful middle-class student as its baseline. The focus soon shifted, however, as the study of working-class youth subculture uncovered not an absent but an *alternative* culture (Willis, 1977). Working-class subculture, especially in the form of youth deviance, came to be seen as a culture of resistance to the dominant political, educational, economic, social and cultural institutions from which the working class was excluded. The working-class subculture serves (Hebdige, 1979: 139) "to embellish, decorate, parody and wherever possible to recognize and rise above a subordinate position which was never of their choosing."

To Hebdige this resistance and embellishment, parody and decoration are manifest in youth "style." Style to Hebdige (1979: 3) is "a gesture of defiance or contempt ... a smile or a sneer ... [it] signals a Refusal." Hebdige focuses on the Punk movement in Britain to illustrate his thesis that lower-class youth subculture and style is a form of political resistance. As Tanner (1988: 342) sums up this argument:

> The Punk dress-code ... does not merely spurn conventional notions of fashion, it subverts it [sic] as well. It transforms inappropriate objects such as garbage bags, razor blades, safety pins into fashion. The overapplication of make-up by young women undermines orthodox notions of femininity, and hair dyed every conceivable color of the rainbow does not conform to the expectation of what a well-coiffed head should look like.

Rather than using Bernstein's "restricted linguistic code," the Punk seems to have transformed all of himself or herself—hair, body, clothes, expression, behaviour and music—into an elaborate code; one sending a loud and clear message that conventional society might well not wish to hear. As for cultural capital, by elevating the trivial and grotesque into fashion and style, the Punks mock and reject both the values and the content of high culture. The Punks thereby perpetuate a tradition of working-class youth deviance as political action. By rejecting the social institutions and values that subordinate them, they reject their assigned place in that society.

But is this what is really going on in youth subcultures? Hunter and Posner (1987: 97) suggest that—whatever it may be in Britain—Punk, at least in North America, is nothing but fashion; the borrowing of the image without any interest in the political message. Tanner (1988), also, suggests two major criticisms of Hebdige's argument. One is that if Punk subculture is a revolt, it is a revolt that "takes place in leisure and consumption rather than at school or work" (Tanner, 1988: 343). In effect, Punk and all of its visual and commercial trappings are commodities available—for sale—to anyone of any class, ethnic or cultural background. This means that in Canada, Punk is a lifestyle that is chosen by young people from a wide variety of backgrounds, is supported by established commercial interests, and is only one of many "styles" available to young people, who frequently move on from one to another of these subcultural styles. Support for this point can be found in Baron's (1989) ethnographic study of Canadian West Coast Punk. He found that this movement was largely classless both in membership and in ideology. The Punks come from various social classes; what they share is a common experience of disaffection and poor performance in school, as well as an attitude of rejection against the adult world. Their ideology is organized in terms of music and dress, rather than class and politics.

Tanner's (1988: 345) second point is that the majority of working-class youth *do not* become members of "expressive youth cultures." Since all working-class youth are subject to the same social, educational and economic conditions, why do different people respond to these conditions in different ways?

Subcultural explanations, Tanner suggests, divert attention from the more common forms of youth deviance, such as minor property crimes and drug- and alcohol-related offences. These forms of deviance are poorly planned, poorly executed, situational and episodic in nature, and "remarkably unworthy of the erudite explanations professed by subcultural theorists" (Tanner, 1988: 346).

While Tanner's critique of Hebdige certainly reflects the Canadian case, it underplays the fact that the political role of Punk is not the product of sociological speculation but a self-proclaimed goal of the Punk "movement." Unfortunately, many of the expressions of that political role, in particular the racism, anti-Semitism and homophobia publicly proclaimed by some of the Punks, are hardly to be commended. Nor is the violence that they often interpret as the enactment of that role.

Finally, if youth deviance is resistance, what are we to make of self-report studies that find that "almost all youngsters commit delinquencies every year" (West, 1984: 87). If deviance is as characteristic of young people as the data suggests, why single out the actions of some young people as resistance and ignore the rest?

Views on Youth Deviance in Canada

In Canada, the study of delinquency and of other forms of youth deviance has gone in a different direction from those found in either the United States or Britain. Unlike the American focus on social psychological, individualistic explanations of participation in deviance, Canadian sociologists and criminologists have tended to look to the structural context within which youth deviance is generated (West,

1984), especially the role of the state. At the same time, the role of the state is not seen as limited only to the reproduction of *class* differences as is the case in Britain.

Why these differences in focus? We already mentioned the greater relevance assigned to the state in Canadian criminology (Chapter One), an outcome of the very direct role and intervention of the state in Canadian society (Panitch, 1977; Friedenberg, 1983). It may be as well that youth pose less of a social problem in Canadian society and are less likely to be seen as "folk devils." In both the United States and in Britain youth social movements, as we have seen, have not only been "cultural" but have also been linked to political or parapolitical action; for example, the Civil Rights and anti-Vietnam-War movements in the United States and the political expression of the Punk movement in Britain. Such political expressions of youth rebellion have generally been lacking in Canada. This is not to say that young people have not been politically active and politically aware, but that young people *as a group* have not been perceived as a threat to social order. Both class and age have been seen as subordinate to ethnicity in Canada's "vertical mosaic." As one example, the violence of the Front de Libération du Québec (FLQ) in Québec during the 1960s has not been seen as a "youth movement" but as a Francophone political movement. West's (1984) comprehensive study of the relationship between "young offenders" and the state fails to even mention that many Québécois, including the young, see the Canadian state as problematic. The "Oka Crisis" of 1990 is another example; it was seen as a Native issue rather than as a class or age issue.

This leads to a built-in contradiction. While West and other "critical" criminologists in Canada look to the political implications of youth deviance, they focus on precisely those forms of deviance that are least political in motivation. So West seeks to set forth a structural, critical view of delinquency as "ideological," yet himself describes delinquency at the very beginning of his book as "juvenile misbehaviour" (West, 1984: xi).

One consequence is that little attention is paid to the deviant and his or her behaviour, and more attention is paid to the state itself: the initiation and pattern of legislation, the actions of the courts and social agencies, the patterns of enforcement and social control. In doing so, Canadian criminologists may be in a position to identify weaknesses in the more single-minded approaches of the Americans and British. American criminologists' individualistic approach becomes a dead end. If deviance is "natural," as Matza (1969) suggests, then there is nothing to explain. As for critical criminology (see Chapter Seven), West (1984: 234) emphasizes that it is "a mistake to see the state, or parts of it, as either monolithically representing solely capitalist interests, or to regard it as captured by socialists since the advent of 'welfarism.' ... The state is itself an arena of contradiction and class struggle." West thus argues for a two-pronged approach. One is the development of more and better ethnographies of young "deviants," especially of different ethnic, racial and linguistic groups. The other is more historical research on the development, application and consequences of legal policies and procedures regarding delinquency. If a Canadian perspective on youth deviance is to develop, it will be by getting a much more complete picture of how and why youth deviance has evolved as it has in Canada.

CHAPTER

6 The Labelling Perspective Approach

The development of the labelling perspective in the early 1960s marked a major turning point in the sociological analysis of deviance. The new perspective became, in a remarkably short time, the dominant approach within the sociology of deviance. This does not mean that all sociologists unquestioningly adopted the labelling perspective; they did not. Rather, this perspective became the major focus of debate, research and thinking about deviance. Many sociologists disagreed with the labelling approach in crucial matters, but they could not ignore it or the changes it brought about in the sociological conception of deviance.

The labelling perspective broke with past approaches to deviance in a number of ways. First and foremost, labelling theorists reflected a new and different attitude towards both deviance and deviants. Howard Becker (1977: 341) expressed this new attitude when he remarked that, "what is really interesting about deviance is not what it is, but what people think it is." Labelling theorists found what people "think" deviance to be so interesting because, as Earl Rubington and Martin Weinberg (1968: v) put it, "deviance is in the eyes of the beholder. ... [Deviance] is defined by what people say and do about persons, situations, acts, or events." This notion that deviance is *defined* "by what people say and do" about it is what we will call the *labelling thesis*, the distinctive claim that differentiates the approach of labelling theorists from the other perspectives discussed so far. In this sense, labelling theorists argued that deviance is always socially relative, that no behaviour is inherently deviant. Deviance is always socially defined and socially created.

Labelling theorists also presented a new, more sympathetic image of the deviant. If deviance is "in the eyes of the beholder," then we, as sociologists, should make no assumption that the deviant is morally or behaviourally different from the rest of us. Labelling theory approached the deviant as an individual having his or her own interests, point of view and sense of identity, rather than as the product of impersonal genetic, psychological or social forces. From this point of view, the deviant is not someone to be condemned but understood.

This emphasis on the relativity of deviance and an appreciation for the deviant was remarkably in tune with the spirit of the 1960s. To a generation that was questioning the received order politically, academically, sexually and morally, the assertion that deviance is only "in the eyes of the beholder" was an attractive thesis. Quite apart from the specific theoretical and empirical contributions labelling theorists made to the study of deviance—which were considerable—it was the somewhat "subversive" attitudes labelling theory seemed to promote that helped lead to its rapid rise in popularity.

In addition to expressing a new set of attitudes towards deviance, labelling theorists also asked a very different set of questions about deviance. Labelling theorists did not seek to fit deviance into some larger conceptual scheme, as had previous sociologists of deviance such as Durkheim or Merton. Nor did they seek to "correct" deviance or suggest ways to prevent crime, as was the case with most criminologists. Their interest was in the deviance itself—in what people did and how they did it—and their research questions reflected this focus.

LABELLING THEORY OR INTERACTIONIST PERSPECTIVE?

Yet, for all its prominence, it is still hard to get a handle on the labelling perspective. Many of the key figures in its development have either denounced or renounced it. Even the term "labelling theory" is in disrepute today, with most supporters preferring the terms "societal reaction" or "interactionist perspective" (Downes and Rock, 1988; Goode, 1984; Rubington and Weinberg, 1968; Schur, 1980). Typical of this approach is Goode (1978: 179) who argues that the term "labelling theory" is a misnomer:

> Labelling is only one subtype of social interaction. It is unfortunate that the term has become popular to describe sociologists who approach deviant behaviour in a certain way. To call interaction sociologists as "labelling" theorists is to use the particular to describe the general.

Still, if the labelling perspective has taught us anything, it is that names *do* make a difference. The term "mental illness" paints a very different picture and suggests a very different set of attitudes than does the term "insanity"; so, too, for the term "mentally handicapped," compared to the term "retarded." The attempt to drop the designation "labelling theory" in favour of the "interactionist perspective" reflects a rejection or reinterpretation of the labelling thesis, as well as an attempt to distance oneself from some of labelling theory's early versions and followers.

Although several major labelling theorists were trained in the interactionist perspective and many of its concepts and methods were adopted from the interactionist tradition, labelling theory stands on its own as a distinctive and separate approach to understanding deviance, by virtue of the questions it asks about deviance. Questions such as, How do people come to be involved in deviant acts? How do some of the people engaged in deviant acts come to be defined as deviant? How are some able to avoid such a designation? What happens to people who are defined as deviant? How do their lives, their senses of identity and their motivations to engage in deviance change as a result of being defined as deviant?

Some labelling theorists choose to answer these questions by making use of the interactionist perspective, but the interactionist perspective is a major sociological perspective, which long preceded the development of the labelling approach and which continues to have many supporters today (Rock, 1979; Charon, 1985). This perspective, usually referred to as "symbolic interactionism," was developed at the University of Chicago in the writings and teachings of the philosopher George Herbert Mead (1934) and the sociologist Herbert Blumer (1969). What is distinctive about interactionism is that it assumes that the links between social structure and individual identity reside in the interpersonal processes of "symbolic interaction" among ordinary people in everyday life. Mead and Blumer asserted that social interaction is "symbolic" because human beings respond neither instinctively nor automatically to each other's acts; rather, we respond to the meanings these acts have for us. By examining how meanings are generated, modified or maintained in the course of interaction, then, interactionists believe they can uncover the core social processes around which both personal identity (what they call the "self") and social structure (in the form of social institutions and social roles) are formed.

This theoretical link between personal identity and social structure corrects one of the chief weaknesses of functionalism—the absence of a "social psychology" that sociologists can use to account for the individual's acceptance and display of social identity and his or her motivation to follow social norms. Most functionalists simply asserted that socialization was sufficient to motivate individuals to follow social norms and to strive to achieve socially approved goals (Parsons, 1951). Interactionists, however, explain behaviour by looking to the social situations within which people find themselves and the shared meanings, definitions, and perspectives generated in the course of interacting with others within these situations.

Is the labelling perspective an interactionist perspective, then? The answer is yes ... and no. Although much of what we call the labelling perspective is derived from the interactionist tradition, the labelling *thesis* itself, i.e., the claim that deviance is defined by what people say and do about it, is not necessarily linked to the interactionist perspective. Indeed, there are other sociological approaches that have influenced the labelling perspective, and adherents of the approach have been characterized not by any specific theory or data, but by a common conviction that it is society that "creates" and defines deviance, that deviance is socially constructed (Plummer, 1979).

THE VARIETIES OF LABELLING THEORY

Both the common assumptions shared by labelling theorists and the significant differences among them are evident when we examine the work of several key figures in the development of the labelling perspective: Howard Becker, Kai Erikson, John Kitsuse, and Erving Goffman. Each of these sociologists seemed to formulate a very similar approach to understanding deviance. Howard Becker (1963: 9), for example, expressed what is often presented by labelling theorists as the most succinct formulation of the labelling thesis:

> Social groups create deviance by making the rules whose infraction constitutes deviance, and by applying those rules to particular people and labeling them as outsiders. From this point of view, deviance is not a quality of the act the person commits, but rather a consequence of the application by others of rules and sanctions to an "offender." The deviant is the one to whom that label has successfully been applied; deviant behavior is behavior that people so label.

Now, consider the following statements by Erikson (1965: 11):

> Deviance is not a property inherent in certain forms of behavior; it is a property conferred upon these forms by the audiences which directly or indirectly witness them. The critical variable in the study of deviance ... is the social audience rather than the individual actor, since it is the audience which eventually determines whether or not an episode of behavior or any class of episodes is labeled deviant.

Kitsuse (1964: 87-88):

> I propose to shift the focus of theory and research from the the forms of deviant behavior to the processes by which persons come to be defined as deviant by others. Such a shift requires that the sociologist views as problematic what he generally assumes as given—namely, that certain forms of behavior are *per se* deviant and are so defined by the "conventional or conforming members of a group."

and Goffman (1963: 2-3):

> Society establishes the means of categorizing persons and the com-
> plement of attributes felt to be ordinary and natural for members
> of these categories. ... The term stigma ... refer[s] to an attribute
> that is deeply discrediting, but it should be seen that a language of
> relationships, not attributes, is really needed. An attribute that
> stigmatizes one type of possessor can confirm the usualness of an-
> other, and therefore is neither creditable nor discreditable as a
> thing in itself.

At first glance, each of these quotes seems remarkably similar; each
emphasizes the relativity of deviance—that neither behaviour nor status is deviant in itself—and each looks to the role of social definition or
labelling in determining who or what is or is not "deviant." Yet this
seeming similarity among labelling theorists hides a number of significant differences. Neither Kai Erikson nor John Kitsuse can be classified
as an interactionist, while the forms of interactionism followed by
Becker and Goffman differ in a number of crucial ways.

Erikson, whom we discussed before (Chapter Four), approached deviance not as an interactionist but as a functionalist. In his discussion
of deviance, Erikson seeks to return to Durkheim's original recognition
that deviance is functional for maintaining the group identity and
group boundary of any community. While functionalists such as Merton
saw deviance in a rather mechanical way as the outcome of specific social conditions, Erikson emphasizes that defining and treating either
behaviour or people as deviant is not automatic. Whether and when an
individual comes to be defined as deviant depends upon the group (the
"audience") and how the group chooses to view or respond to the individual's behaviour. Erikson's interest, however, is not really in the deviant but in the group itself and the social processes put into play to
deal with deviance. These are not always processes to restrict the deviance or punish the deviant; to the degree that deviance is functional
for the group, Erikson argues, it may actually encourage or call forth
the deviance. Like Durkheim, Erikson asserts that society creates deviance in order to fulfil certain functions beneficial to the group.

Kitsuse, too, shows little interest in the actual deviant behaviour or
actor. His interest is in how the rest of us impute deviance to some individual. That is, his concern is with socio-cultural conceptions of deviance—the labels themselves—and how we apply these labels, rather
than with who is being labeled or why. In his research on how we define
or "impute" others as deviant, for example, Kitsuse argues that the
functionalist notion that there is widespread normative consensus concerning deviance is wrong. Instead Kitsuse (1964: 101) suggests, "a sociological theory of deviance must explicitly take into account the variety
and range of conceptions held by persons, groups, and agencies within

the society concerning any form of behavior." Kitsuse's interest in the set of conventional assumptions and expectations that affect our interactions with others has more in common with the ethnomethodological perspective (see Chapter Eight) than it does with the interactionist perspective (Rains, 1975).

As for Becker and Goffman, while both can be characterized as interactionists, their views on deviance differ considerably. Like Becker, Erving Goffman was trained at the University of Chicago, and he adopted much of the symbolic interactionist approach into his own work. But Goffman's interactionism differs from that of the symbolic interactionists in many ways. For example, symbolic interactionists like Blumer or Becker take identity or the self to be the *outcome* of interactions among people. For Goffman, the self is a resource, a symbolic presentation, which is *used* in interaction. In his work, Goffman emphasized that, all things being equal, we each honour and respect the self the other portrays. But in the case of mental illness or stigma we are dealing with an identity that has been "spoiled." What effect will this have on interaction? How do interactants take into account or purposely fail to take into account this stigma?

Take the interactional subtleties and nuances that determine whether and how we come to treat others as deviant or even just as "different." We do not automatically act on our perception of the other as deviant, as Goffman emphasized in the case of such "stigma" as bodily deformities or handicaps which may make many people uncomfortable. In interacting with the stigmatized, for example, we may find that we do not want to draw attention to their deformity, but we also do not want to show a lack of consideration by ignoring it, or make demands that the handicapped may not be able to meet. As a consequence (Goffman, 1963: 18):

> Each potential source of discomfort for [the visibly stigmatized] when we are with him can become something we sense he is aware of, aware that we are aware of, and even aware of our state of awareness about his awareness; the stage is then set for the infinite regress of mutual consideration that Meadian social psychology tells us how to begin but not how to terminate.

The mutual awareness of physical "spoilage," as Goffman points out in the quote above, undercuts *our* ability as "normals" to engage in ordinary interaction. This is even more so for the stigmatized. They are put in a position where they have much more to gain or lose from interaction than does the ordinary, everyday individual. Yet the very stigma that make interaction more fateful diminish the individual's ability to control interaction. This dilemma, in which one's own body restricts one's self, is what Goffman finds fascinating about the role of stigma. Yet this is not really "about" deviance at all; it is about how we use moral or other ideas and ideologies about the self to order and control interaction in everyday life.

Of the four sociologists being discussed, Becker's approach to deviance has the closest affinity with the symbolic interactionist tradition. Becker's work clearly shows its roots in the Chicago tradition and in symbolic interactionism. Becker's research on deviance, for example, continues the tradition of ethnographic research dating from the era of W. I. Thomas and Robert E. Park, while his theory shows the influence of Herbert Blumer and Everett Hughes.

Because Becker's version of labelling theory has been the most systematic and broadest in scope, it has served as a model of the labelling approach and helped direct labelling theorists towards the interactionist camp. But even in Becker's work significant differences can be found from the traditional interactionism of Blumer. Implicit in Becker's discussion of deviance is a recognition that interaction is not always based on consensus, that there is not always a mutual agreement on the meaning of acts and the definition of the situation. Becker's approach raises the issue of the crucial role played by *power* in the creation, application and impact of rules and sanctions. Deviance, as Becker stresses in the quote above, is the *successful* application of rules and sanctions. Labelling someone as deviant and punishing them for this deviance *may* be a consequence of their deviant behaviour, but not all people who have engaged in deviant behaviour get caught, nor have all who get punished engaged in deviance.

Becker's approach, then, raises a whole set of important research issues: How are some people able to avoid getting caught? What resources are available to them to keep their deviance secret? Do some people or categories of people have disadvantages (such as race) which increase the likelihood that they will get caught? What role do power, influence, social class or knowledge of the "rules of the game" play in determining who does or does not get caught? What such questions show, Becker argues, is that the labelling process is independent of the process of engaging in deviance and must be studied separately. Being labelled deviant, Becker (1963: 11) says, "is the product of a transaction that takes place between some social group and the one who is viewed by that group as a rule-breaker."

Although labelling theorists such as Becker addressed these issues, they have tended to limit themselves to what we can call a microsociology of power, leaving an impression that the workings of agents of social control are a consequence of the particular situation a person may find themselves in—even the individual whim of agents of social control—rather than significant social processes and structural features of society (Schur, 1980). Many sociologists interested in the issues related to power in the study of deviance have found the critical perspective (discussed in Chapter Seven) to be more useful than the social psychological analyses of the labelling and interactionist approaches.

Nevertheless, despite the limitations of the approach which later became evident, labelling theorists made a number of significant contributions to the study of deviance. In particular they are: Becker and Goffman's application of the career model to deviance; Becker's transactional model; Edwin Lemert's examination of the "secondary deviance" that emerges after labelling; and Becker's concept of moral enterprise. Basic to all of these components of the labelling perspective, however, is the rejection by labelling theorists of what Becker called "conventional sentimentality" when looking at deviance.

DE-MORALIZING THE STUDY OF DEVIANCE

Asking *how* individuals come to be engaged in deviant behaviour, labelling theorists assert, is not the same as asking *why* they are so engaged. This difference in the question being posed is central to the development of the labelling perspective. Asking "why" presupposes a moral position on the behaviour in question; "why" is only at issue because the behaviour is taken to be deviant. Few people wonder why a man or woman develops a preference for heterosexual sex, why a passenger pays the fare on boarding a bus, why most high school students attend classes regularly, why most people who drink do so in moderation. Such "conformist" behaviour is taken for granted, assumed to be the outcome of successful socialization into a society's normative order. Not considered deviant, these behaviours seem to require no explanation.

Asking "why," then, implies a moral stance or set of biases towards behaviour considered to be deviant. The trend in sociological theories of deviance that we have considered so far has been towards the development of a "de-moralized" stance on deviance, that is, one that leaves aside or "brackets" moral questions and assumptions in order to examine deviance in the same way that any other form of behaviour would be studied. Durkheim began this trend by arguing that deviance is "normal"; not in the sense of being acceptable to society or to all individuals, but in the sense of being inevitable and even beneficial. Merton took this a step further by arguing that the deviant, too, is normal, that normal people placed in a situation of social strain respond in ways considered deviant. Howard Becker's approach to deviance is more rigorously "de-moralized" still. As Becker (1963: 176) puts it, "We ought to see [deviance] simply as a kind of behavior some disapprove of and others value, studying the processes by which either or both perspectives are built up and maintained." Becker asserts that when we shift our questions about deviance from "why" to "how" we uncover social process instead of moral process: we discover that deviant behaviour itself is part of a process. It is ongoing social behaviour which develops in certain ways, undergoes change and may either disappear or become fixed

THE CAREER MODEL

This issue of process—of change—is crucial to Becker. But Becker is not concerned with broad social changes; such changes, after all, are not apparent in the course of the kind of ethnographic research sociologists of deviance typically undertake. The processes Becker seeks to explain are those that affect the individual in the course of his or her life: changes in attitudes, in identity, in motivation and in behaviour. Structural conditions may explain broad social changes, but cannot explain the specific details and circumstances of an individual's life. In contrast, Becker examines the individual's own experiences and circumstances that give rise to them as the source of any explanation of deviance. This, too, is a crucial assumption of the labelling perspective.

Because Becker does not assume that deviant behaviour is inherently different from conventional behaviour, he avoids using a special model or theory to account for deviance, such as Merton's concept of "anomie" (Chapter Four). Instead, Becker makes use of the career model which had been developed by Everett Hughes to examine conventional careers. Unlike the term "job," which refers to some specific task someone does, the concept of career implies a lifelong sequence of changes in activities and experience. For example, a career sequence might involve training, recruitment, a series of promotions or transfers, and finally, retirement. The career model examines how each new stage or phase differs from the one preceding and the contingencies that lead an individual to move from one stage to another. Each stage is not viewed as a preliminary to or a precursor to the next, but as a distinct set of experiences involving distinctive identities and motivations. Hughes and Becker (Becker, Geer, Hughes and Strauss, 1961), for example, looked at the role of medical school in the career of the physician and found that medical students organize their activities and deal with the problems they face in terms of their current experiences as students, rather than in terms of their expectations about what life as a doctor will be like. Students study what they need to know to pass exams rather than what they think they will need to know to practise medicine.

This approach treats deviance, too, as the outcome of a sequence of changes in an individual's experience and circumstances. Applied to deviance, the career model "points specifically to a process that begins rather than ends with a person's first deviant experience" (Rains, 1982). As with conformist careers, both motivation and identity emerge in the course of participating in deviant activities. As Becker (1963: 42) expresses this basic principle of the labelling approach: "Instead of the deviant motives leading to the deviant behaviour, it is the other way around; deviant behaviour in time produces the deviant motivation."

Becker illustrates his approach to deviance in his study of marijuana use among jazz musicians. Two crucial aspects of marijuana use are discussed by Becker: motivation and the social definition of marijuana's effects. Merton's theory confounds these two separate issues. For Merton the drug's primary effect, the sense of escape from reality, is also the motivation for use. Becker's work argues that these two are quite separate and distinct issues. In contrast to Merton's description of the retreatist as an asocial outcast from reality who has given up on society's values, goals and means, Becker found that:

- Marijuana is not used by jazz musicians as an escape from reality but as a mode of participation in the jazz subculture.
- Marijuana use is not asocial behaviour but is learned behaviour; it is socially organized and socially passed on.
- Marijuana use does not imply giving up on values, goals and means, because marijuana use is part of the jazz subculture's system of values (becoming a better musician), goals (getting high) and means (preferences for particular types of marijuana, use of various drug paraphernalia, and appropriate techniques for getting high).

Becker differentiates among "beginners," "occasional users" and "regular users." Beginners do not come to use marijuana because of any consistent set of dispositions, such as a desire to escape from reality. They begin to use marijuana as a consequence of the contingencies related to participation in the jazz subculture. They will use marijuana *if* they have *access* to people making use of the drug; *if* these others are willing to *supply* them with the drug; *if* they themselves are willing to *use* the drug; and *if* they can *overcome their fears* of engaging in illegal behaviour. Since jazz musicians typically smoke marijuana when they get together, much as others use alcohol, access and supply are not a problem once an individual is accepted into their circles. While some are afraid to try a drug whose use is illegal, its regular and routine use by most of the musicians soon overcomes fear of the law.

Willingness to try the drug is a consequence of curiosity, Becker suggests, rather than a desire to experience specific effects. Since the non-users have never experienced the effects of the drug, it is not a desire for these effects that motivates them but a curiosity about the effects the drug will have on them. First-time users are often disappointed, however. In their interviews, many users told Becker that they had experienced no effects at all the first time they tried the drug. Despite popular mythology among both those who would legalize marijuana and those who would see its use further criminalized, the effects of the drug are not obvious, particularly to the new user. This may be either because the marijuana smoke was not inhaled properly or because the new user, not knowing what to expect, does not recognize the effects or connect them to the marijuana. There is nothing either natural or inevitable in getting "high." Perceiving the effects of the drug, Becker insists, must be learned.

Once someone has tried the drug and learned to perceive the effects, they will not continue to use the drug unless they consider those effects to be pleasurable. The contemporary ideology of drug use implies that the effects of drugs are always pleasurable. Becker's research showed, however, that for many who tried marijuana, the effects were not at all enjoyable. Still, most of those who did not find the effects enjoyable eventually became marijuana users anyway. Why? Because, again, they *learned* to enjoy the effects. Like learning to perceive the effects, learning to enjoy the effects, too, is a social process.

Each movement from one level of use to another, such as that from beginner to occasional user and from occasional user to regular user, has its own motivational sequence. Moving from beginner to occasional user requires a new motivation. Once one has learned to experience the effects, curiosity is no longer a suitable motivation. One has to have learned to enjoy the effects. As for movement from occasional user to regular user, this, Becker suggests, is a consequence of a change in the level of supply; the more often the drug is available the more it will be used. Only after a drug has been tried can its effects become a motive for continued use.

Becker's use of the career model indicates a clear shift away from a focus on deviance as a category of behaviour, such as crime, delinquency or suicide, to an interest in the deviant as an individual. This does not mean that deviance can only be understood from a psychological point of view, as a consequence of the individual's personality, character, temperament or early childhood experiences. Rather, the individual is seen as engaged in an ongoing process of interaction with others during which deviant identity and deviant motivation emerge.

This last point shows the limitations of the career model. By itself, the career model is not a theory of deviance. Participation in a deviant career involves more than the individual's own experiences and motivations. Once people have been labelled deviant, their identity and motivation are no longer based on *their* experiences but on how *others* define and treat them. A deviant career is not the same as a conformist career because of the most significant set of contingencies of all: getting caught, labelled deviant and punished.

For this reason, being a prostitute is not the same as being a bus driver; the prostitute must always take into account the negative moral evaluations and actions of others. The prostitute must also come to terms with these moral evaluations and must learn to neutralize or to discard them. This means, as Erving Goffman (1961) suggested, that the career of the deviant is different because it is always a "moral career." The stigma that results from being defined as deviants alters how others treat them. Goffman applied this insight to what he called the moral career of the mental patient. He examined how people admitted to a mental hospital come to take on the role, identity and status of a mental patient. In Goffman's approach, the fundamental issue is not how people become mentally ill, but how they come to take on the role of mental patient and come to think of themselves as mentally ill.

THE TRANSACTIONAL MODEL

Although the career model seems to have nothing to do with *labelling*, this model is at the heart of the interactionist version of labelling theory. The career model as used by interactionists is a model of the "self." This social "self" is not seen as some permanent, essential quality of the person, but as emergent. As new experiences, new interests and new needs alter the individual's motivation, perspectives and identity, they alter the self as well. What the career model does is link these new contingencies to social circumstances: a new job, a promotion, marriage and so on.

Yet contingencies are not random and individual; most are predictable and socially shared. Students in medical school, for example, will undergo a similar set of experiences, have similar problems and develop similar solutions (Becker, Geer, Hughes and Strauss, 1961). It is this shared set of contingencies and the development of shared solutions that make it possible to speak of a "career," for the career, too, is "emergent." Entering medical school does not make someone a doctor; students must pass through a sequence of stages and contingencies before that happens.

Similarly, trying marijuana does not make someone a "user." Many people engage in brief or transitory episodes of crime or deviance such as shoplifting, for example. But how does someone go from occasional episodes of shoplifting or petty theft to becoming a professional thief? Put differently, the career model raises the issue of how *commitment* to deviant activity and deviant identity emerges. This model illustrates that the emergence of such commitment is not inevitable but is *contingent*, and that one of the most important of these contingencies is whether *others* treat or define the individual as deviant.

Goffman (1961) was the first to describe the contingencies involved in labelling someone deviant when he examined the process of labelling patients as mentally ill. The labelling process is not some automatic operation in which we simply apply labels to people who are "clearly" deviant. The husband, wife, son or daughter of someone who comes to be labelled as mentally ill may undergo years of suspicion, confusion, accommodation, denial, hope and despair before finally coming to decide that their relative is "mentally ill." Being labelled deviant, then, is as much a contingency in someone's deviant career as is any other possibility.

William Chambliss's (1973) well-known study of the "Saints" and the "Roughnecks" uncovered similar contingencies in the labelling of boys as juvenile delinquents. These were two groups of high school students, both of whom were involved in delinquent activities. One group consisted of upper-middle-class boys Chambliss nicknames the "Saints"; the other group consisted of lower-class boys, and Chambliss refers to these boys as the "Roughnecks."

Both sets of boys were engaged in similar sorts of deviance: skipping school, drinking, vandalism and theft. The Saints also engaged in drunken and reckless driving on the weekend, while the Roughnecks were more likely to get into fights. Yet, says Chambliss, during a two-year period of observation the Saints were never officially in trouble with the police while the Roughnecks were regularly in trouble with both the police and members of the community.

The Saints were occasionally caught by the police doing some "mischief," but the police basically saw them as "good boys just out for a lark" (Chambliss, 1973: 26). There were two major reasons for this. One was that the delinquent acts of the Saints were rarely *visible*. They drove away from the neighbourhood when they skipped school and much of their drinking, vandalism and reckless driving was done in a nearby city rather than in their own community. Also, on those occasions when they were caught by the police, their *demeanour* towards the police was apologetic and polite. The police were therefore disposed to give them another chance and hope they had learned their lesson.

As for the Roughnecks, the police were convinced, despite the lack of hard evidence, that these boys were engaged in criminal activities. The Roughnecks hung around a neighbourhood drugstore when skipping school, where they were easily visible to the community, to teachers and to the police. They seemed thereby to flaunt their blatant truancy at the community. They also made rude remarks to passersby and regularly got into fights which were highly visible. Their demeanour towards the police was one of "hostility and disdain" (Chambliss, 1973: 29) and the police felt little or no sympathy towards them.

Visibility and demeanour are two sets of situational and interactional contingencies. They reflect, however, different sets of *resources* available to the boys with which to achieve their goals and to avoid getting caught. For example, the middle-class Saints had cars available to them with which to get away from the community, while the lower-class Roughnecks did not. Chambliss argues that this difference is *structural*; that it reflects the class structure of American society. In this respect the police were biased, already predisposed to seeing the middle-class boys as "good kids" and the lower-class boys as "delinquents": not because of some sort of conspiracy to let middle-class kids get away with what lower-class kids get punished for, but, as Chambliss (1973: 29) puts it, because of the police's experience, "with irate and influential upper-class parents insisting that their son's vandalism was simply a prank and his drunkenness only a momentary 'sowing of wild oats'— and experiences with cooperative or indifferent, powerless, lower-class parents who acquiesced to the law's definition of their son's behavior."

These differences were not only matters of definition but of fate. Seven of the eight Saints finished college and became "respectable," middle-class members of society. The story with the Roughnecks was very different. Two of the boys received athletic scholarships to college and ended up as high school teachers and coaches. Three others ended up with criminal careers, two serving sentences for murder in state penitentiaries, while the third was involved in illegal gambling. The seventh apparently became a truck driver. Chambliss (1973) argues that the community's response to the Saints and the Roughnecks was one of "selective perception and labelling." The labelling of the Roughnecks served to *reinforce* the community's perception of them as troublemakers and criminals. The boys, too, Chambliss (1973: 31) asserts, developed self-images as deviants, chose friends who reinforced that image, and "became willing to try new and more extreme deviances." Here, again, the convergence of community and self-label served to reinforce the deviance. As for the Saints, by being able to avoid any labelling as deviant, they were able to continue with their academic career paths and give up their adolescent deviance with no repercussions for their later lives.

Chambliss is making two points in his discussion of the Saints and the Roughnecks. One is that being labelled deviant—or being able to avoid that label—and the various circumstances that contribute to either outcome, are crucial contingencies which in large measure determined whether or not any one of the boys got locked into a life of deviance. The second point is that this does not occur at random; it reflects the structural characteristics of the society, in this case its class structure, but it can also reflect the racial or ethnic characteristics of the society.

Becker systematized this view of labelling as contingent in his transactional model of labelling. Some people engage in deviant behaviour without ever getting caught, labelled or punished. They are not seen as deviant in the eyes of the community and do not suffer the negative consequences of being labelled. To all intents and purposes, they live the outward lives of conformists and their deviance remains secret. It is only when someone *is* labelled deviant that the various social processes designed to control deviance and punish the deviant come into play. The results of these transactions are summed up by Becker in Figure 6.1.

	Obedient Behaviour	Rule-Breaking Behaviour
Perceived as deviant	Falsely Accused	Pure Deviant
Not perceived as deviant	Conforming	Secret Deviant

FIGURE 6.1   Becker's Model of Deviant Behaviour

Source: Becker (1963)

There is another possibility raised in Figure 6.1: some people who have not engaged in deviant behaviour may nevertheless be falsely accused and punished. These people *will* suffer all of the consequences of being labelled deviant. The case of Donald Marshall can serve as an example. Marshall, a Nova Scotia Micmac Indian, was accused in 1971 of the murder of a young black man. Despite his claim of innocence, Marshall was convicted. Subsequent investigation showed that it was his accuser, Roy Ebsary, who had actually committed the crime and that the police were clearly biased in their dealings with Marshall (Harris, 1990). Indeed, the police had eyewitness testimony that it was Ebsary who had committed the crime in 1971, but Marshall remained in prison for eleven years until Ebsary confessed. Even after Marshall was finally acquitted, the court blamed *him* for having originally been found guilty. A Royal Commission set up by the Nova Scotia government later found evidence of bias and incompetence in the working of the police, the RCMP, the courts and Marshall's own lawyers. As the commission put it (quoted in Harris, 1990: 407):

> The criminal justice system failed Donald Marshall, Jr. at virtually every turn from his arrest and wrongful conviction for murder in 1971 up to, and even beyond, his acquittal by the Court of Appeal in 1983.

The Donald Marshall case and others like it raise a number of very important issues. Are some people more likely to be singled out and accused of deviance than others? Are racial, ethnic or other biases and stereotypes used by authorities in determining who is deviant? How significant are the falsely accused in distorting our image of the "typical" deviant?

Remaining with the example of natives for a moment, natives make up a disproportionate number of inmates in prisons in Western Canada. In 1985, natives accounted for 61 percent of admissions to federal custody from Saskatchewan, 34 percent from Manitoba, 22 percent from Alberta and 13 percent from British Columbia (McKie, 1987: 3). This compares with 3 percent in Eastern Canada. Rates were even higher in admissions to provincial prisons: 64 percent in Saskatchewan, 54 percent in Manitoba, 30 percent in Alberta and 16 percent in British Columbia (McKie, 1987: 4). While these figures do not in themselves prove that natives are being falsely accused, the very high proportion of prison inmates coming from such a small proportion of the population suggests that, at the very least, natives in Western Canada are at much higher risk of being accused and found guilty than are non-natives. Clearly this warrants investigation to see whether the criminal justice system in Western Canada is biased in its dealings with native people.

As for Donald Marshall, the clear miscarriages of justice in his case, which led him to spend eleven years in prison and to be blamed for his own false conviction, resulted in his being awarded substantial monetary compensation, a lump sum payment of $199 872 and $1875 a month for the rest of his life. But this is not some fable with a happy ending. Monetary compensation cannot erase what was done to Donald Marshall in the courts, in prison, in the eyes of the community or in his own heart. That legacy, which includes substance abuse, has not disappeared.

Because Marshall was falsely accused, we tend to see his case as tragic, but there are always consequences to being labelled. Matters do not end once someone is labelled deviant; indeed, labelling theorists argue that being labelled is only a new beginning.

SOCIETAL REACTION AND DEVIANT STATUS

Most of the emphasis in the labelling perspective has been on identifying the processes that lead to the labelling of someone as deviant. Far more attention is paid to the process of "becoming" deviant than to the consequences of being labelled (Spector and Kitsuse, 1977). Nevertheless, the initial point made by Becker, and even earlier by Edwin Lemert (1951), was that labelling someone is a crucial moment in the process of creating deviance. It fundamentally alters the nature of the interactions between the individual labelled deviant and conformists; subjects the individual to the whims of social control agents; and forces the individual to reorganize his or her life and identity. The labelling perspective, then, does not leave off its analysis at examining who is labelled as deviant and why. Labelling theorists insist that labelling itself puts into play a whole variety of social processes which have a fateful impact on the life of the deviant.

The response or adjustment of the individual to the deviant label and the negative social reaction that goes along with it is often referred to as "secondary deviance" (Lemert, 1951). "Primary deviance," as used by Lemert, refers to the "original violations" that lead an individual to be defined as deviant. Primary deviance, then, puts into play a process of "societal reaction." As for secondary deviance, this refers to the situation (Lemert 1951: 76), "when a person begins to employ his deviant behavior or a role based on it as a means of defense attack, or adjustment to the overt and covert problems created by the consequent societal reaction to him."

Secondary deviance involves the individual reorganizing his or her life and identity in terms of the deviant status. This reorganization can take many forms. The thief may engage in "neutralization" to explain away the deviance by arguing that everyone steals when they can get away with it or that no one is hurt except the insurance companies. Another form of secondary deviance has to do with how individuals organize their everyday activities. Drug addicts organize their lives around a set of activities designed to allow them to obtain and use the drug. Some people may engage in political or group activities designed to legalize or legitimate their deviance.

Until a person has been "caught," labelled or defined as deviant, there are various options and contingencies available to them. They may be able to continue to avoid getting caught, in which case their deviance remains secret and they are forced to suffer none of the negative consequences of being labelled. They may also *stop* and return to conformity, thereby again avoiding both the labelling and the subsequent social reactions. Or circumstances may change and their behaviour may no longer be seen as deviant, in which case they can come forward or admit to their activities.

People engaged in deviant behaviour are aware of the negative reactions with which others will respond to what they are doing. The identity taken on when someone becomes a prostitute or a thief is an identity that they *know* is evaluated negatively by society at large. They know as well that they may be punished for doing what they do or being what they are. Such people are therefore forced to organize their activities around knowledge of this fact. At a minimum, for example, they will organize their activities so as to avoid getting caught.

Once having been labelled, however, the range of options becomes much narrower. The resulting deviant status fundamentally alters the lives of these individuals. Going to prison or being admitted to a mental hospital are contingencies that come into play only *after* a person has been labelled. In addition, people who have been labelled as mentally ill, as murderers or as child molesters, find that they now have a "master status" (Becker, 1963) that affects how other people see them and deal with them in the future. Calling someone a "child molester" is not only to describe their behaviour in supposedly objective terms, but to classify them as one of a group of people the rest of us find morally repulsive. The fact that the "child molester" may have been a brilliant student in university, is now an excellent physician, a loving husband and a dutiful son, would all be considered irrelevant by most people. All that counts to most of us is that he molests children. That is why the deviant label is a master status; it tells us everything most of us think we need to know about the person. Because these labels become a matter of official records, they are hard to remove, and people may find themselves unable to return to conformity and therefore "locked in" to a deviant lifestyle. Applied to groups rather than individuals, labelling creates categories such as "homosexuals," "prostitutes," "mental patients," "murderers" and "child molesters," which ignores individual circumstances and individual differences.

Someone who is labelled deviant need not necessarily accept the label, however. They may make use of what Sykes and Matza (1980) call "techniques of neutralization" to reject a view of themselves as deviant, criminal or morally in the wrong. Sykes and Matza identify several types of neutralization:

- *The denial of responsibility*: in which the deviant argues that he or she is not really responsible for his or her actions, but lays the blame on others such as relatives, friends or authorities. Examples would be the alcoholic who drinks because his wife "puts too much pressure on him" or the delinquent who claims to have come under the "bad influence" of his friends.

- *The denial of injury*: in which individuals engaged in deviance may insist that "no one is really hurt" as a result of their actions. Sykes and Matza (1980: 212) argue that these individuals will try to minimize the effect of their actions by redefining the acts; for example, defining gang fighting as a private quarrel.

- *The denial of the victim*: in which the deviant actor insists that the victims are not "really" victims because they "deserved" what they got. Shoplifters, for example, may claim that their actions are a form of protest over the "unfair" high prices being charged by a store.

- *The condemnation of the condemners*: where the individuals may claim that, compared to the secret crimes committed by supposedly legitimate individuals or corporations, their own misdeeds are minor. A thief, for example, may argue that corrupt police officers steal far more from the public than he does.

- *The appeal to higher loyalties*: this technique of neutralization involves "sacrificing the demands of the larger society for the demands of the small social groups to which the [deviant] belongs" (Sykes and Matza, 1980: 213). The terrorist, for example, will acknowledge that his or her behaviour *is* violent and *does* hurt innocent people, but argues that it is still necessary and morally right because of the greater good to which it will lead.

MORAL ENTERPRISE

The issues we have discussed to this point have, in various ways, dealt with those individuals who come to be labelled and treated as deviant. Yet if, as Becker (1963: 9) asserts, social groups "create deviance by making the rules whose infraction constitutes deviance, and by applying those rules to particular people," we must pay attention as well to those who create the rules and to those who enforce them. If contingencies play a role in determining who is being labelled, then one of the most important contingencies will be *who* wants to label them and why. This is what Becker covers in his discussion of the "moral enterprise."

We first looked at the concept of the moral enterprise in Chapter Four when we considered the role of William Lyon Mackenzie King in the criminalization of opium use in Canada. As you may recall, the term "moral entrepreneur" refers to an individual who engages in a public campaign to criminalize some form of behaviour previously largely accepted or tolerated. Moral enterprise is always involved in deviance, Becker (1963: 162) says, because:

> Before any act can be viewed as deviant, and before any class of people can be publicly labeled and treated as outsiders for committing the act, someone must have made the rule which defines the act as deviant. Rules are not made automatically. ... Someone must call the public's attention to these matters, supply the push necessary to get things done, and direct such energies as are aroused in the proper direction to get a rule created.

Although Becker refers to "social groups who create and apply rules," he describes this process in terms of individuals having a distinctive personality type. The moral entrepreneur, says Becker, is a "crusader," a moral reformer who believes that he or she has right on their side and who is determined to eliminate some social evil. Such a person, says Becker (1963: 148), "operates with an absolute ethic," is willing to use any means to achieve the goal, and tends to be self-righteous.

Yet, after identifying the moral entrepreneur as a personality type, the examples that Becker gives describe the role of groups rather than individuals in moral enterprise: the Federal Bureau of Narcotics in the prohibition of marijuana use; the Women's Christian Temperance Movement in the prohibition of alcohol use; and psychiatrists in the creation of sexual psychopath laws. There is, then, a gap in Becker's theory of moral enterprise. He is unable to relate the particular individuals or groups he describes as moral entrepreneurs with the particular form of behaviour they seek to criminalize. In the case of the Federal Bureau of Narcotics, for example, Becker (1963: 138) tells us, "while it is, of course, difficult to know what the motives of Bureau officials were, we need assume no more than that they perceived an area of wrongdoing that properly belonged in their jurisdiction and moved to put it there." But surely the motives of the Federal Bureau of Narcotics are precisely the crucial issue in understanding its moral enterprise. Dickson (1968), for example, claims that the Federal Bureau of Narcotics was not acting out of a moral conviction that marijuana use is a danger to American society, but out of a concern with its own organizational interests. The Bureau used the issue of marijuana to convince the public that there was a drug "problem" in the United States, to raise its stature in the public eye by showing that it could identify and control the problem, and to argue for increased budgets.

Ian Taylor has criticized Becker's notion of the moral entrepreneur on several grounds. First, he argues that Becker's use of the term is too general (Taylor, 1983: 126): "it speaks of campaigns that are successful by virtue of their importance to a culture," rather than identifying specific interests in terms of which groups clash. Taylor (1983: 126-27) also accuses Becker of being too individualistic, allowing "considerable power and influence ... to committed individual moral entrepreneurs," rather than identifying the structure and distribution of power in the society which allows one group to define and treat the other as deviant. Finally, Taylor argues that Becker's approach is too subjective, assuming moral enterprise is the outcome of individuals' "prejudices, preferences, fears, desires, etc." (Taylor, 1983: 126-27). To Taylor, moral enterprise is better seen as "ideological work." Moral enterprise emerges at times when there are serious social, economic or political problems. It is used, largely by the radical Right, to provide people with an explanation of what is going wrong in the society around them or in their own lives. This explanation directs attention away from the real social and economic causes of the problems and instead blames the "deviant," calling for greater restraints on individual liberties and a more authoritarian political form. The deviant then becomes the scapegoat for society's ills.

We have now covered the major elements of the labelling perspective. It should now be clear that the labelling approach provided neither an integrated theory nor an explanation of deviance. It did raise new and significant questions, and provided new descriptions of specific forms of deviance. Labelling theorists such as Becker (1973), Kitsuse (1980) and Lemert (1982) would agree with this. They argue that their original goals were limited and that they had no intention of developing a general theory of deviance on the basis of the process of labelling alone. This may be true, but if they were misunderstood the fault often lies in their own writings and analyses, which were often ambiguous and contradictory (Lemert, 1982). And if their critics failed to recognize their modest ambitions, it may well be because those ambitions did not seem, during the 1960s, to be so very modest at all. Certainly this is the case if we look at the labelling account of mental disorder and the labelling theorists' assault on the medical model of mental illness.

MENTAL DISORDER AS A SOCIOLOGICAL ISSUE

Despite decades of research and professional practice, mental disorder remains a subject of intense dispute and controversy (Gallagher, 1987; Grusky and Pollner, 1981; Scheff, 1984). What mental "illness" really is, what causes it and how it is to be treated have all been matters of dispute among mental health professionals themselves. Is mental disorder a psychic disorder, a medically treatable illness like pneumonia, a constitutional condition like drunkenness or a genetic defect like Down's Syndrome? Is it best treated with psychotherapy (in its many forms), drugs, psychosurgery, "rebalancing" body chemistry, community reintegration, hypnosis, electroconvulsive shock therapy or benign neglect? Or is mental illness itself nothing but a myth (Szasz, 1961), an excuse for a modern-day witch hunt?

It would be audacious and arrogant for sociologists to assume that we have the answers to the questions that have been bedevilling mental health practitioners for so many years. It is neither our role nor within our competence to provide solutions to these questions. Instead, sociologists direct themselves to an entirely different set of issues: How is mental disorder socially defined; i.e., what attitudes, values and beliefs about "normal" behaviour affect our perceptions and treatment of the "mentally ill"? What social processes come into play when someone is identified as mentally ill? How do "the rest of us" respond to this person?

The nature and scope of appropriate sociological interest may be clearer if we turn aside momentarily from the morally loaded topic of mental disorder to look at other sociological issues related to medicine. Sociologists are not competent to say whether a particular patient in a hospital requires surgery, but we can examine the social organization of surgical wards, the differences of role and status among staff, how treatment of patients may be affected by non-medical factors such as the social class, age or gender of the patient, how staff interact with the patients and the relatives of patients and so on. Indeed, the sociology of medicine is an extraordinarily rich and fertile field for research.

Further, because mental disorder *is* so morally loaded an issue, there is even more for the sociologist to look at. Whatever the *origin* of mental disorder, its manifestation often involves social norms and cultural values. An example may make this clear. Tourette's Syndrome, while it is not considered a form of mental illness today, nevertheless raises fascinating questions related to mental disorder. As Oliver Sacks (1987:92) describes this syndrome:

> [It is] characterized by an excess of nervous energy, and a great production of and extravagance of strange motions and notions: tics, jerks, mannerisms, grimaces, noises, curses, involuntary imitations and compulsions of all sorts, with an odd elfin humour and a tendency to antic and outlandish kinds of play.

There is no question that Tourette's Syndrome is neurological in origin, constituting either a "disturbance" of the thalamus, hypothalamus, limbic system and amygdala or an excess of dopamine in the brain (Sacks, 1987). Yet notice that Sacks's catalogue of symptoms above mentions "curses." One patient he discusses, for example, would involuntarily shout "fuck" or "shit" at various times. Now, while the syndrome itself is neurological in origin, shouting "fuck" or "shit" is not. These are not sounds, they are words in a particular language, having a broad set of culturally defined connotations, none of which arise organically in the brain but are a product of our society. So, for example, someone who shouts "merde" is not suffering from some different organic disorder than is someone who shouts "shit." The shouting may be neurological; what is shouted out is not. Nor is the societal response. How would you or most people respond to a man who, when passing an attractive woman on the street, suddenly shouts out "fuck"? You might well consider such a person to be seriously disturbed. Sacks mentions that, as recently as 1971, Tourette's Syndrome was considered a rare condition. Now it is known to be far more common than once thought. This means that many people who had Tourette's Syndrome in the past were not recognized as having that condition but were treated as having some other problem, possibly mental illness.

The example of Tourette's Syndrome illustrates several points. Even if a disorder is constitutional in origin, its manifestation is sociologically relevant to the degree that it makes use of social and cultural definitions to express itself, as is true in Tourette's Syndrome but is also true in many forms of mental disorder. To the degree that the rest of us disapprove of these manifestations, we will then define and treat the individual as deviant because of them: while Sacks's patient's condition was neurological in origin and harmless to others, he was frequently fired from jobs because of the behavioural manifestations of his condition.

Sacks's account of his patient (whom he calls "Ray") takes an interesting and highly relevant twist. Sacks was able to control Ray's uncontrolled and "extravagant" behaviour using a drug (Haldol) to lower dopamine levels. This worked, but Ray found himself to be "sober, solid, square" when using the drug. He was no longer lively and witty in conversation, no longer quick and agile when playing ping-pong, no longer energetic and creative when playing music. Being "normal" or "well," in other words, has its costs, too. As a consequence, Ray decided to take his medication during the week, but not on weekends. To Ray, the return to Tourette's Syndrome on the weekends was liberating and exhilarating, although that is only true because he could take his medication again on Monday morning. He was not therefore condemned to either extravagance and creativity, or conformity and mediocrity.

This last point is relevant to our discussion because it points out the relativity of notions of "sickness" and "health," the "normal" and the "abnormal." It was precisely this relativity that made mental illness seem so perfect a subject for the labelling theorists, at first. Just how *do* we decide who is normal or abnormal? This issue was illustrated in the following anecdote recorded by Gellner (1975: 431):

> A well-known eccentric in Edinburgh ... used to accost passers-by on Prince's Street and ask them—are you sane? If any replied Yes, he would retort—ah, but can you *prove* it? And, as they could not, he proceeded triumphantly to show them that *he* at any rate could prove his sanity, by producing his own certificate of discharge from a mental hospital.

The passersby did not know how to prove their sanity because we do not test each other for "normality" in everyday life. We simply take it for granted. We assume others are normal unless they otherwise display themselves as abnormal. It is not normality that stands out, but abnormality.

Since most people do take "normality" for granted, the question is, how do some people come to be seen as abnormal? Labelling theory, which views both normality and abnormality as socially produced and maintained, looks to the processes that lead people to differentiate the abnormal from the normal. Since these sociologists see both normality and abnormality as being produced out of how others react to behaviour, there is no assumption made that some behaviour is either normal or abnormal in itself or that it is necessarily the behaviour itself that leads to the definition. Rather, the outcome is a consequence of the social relationships within which processes of "normalizing" or "abnormalizing" are embedded.

THE LABELLING APPROACH TO MENTAL DISORDER

In the first flush of enthusiasm for the labelling approach, mental illness—especially schizophrenia—seemed an ideal subject. It was dealt with by several sociologists considered crucial to the development of the labelling approach, including Erving Goffman (1961), Edwin Lemert (1967), and Thomas Scheff (1966), and six of the first eleven articles reprinted in the first major sociology of deviance text to make use of the labelling perspective (Rubington and Weinberg, 1968) were on some facet of mental illness.

Few argue with the notion that getting caught, labelled and punished has a profound effect on the life of a thief or a murderer. But in the case of mental disorder the labelling theorists seem to be claiming much more: that the "disease" of mental illness is itself *nothing but a label*. Indeed, they argue that being mentally ill is not a consequence of constitutional or psychic factors but a role that one learns *after* being labelled. This has been the strongest statement of the labelling point of view; it has also posed a challenge to the dominant medical and psychiatric view of mental disorder, a view shared by the majority of ordinary people and non-speciaists in psychiatry, including sociologists. The labelling perspective on mental illness is not a theory of mental disorder *per se*, but an analysis of the mental patient as the victim of social control.

Although Thomas Scheff (1966; 1975; 1984) developed the most systematic version of the labelling approach to mental disorder, he based his analysis heavily on the earlier work of Erving Goffman. Before looking at Scheff's systematic labelling theory of mental disorder, then, we will begin by looking at Goffman's analysis of mental patients in the hospital.

Despite his significant contributions to the labelling approach, Erving Goffman's interest was not in understanding or explaining deviance but in examining the "self" as the outcome of interactional processes. By the "self" Goffman (1961: 168) referred to the individual's presentation of character, personality, reputation, worth, competence and similar "personal" qualities to others:

> The self can be seen as something that resides in the arrange-
> ments prevailing in a social system for its members. The self in
> this sense is not a property of the persons to whom it is attributed,
> but dwells rather in the pattern of social control that is exerted in
> connection with the person by himself and those around him. This
> special kind of institutional arrangement does not so much support
> the self as constitute it.

The self, then, does not reside within individuals but outside them,
in their interactions with others and the social relationships within
which they find themselves with others. This "presentation of self" *is*
the self, insofar as anything is.

One important implication of this view of the self is that the sociologist can make no claims or statements about any "true" or "real" self
that resides in the individual. There is no "real" you—at least no "real"
you that is accessible to the observing sociologist—only a set of roles
that you act out. The sociologist, then, should examine the roles being
acted out and the circumstances within which they are being acted out
without making reference to any underlying psychological states, dispositions, traits, motives and so on. This is the case whether the sociologist is examining interaction in a classroom, in a restaurant or in a
mental hospital.

A second implication is that changing patterns of social arrangements change the nature of the self that is acted out. By looking at different types of social arrangements we can identify different types of
self and role. Since the social arrangement that characterizes the mental hospital is that of a "total institution," the self and role acted out by
mental patients will be one appropriate to such a total institution.

By a total institution, Goffman refers to the type of social arrangements typical of hospitals, prisons, boarding schools, army barracks and
orphanages. Goffman identifies two distinct features that "totalize"
such institutions. First, the nature and range of interactions with others are sharply limited, both in the sense that people tend to live and
spend most of their time within the institution, and in the sense that
interactions with others outside the institution are cut off. Moreover,
interactions are highly structured in terms of where, when and with
whom one can interact. A prison illustrates this feature particularly
well. Second, the institution provides the individual with a "total" self.
The "old" self with which people enter such an institution is systematically stripped from them through what Goffman calls "mortification rituals." During these humiliating and degrading rituals, the cherished
identity of the individual is ridiculed and reviled. The "boot camp" at-
tended by new recruits to the military is a particularly apt example. At
the same time, individuals are provided with a new, institutionally defined "self." The institution provides the individual with a new identity

to replace the old one; systematically building up this new identity through its monopoly over interaction and social relationships. The new self becomes a total self, in which all the symbolic images are provided by the institution and where all the others to whom this self is displayed are themselves participants in the institution.

As Goffman describes it, the mental hospital is the most "total" of total institutions. Just as in a prison, most of the patients are institutionalized against their wills. But in a prison there are limits on the ability of the institution to impose a total self on the inmate. Prisoners have their own system of status and honour, of privileges and disadvantages, of rewards and punishments, independent of and often inverting those the authorities attempt to impose. Above all, the prisoner is not seen as different from who he was before, as is the case with the military recruit, but as a prisoner *because* of who and what he was outside and may well still be. In a mental hospital not only are "outside" identities seen as irrelevant, they are derided as morally reprehensible, and individuals are expected to join in the rituals of ridding themselves of these reprehensible identities.

But if being a mental patient implies a view of the self that is so morally reprehensible, how then do people come to take on this identity? How does one become a mental patient? For Goffman, the easy answer, that people come to be mental patients because they are mentally ill, is the least useful. There are many people *outside* of mental hospitals who are as mentally disturbed or perhaps more disturbed than those who end up being committed to an institution. Thus, the factors, reasons or causes used as an explanation of how a person came to be mentally ill do not also explain how they came to be a mental *patient*.

MORAL CAREERS AND THE SELF

As discussed above, Goffman made use of the career model and the notion of career to get around this difficulty. As Goffman (1961: 135) puts it:

> In the degree that the "mentally ill" outside hospitals numerically approach or surpass those inside hospitals, one can say that mental patients distinctively suffer not from mental illness, but from contingencies.

One particularly clear example of what Goffman means by contingencies is the central role he assigns to the act of "betrayal." Goffman asserts that the contingencies surrounding betrayal play a significant and peculiarly central role in the process of becoming a mental patient. Goffman points out that most mental patients are not willingly committed to a mental institution. Many have to be tricked into allowing themselves into such an institution, others have to be taken by force. Usually, it is the closest relatives who have someone committed. This sets up, in most cases, a scenario of betrayal.

This is not just a bare fact; it is one of the dynamics that underlie the process of becoming a mental patient. Betrayal is *how* one ends up as a mental patient. It is also the first of the mortification rituals the inmate undergoes in becoming a mental patient.

The act of betrayal cuts the patient off from those outside the hospital. The very people to whom the patient was closest and to whom she[1] would normally turn in time of crisis or would miss the most are the very people who put her in this situation. The animosity, anger, outrage, frustration and humiliation of the patient engendered by the betrayal cuts the patient off from them. It suggests to the patient that these people and her relationship with them were not what she thought them to be.

In addition, the fact of betrayal suggests to the mental patient that in order for others to do this to *her*, she cannot really be what she always took herself to be. In this sense betrayal begins the process of identity dissolution, of losing faith in the reality of her own sense of herself.

Moreover, because this betrayal was for "her own good" the patient is not granted the moral right to display—or even to feel—anger or outrage. The patient is expected to come to swallow the betrayal and show signs of gratitude. This cuts the patient off from *herself* and prevents her from having a right to her own emotions. Another step in the dissolution of the self.

At the same time, there is an enormous difference in the notion of physician or even burglar as a career and the notion of mental patient. The career of mental patient is, first and foremost, a *moral* career. Being a mental patient implies a standard set of expectations about the personality, character, reputation, worth and competence of people in which all other considerations are subordinated to what is in effect a moral master status. This does not imply a sequential development of identity but a sharp, complete break between who you were and who you (now) see you really are.

In the mental hospital, the patient must learn three related yet independent roles and must exercise some degree of proficiency in each. The first role is the general patient role, particularly the role of the "non-person," which is an important part of the role that any patient has in any hospital. The ability of the patient to act out this general patient role is essential to the patient being defined or understood as a "good patient," with all of the moral repercussions carrying over to the perceptions on the part of staff of the individual's performance in the other two roles.

The second role is that of the mentally ill person. In this role, the patient must come to act out the views, perceptions and expectations of the staff for a "typical" mental patient of his or her type.

The third role is that of the "normal" person that the mental patient ought to be striving to become. The mental patient must not only understand who he or she is, to act out the role of mental patient with all the intricate rewards and punishments supplied by the hospital, but at the same time must be learning how and when to exhibit those signs of normalcy, as that is defined by the staff.

The ultimate irony of the mental hospital, as Goffman shows, is that such institutions are particularly unsuited to the learning of "normal" roles and the consequent development of an identity as "normal," "recovered" or "cured." This is, Goffman contends, because interaction within the mental hospital is anything but "normal."

Within a mental hospital, interaction differs markedly from the typical communicative acts found in everyday life. For the most part, patients have little interaction with staff; much of their interaction is with other patients. The interactional behaviour displayed by such patients, and the self they consequently display, is by definition, if not always in practice, psychotic. One can and does learn from other patients new and previously unimagined ways of being "mentally ill," but they are poor role models from whom to learn behaviour appropriate to everyday, "normal" life. It is their inability to display appropriate behaviour, after all, that has led many of them to being placed in a mental hospital.

Interactions with physicians or psychiatrists are communicatively "over-determined," again, in ways that deviate sharply from the ordinary interactions found outside the hospital. In the mental hospital physicians have full and complete monopoly over interaction with patients. It is the psychiatrist who defines the situation and assigns both an identity and a status to the patient. Moreover, every action of the patient, every gesture, expression, hesitation, stumble, etc., is seen by the physician as *meaning something*. The patients' behaviour is seen as symptomatic of their mental status and, as Goffman (1967: 138) notes, to a physician, such a symptom "is merely a licence to start digging." Thus both the scope and relevance of communication given off by the patient is defined and controlled by the physician. Paradoxically, this makes the patient's control over her own actions and expressive display far *more* significant in the hospital than it would be in everyday life interaction. Yet, given this combination of greater significance and less control, the inevitable consequence is a much higher level of failure. Mental hospitals are conducive neither to sane nor competent interaction.

By the end of *Asylums*, Goffman presents a view of the mental patient as literally self-less, and thereby at the mercy of whatever benevolences or terrors those charged with her choose to apply (Goffman, 1961: 386):

> Mental patients can find themselves in a special bind. To get out of the hospital, or to ease their life within it, they must show acceptance of the place accorded them, and the place accorded them is to support the occupational role of those who appear to force this bargain. This self-alienating moral servitude, which perhaps helps to account for some inmates becoming mentally confused, is achieved by invoking the great tradition of the expert servicing relation, especially its medical variety. Mental patients can find themselves crushed by the weight of a service ideal that eases life for the rest of us.

Note that Goffman's discussion of the mental patient "brackets" or puts aside the issue of whether someone "really is" or is not mentally disturbed. Goffman's interest is not in deviance *per se* but in the moral displays of self that underlie all interaction, and the forms of social organization that call forth, inhibit or facilitate such displays. For Goffman, "all interaction is a moral enterprise involving the attribution of human character" (Hepworth, 1980: 85). The mental hospital is simply one kind of "place," one where it is insanity and the care of the insane that are displayed (Goffman, 1971).

Compared to Thomas Scheff's *theory* of mental illness, Goffman's work is more limited. Scheff goes beyond Goffman in two significant ways: (1) Scheff presents an alternative view of mental disorder itself, one that counters the dominant medical model of mental illness; and (2) he develops a systematic theory of becoming a *chronic* mental patient, which takes into account both the contingencies that precede and those that follow hospitalization. Yet in several crucial ways Scheff's approach is more limited than Goffman's. Scheff does not, as does Goffman, integrate his discussion with a more general theory of social interaction and social organization. Nor does Scheff, as does Goffman, generate a model of individual identity, action and motivation on which to ground his theory. This means that he lacks a "social psychology" to account for how and why individuals behave as he asserts they do.

SCHEFF'S LABELLING THEORY OF MENTAL ILLNESS

Thomas Scheff's theory of mental illness provides an example of what Goode (1984) calls the "hard" version of labelling theory. In effect, Scheff denies the reality of the medical model of mental disorder as an illness. The medical model assumes that mental disorder is an illness in the same way that heart disease, cancer or the flu are illnesses. According to this model, the various mental disorders have physiological causes and they can be objectively diagnosed and treated by a properly trained physician, with treatment leading either to a cure or to remission.

In opposition to the medical model, Scheff defines the "symptoms" of mental disorder as the violation of "residual rules" (Scheff, 1984: 188):

> Every society has myriad explicit rules and understandings about appropriate behavior, perceptions, feelings, and thoughts. For every explicit rule [e.g., stay on the right side of the road], however, there are probably many more rules that are so taken for granted that they are never stated or even thought about ... [such as] that in conversation one may look at the eyes and mouth of the speaker but not gaze only at his/her ear. When a person's behavior is disruptive or upsetting and we cannot find a conventional label of deviance [crime, drunkenness, etc.], we may resort to a miscellaneous or residual category. In earlier societies, witchcraft or spirit or demonic possession were used. In our society, our residual category is mental illness.

Note that Scheff does not dismiss a possible constitutional cause for the residual rule-breaking; he simply ignores it. The issue for Scheff is not *why* people do this but how we *respond* to it. This is consistent with Goffman's moral career model, which assumes that many more people engage in behaviour that could get them labelled "mentally ill" than actually receive this label. The question, then, is why are some labelled and what happens to them as a result?

Scheff argues that there are two sets of societal reactions to residual rule-breaking: the individual engaged in rule-breaking may be "normalized," in which case he or she will not be seen as mentally ill; or the individual may be "labelled," by which Scheff means stigmatized and segregated. In this latter case, Scheff argues, the result may be a career of deviance, i.e., a history of repeated admissions to mental institutions.

Scheff sets forth his theory in nine propositions (1984: 189):

1. Residual rule-breaking arises from fundamentally diverse sources.
2. Relative to the rate of treated mental illness, the rate of unrecorded residual rule-breaking is extremely high.
3. Most residual rule-breaking is normalized and is of transitory significance.
4. Stereotyped imagery of mental disorder is learned in early childhood.
5. The stereotypes of insanity are continually reaffirmed, inadvertently, in ordinary social interaction.
6. Labeled deviants may be rewarded for playing the stereotyped deviant role.
7. Labeled deviants are punished when they attempt to return to conventional roles.

8. In the crisis occurring when a residual rule-breaker is publicly labeled, the deviant is highly suggestible and may accept the proffered role of the insane as the only alternative.

9. Among residual rule-breakers, labelling is the single most important cause of careers of residual deviance.

We will not consider all the different aspects of Scheff's theory here. Note, however, that the most important assumption of all, that the symptoms of mental illness are simply "residual rule-breaking," is not presented by Scheff as a proposition but as a statement of fact, the foundation for all his other propositions.

In his criticism of Scheff's "hard" labelling approach, Goode (1984: 274) suggests that, contrary to Scheff's assertions in propositions 6 and 7, "conventional, 'normal' individuals are rooting for the rule breaker's recovery to normalcy." Goode also expresses doubt that labelling is the critical or single most important factor in "stabilizing" the career of remission and relapse among mental patients.

There is a also a major built-in contradiction in propositions 4 and 5. The notion of "stereotyping" used by Scheff suggests that mental disorder is not merely some grab-bag category into which we dump any behaviour that violates "residual rules," but is a very specific set of behaviours that we readily define as "insanity," just as we define other specific behaviour as "bank robbery." Few us us have ever seen or experienced a real bank robbery, yet thanks to everyday knowledge and the media we know what we mean by the term, and would easily recognize what was going on were we to find ourselves in one. In the same way, we know what mental illness "is" from everyday knowledge and from the media. Indeed, unlike a bank robbery, most of us *have* seen someone we consider to be mentally disturbed.

Goode (1984: 275) argues for a "soft" labelling approach to mental illness. He describes this approach as recognizing that, in addition to any objective psychiatric state, contingencies affect "how and why" someone gets to be labelled as mentally ill. But it has proven very difficult to do research to either confirm or invalidate either version of the labelling theory of mental disorder. The reason is that the labelling argument does not deal with causes and effects, but with complex social processes which come between the presumed "causes" and the identifiable "effects." As pointed out above, it is irrelevant to this argument whether schizophrenia is "really" caused by a neurochemical imbalance, by a genetic defect or by the tides of the moon. It is how we label, define and treat schizophrenics that is the issue. Moreover, doing research in hospitals with schizophrenics begs the question since it does not tell us why some people are not in hospital nor why these *are*.

PSYCHIATRIC DIAGNOSES AS LABELLING

The most powerful empirical critique of the medical model of mental illness was developed by David Rosenhan (1973; 1975). Rosenhan, a psychologist, concentrated on the issue of diagnosis in its broadest terms: how do psychiatrists determine the sanity or insanity of a patient? In his study, Rosenhan (1973) and several associates were admitted to twelve different mental hospitals after telling staff psychiatrists that they were hearing voices saying "empty," "hollow" and "thud." Once admitted, they tried to act as "normally" as possible, no longer claiming to hear any voices when asked.

Rosenhan's goal in this research was to see how the pseudopatients would be diagnosed by the psychiatrists, whether the psychiatrists would uncover the deception during the diagnostic interview, and whether the normal behaviour of the pseudopatients after admission would lead either to a discovery of the deception or to the decision that the patient was now "sane." In none of the cases was the deception discovered. In 11 cases the pseudopatients were diagnosed as paranoid schizophrenic, and in one case as manic depressive. In every case the pseudopatients were admitted to a psychiatric ward for a period ranging from 7 to 52 days. Discharge in each case was not based on the pseudopatient's apparent or achieved "sanity" but because the schizophrenia was "in remission."

In a second, related experiment, the staff at one hospital was told that one or more pseudopatients would attempt to be admitted over a period of three months. The staff were asked to keep a record of each patient in which they rated the likelihood that the patient was a pseudopatient. By the end of the period, 41 patients were suspected by at least one staff member of being a pseudopatient, but not one pseudopatient had been sent by Rosenhan during this period.

There are two particularly significant points made by Rosenhan in describing his experiments. One is his assertion that no criteria exist in psychiatric practice for "sanity" and that, as a consequence, no real criteria can exist for insanity. Just as the pseudopatients could pass as "insane" with no difficulty, so, too, real patients could be suspected of being "sane." The crucial difference is not the behaviour of the patients but the expectations of the psychiatrist. This suggests that mental disorder is not an objective "illness" that can be "diagnosed" like a physiological illness and that the "diagnosis" is really a labelling process.

The second point is that psychiatric wards are set up in such a way as to support the psychiatric label of insanity and prevent the possibility of displaying "sanity." Staff in the hospital take for granted that the patient is insane. Consequently every act, every gesture and every conversation is interpreted in light of the patient's illness. As an example, all the pseudopatients took notes publicly when engaged in conversation with the staff. In normal, everyday life, if someone were taking notes while you spoke, you would most likely question them, asking them why they were taking notes. None of the pseudopatients were asked by the staff why they were taking notes. The staff took for granted that they knew why the patients were taking notes: because they were "insane."

In effect, Rosenhan argues, it is almost impossible to display sanity in a psychiatric ward because the staff is predisposed to interpret behaviour as displays of insanity. In a mental hospital, says Rosenhan, the labels are "sticky."

Rosenhan's experiments are a powerful critique of the medical and psychiatric ideology of mental illness, but exactly what sort of critique is it? Is he arguing that mental illness is not "real," that the application of the label as mentally ill occurs at random, or simply that psychiatry has not yet developed sufficiently objective diagnoses?

Rosenhan is *not* saying that people who are in mental hospitals are not "really" crazy. He is saying that objective criteria do not exist among psychiatrists to determine or recognize if one is "sane." And if one has no criteria for sanity, then one has no reliable criteria for insanity. Sanity or insanity are not determined on objective, scientific, professionally established grounds, but on the basis of a subjective assessment, of past experience, the evidence presented by others and the patient's presentation of self.

Again, this is a criticism of psychiatric ideology, but is it really a criticism of psychiatric practice? If, as labelling theorists seem to be telling us, the labelling of the mental patient is always subjective, then psychiatric diagnoses may be "right" (in the sense that the patient clearly needs help) even if the reason for the diagnosis is not the one assumed by the psychiatrist. Of course, such psychiatric labelling *can* be abused, and there are many individual cases in which they are manipulated to label persons as mentally ill who ought not to to be so considered. Rosenhan's own research, which involved the manipulation of the presentation of self, is a case in point. But how much does that really tell us about the typical case of someone who desperately needs and wants help?

Do any criteria exist for determining if someone is sane or insane? If no criteria whatever exist for determining who is sane and who is insane, then the application of the label "insane" would be perfectly random. This is not the case. There tends to be widespread consensus as to who is mentally ill, not only among psychiatrists, but also among ordinary people in everyday life. If anything, ordinary common sense sees far more people as mentally disturbed than do psychiatrists, and far more people would be classified as crazy if it were up to the ordinary members of the public. Over the past few years one of the authors has asked his students to describe someone whom they consider mentally ill and the grounds for their assessment. He has purposely refrained from any technical discussion of mental illness until after receiving the completed assignments. The responses have been fascinating. Students have described as "crazy" a friend who spends too much on clothes, an aunt who cleans her home daily, someone who playfully splashed a friend with ketchup during a snack. Whatever the diagnostic deficiencies of psychiatric ideology, it is more restricted and rigorous than common-sense notions of what is normal or abnormal behaviour. Put differently, despite Rosenhan's criticism of psychiatric diagnosis, the attempt to establish and maintain *some* form of consistent and objective diagnosis on the basis of which to treat patients is far preferable to relying on the whim of the community.

THE CRITIQUE OF LABELLING THEORY

Looking back on it now, the labelling approach to mental illness suffered from three weaknesses. One, appropriately enough, was an historical contingency: the deinstitutionalization of the mental patient. Since the time in which Goffman, Scheff, and Rosenhan did their research, the treatment of mental illness has relied less and less upon placing patients in psychiatric wards. Instead, patients have tended to be placed on a regimen of drugs and released into the community. This has profoundly altered the relationship between the patient and the "agents of social control" in ways that have not necessarily benefited patients at all (Scull, 1977). Still, even with deinstitutionalization, over 25 000 people at any given time are patients in Canadian psychiatric institutions (Menzies, 1991: 198). Even within such institutions, however, treatment largely consists of the use of drugs.

A second factor that has significantly affected the credibility of the labelling approach to mental disorder is the recent claims of the dicovery of both a biochemical link to mental disorder and a putative genetic "cause" of mental disorder (Scheff, 1984). Again, while this does not necessarily affect the "soft" labelling approach, if confirmed it would be a decisive blow to the "hard" approach of Scheff. It would then be difficult to argue that mental disorder is nothing but residual rule-breaking.

The third factor has to do with the nature of the labelling argument itself. Labelling theory is not and was never intended to be a complete theory of deviance. Rather than *explain* mental illness, for example, labelling theory works best at describing some aspects of the *social organization* of mental disorder in North American society. It tells us how systems of social control are organized to process deviants and what happens to people caught up in these processes. It does not, however, tell us *why* these particular systems of social control are organized in the first place. Goffman tells us some of what happens in a mental hospital, but he does not tell us—as does Foucault (1973; 1976)—the origins of our notions of "madness" or why the asylum came to be seen as the place where the insane should be isolated from the rest of society and treated by specialists.

The labelling approach, especially in its interactionist form, really comes down to an attempt to answer these questions: How do individuals come to be classified as deviant and what effect does this have on how others treat them and on their self-identity? In themselves, these do not seem to be particularly contentious questions today. Yet labelling theory was inundated with a flood of criticism by the early 1970s. Some critics saw labelling theory as too "psychological" and too relativistic, thereby threatening cherished sociological concepts of society as consensual in terms of "norms" and "values" (Gibbs, 1972). Others saw it as inadequately relativistic and too modest in its claims about the importance of social definitions (see Chapter Eight). Still others saw it as too limited, ignoring the broader social, political and economic contexts within which deviance is defined and maintained and within which laws are enforced (see Chapter Seven). By the mid 1970s, labelling theory found itself in a peculiar position, then. Not of being seen as wrong, but rather as being seen as "right" but trivial. With the exception of a few critics (Gove, 1980), later perspectives on deviance have simply incorporated some components of the labelling approach while insisting that much more is involved in deviance than simply labelling.

While we would agree with this evaluation of the labelling perspective, there is still, it seems to us, a special place for labelling theory when examining deviance of a very special kind: symbolic deviance. By "symbolic deviance" we mean circumstances in which the processes of social control are put into play but in which *no actual deviance occurred*. The Salem Witch Trials discussed by Kai Erikson are a case in point. Normally, the labelling process is actually a rather technical matter. For example, a police officer deciding that some person's behaviour is "suspicious," or that a young person is "really" a delinquent rather than a good kid having some fun, is based on some fairly predictable and understandable criteria. But when there are no norms, rules or laws actually being violated, the "deviance" to which the community responds is purely symbolic, although the punishment inflicted on the supposed deviants may be very real. Under these circumstances, which are far more frequent than people realize, the labelling process is transformed from a technical issue to a symbolic display of the interests, biases, assumptions, hopes and fears that underlie our notions of what is or is not deviant. Examples would be the search for "secret" Communists during the McCarthy era in the United States, the Soviet treatment of dissidents as "mental patients" until quite recently, and the claim by the federal government that there existed an organized and well-planned "conspiracy" to topple the Québec government during the October Crisis in 1970. It is in examining such instances of deviance that the labelling perspective can still make significant contributions. Note, however, that such symbolic deviance often tends to have a political character. This means that the labelling theorists would have to turn away from their almost exclusive focus on the definition of the "situation" and, like Foucault (1973; 1976), look in more detail at the cultural, political and conceptual contexts within which some form of behaviour or some category of person takes on the symbolic attributes of deviance. That this is beginning to happen is suggested in the work of, for example, Denzin (1989), Plummer (1981a) and Rock (1973). Where it will lead remains to be seen.

NOTES

1. In order to avoid the complexities of writing "him or her," "he or she," we will use the feminine pronouns in this example.

CHAPTER

7 Critical and Feminist Criminologies

The 1960s and the early 1970s were a period of political and social turmoil in many advanced industrial societies. In Canada this was the era of rising Québec nationalism and of Trudeaumania; of episodes of student protest and of experimentation by young people with "alternative" lifestyles; of intense controversy about our relationship with the United States and of the wholesale invasion of Canada by American "culture." This social and political turmoil was also reflected in the rise of new ideas and new debates in the social sciences. New ideas in the philosophy of science seemed to undermine the claims of the natural sciences to be completely independent of historically and culturally formed assumptions and biases. Perhaps the most striking effect of these upheavals on sociology was the rise of perspectives that called on social scientists to be actively involved in changing the social conditions they studied. This went counter to the struggle of sociologists, from the time of the Chicago School in the 1920s, to distance themselves from earlier generations of moralists and social reformers, and to argue that sociological analysis should be "value free" and scientifically objective. The new ideas and questioning of authority arising from political and social unrest contributed to the development of subjectivist, radical, critical, Marxist and feminist sociologies which challenged earlier perspectives on political, as well as theoretical and empirical, grounds. Each of these new approaches developed alternative accounts of deviance which we take up in this and the following chapter.

The terms "critical," "radical," "conflict" or "Marxist" have all been used to describe analyses of deviance that focus on the differences in the distribution, use and vulnerability to power. Earlier theories of deviance identified a variety of causal factors: urban conditions for the

Chicago School; cultural values and stratified opportunities for Merton; symbolic resources for labelling theorists. While differences in social resources and uneven power relations were incorporated into these explanations, they were not the central focus of the perspectives. By contrast, critical theorists argue that power is pre-eminent as an explanation of deviance and social control.

Despite this common foundation, there are many, often subtle, differences among varieties of conflict and critical analysis. For example, the conflict approach often adopts a perspective derived from the German sociologist Max Weber (1978), which emphasizes the independent role of bureaucratic and government organizations, while Marxists place class relations in the forefront (Hinch, 1985). Marxists, in turn, differ among themselves about the precise nature of social classes, the relationships between economic and non-economic elements in society, the nature of ideology and so on.

Critical criminologists are engaged in multiple tasks: they seek to provide a critique of past criminology, to relate the issues relevant to crime and deviance to the "broadest sociological and philosophical concerns" (Gouldner, 1973: x), and to provide an alternative criminology which actively promotes human emancipation. These new critical theorists look at the pattern whereby power is distributed in a society, the socialization processes that reproduce this distribution, the organizational relations that maintain it, and the ideologies that serve to legitimate it. They insist that understanding deviance requires an understanding of these patterns.

Conflict theory shares some of the assumptions of critical theory, without sharing either its social psychology or its goal of emancipation. Conflict theorists reject the functionalist assumption of consensus on norms and values and assume instead that society is composed of sets of competing interest groups. They argue that society is therefore characterized, not by consensus, but by conflict: conflict over norms, over group interests, over economic resources, power and status; indeed, over all of those things that are in some way important to people. That means conflict, too, over what ought to be considered deviant or criminal and what ought to be done about it. As Jim Thomas (1982: 300) explains:

> Conflict theories hold that deviance ... is a natural state of social affairs [which] is at root a reflection of unequal power distribution. ... [D]eviance is a conflict between at least two parties, one the superordinate, who makes and enforces the rules, and the other the subordinate, whose behaviors violate those rules.

Since this approach views conflict as inevitable, it see social order as, at best, merely a temporary balance of power among competing groups (Turk, 1985). This is one area where conflict theory differs dramatically from critical theory. Emancipation, which implies equality, social justice and an end to conflict, is not considered feasible within the conflict perspective. Austin Turk (1985), in his summary of the conflict perspective, notes that it is primarily an empirical approach, which looks for statistical regularities and which rejects speculative or normative considerations. The insistence by critical theorists that sociologists ought to be directing their activities towards the achievement of emancipation is precisely the sort of normative consideration that is rejected by conflict theorists.

The more general term "radical" criminology refers to a potpourri of different Marxist perspectives and other, so-called "reformist," perspectives. Some of the radical sociologists or criminologists see their goal as changing society (Quinney, 1974; Chambliss, 1978), others as reforming some specific aspects of society. Some seek to fundamentally alter the structure of social relationships, others, to make those relationships more equitable (Downes and Rock, 1988; J. Thomas, 1982). What these particular sociologists seem to share is a dissatisfaction with the present ordering of society and an insistence that the only "real" deviance is the deviance of the powerful (Reasons, 1982). Their attitude is well summed up in Steven Box's (1983: xi) comment that "crimes of the powerful can only be ignored at the risk of enormously increasing our chances of being victimized by them."

Still another set of critiques with which we will deal in this chapter is derived from feminist perspectives. Feminists argue that sociology is biased in a number of ways. First of all, sociology neglects to pay sufficient attention to the place of women in society, and what attention is paid tends to view women from a male-centred point of view. Women are not portrayed as active members of society, participating equally in social activities, having experiences, goals, needs, desires or fears of their own. Their actions are always subordinated to male concerns. For example, Kingsley Davis's analysis of prostitution (Chapter Four) is based on the perceived "needs" of the male clientele rather than the circumstances of the prostitutes themselves. Prostitution is then seen as "caused" by balancing these individual male needs against impersonal systemic and institutional needs, rather than by an economically and sexually exploitive system which degrades women. Feminists argue that the personal and social degradation experienced by prostitutes is only an extreme form of the more ordinary forms of degradation faced by most women every day. To take another example, the argument over the reliability or validity of official rape statistics ignores the real impact rape has on the victims, how it fundamentally transforms (or deforms) their lives. It ignores as well the social and personal circumstances that surround any particular instance of rape, which result in many rapes being neither reported nor officially recorded. In addition, examining rape as a form of deviant behaviour ignores the ways in which society is structured to promote rape, the way in which rape reflects significant social divisions and group interests. Finally, legalistic definitions of rape focus only on the particular rapists and on their specific victims rather than on how the fear of rape affects all women. Feminists argue that a prevalent fear of rape is one of the factors that prevent many women from being full and active participants in society.

Few of these new criticisms, then, fall neatly into clear-cut categories we can identify as critical theory or conflict theory, but are inspired by the sorts of issues these perspectives raise, and they view the issue of power as crucial to understanding deviance.

THE DEVELOPMENT OF CRITICAL CRIMINOLOGY

Critical, radical and Marxist criminology commenced with a series of critiques of established perspectives on deviance. One of the first of these critiques was that of Alexander Liazos (1972) who directed his criticism particularly towards labelling theory. Liazos argues that labelling theory has three fundamental weaknesses (Liazos, 1972: 9-11):

- By focusing closely on the deviant acts engaged in by individuals, these actors are portrayed as essentially deviant and different from the rest of us.

- By focusing on individuals and acts usually defined as deviant, the labelling theorists ignore many other—sometimes more serious—forms of deviance which rarely come to the attention of the public.

- By emphasizing transactional and interactional processes among individuals, labelling theorists ignore the role of power in deviance and the ways in which power can be used either to define others as deviant or to avoid being defined as deviant oneself.

There are many ways in which people are the same, many ways in which they conform, and many times when they are not engaged in deviant activities. These are ignored when our focus is on deviance, when we examine how these people become prostitutes or drug users or mental patients or thieves. Although labelling theorists such as Becker claim to be on the side of the "underdog," their acknowledgement that sides exist places further stress on the deviant as different. Liazos, like Lofland (1969), suggests that the very term "deviant" should be eliminated. The use of the term "deviant" already labels those being studied and sets them apart from others. In response, we should note that sociologists must use some term to describe what it is they are studying and merely substituting one term for another would solve nothing. More practically, Liazos argues that if sociologists examined a broader range of deviant acts, including white-collar crime and corporate crime, it would be obvious that there is nothing either special or different about those who engage in deviant behaviour. Instead, deviance would be seen as an inevitable outcome of the ways in which our society is structured.

Liazos suggests that sociologists shift their attention from the "exotic" study of what he described as "nuts, sluts, and preverts," towards hidden deviance, such as corporate and political deviance. At the same time, sociologists and criminologists should shift their focus away from personal violence to the impersonal violence committed by corporations and the state through unsafe working conditions, pollution, the use of toxic substances and the manufacture of unsafe or hazardous products. Ultimately, such "covert institutional violence," as Liazos refers to it, threatens the public much more than the actions of muggers, armed robbers or contract killers. The recent fires at tire storage dumps in Ontario and Québec and the fire at a PCB storage facility near Montréal demonstrate the dangers of corporate irresponsibility and inadequate government enforcement of its laws. Luckily, no one seems to have come to any harm in these episodes, but the terrible loss of 3300 lives from the explosion and leak of poisonous gas at the Union Carbide pesticide plant in Bhopal, India, in 1984 shows the very real danger posed by corporate negligence and a casual disregard for the laws.

What is required, Liazos suggests, is both an investigation of crimes *by* the powerful, such as the Watergate break-in and subsequent cover-up in the United States, and an investigation of the ways in which the very definition of crime expresses power relationships in a society. Deciding whose side "we" are on is not enough. We must try to understand why there are "sides" in the first place and what these sides really are.

A broader critique of the entire tradition of the sociology of deviance was undertaken by British sociologists Ian Taylor, Paul Walton and Jock Young (1973). Taylor and his co-authors argued that all preceding perspectives on deviance were flawed by their ultimate adherence to a set of unexamined premises. These premises arise from trying to develop explanations of social phenomena in the same way as natural scientists explain natural phenomena. This leads sociologists to assume the objective existence of a society or a culture that is stable, that is organized around some generally agreed-upon values, and that is the basic, determining cause of a people's beliefs and behaviour. From such a point of view deviance is a "residual" phenomenon resulting from faulty socialization, value strain or special interactive processes leading to stigmatizing and labelling.

Taylor, Walton and Young argue that this is really a view of deviance from those at the top of the social order, for whom deviance is either a nuisance or a threat. Such views do not allow us to understand deviance either in terms of the deviants' own interests and interpretations, or in terms of the ways various institutional arrangements and social conflicts contribute to the phenomenon. The sociologist's lack of attention to the implicit assumptions underlying his or her understanding of deviance results in the co-optation of the discipline as part of the mechanisms of social control, providing techniques and justifications for the suppression of deviant individuals and groups. Such sociologists, as well as criminologists, do not study crime, they seek to control or prevent it. In contrast, Taylor, Walton and Young call for the development of a new social theory of deviance, a call that has served as an incentive to much of the subsequent development of critical criminology.

A third early critic of sociology's analysis of deviance and social control, Richard Quinney (1975: 191-92) sums up the past treatment of law by social scientists in a similarly sweeping manner: "The legal order has thus been viewed in the social sciences as a necessary force to assure order in capitalist society." As a consequence, sociologists have not sought alternatives to the existing legal order.

Quinney subsequently attempted to develop a coherent Marxist approach to crime, law and social control (1977), one that paid particular attention to the role of the state.

CRIME, CAPITALISM AND THE STATE

For Marxists such as Quinney, capitalist societies are rather peculiar in that they combine inequalities in wealth and property with methods of social control that depend far more on assent and acceptance than on force and fear. In pre-capitalist societies, social inequalities in wealth and property were backed up by punitive methods of social control and by force of arms. In Western Europe, property rights allowing trade, investment and speculation led to the development of markets, capitalistic enterprise and, ultimately, a powerful class of capitalists increasingly able to influence kings and governments. In this historical context the state became charged with responsibility for maintaining those social arrangements necessary for the persistence of capitalism as an economic system. That is, to safeguard private property and the conditions conducive to its profitable growth. At the same time, the state came under pressure to ensure the political stability and legitimacy of the social order as a whole.

This leads to a built-in contradiction in the workings of the state. The functioning of the state in maintaining the capitalist economy accounts for the overall bias of the legal framework in upholding the rights of capitalists. The functioning of the state in relation to legitimacy and political stability accounts for the genuine opportunities that allow working people, consumers and other subordinate groups to protest and fight for their interests. The legal system and other social control bodies cannot be used purely in defence of the privileges of wealthy capitalists without undermining the social, ideological and political basis of capitalism. Consequently laws and agencies charged with their enforcement develop some degree of independence and neutrality in relation to the inequalities of wealth and power resulting from capitalist economic development. How laws develop and how law enforcement and other control agencies operate, then, depends upon the relative strengths and successes of different class groups in asserting and defending their interests in the political system.

Quinney attempts to delineate the kinds of crime that develop in the political-economic context of industrial capitalism. Crimes of "domination" and "repression" are carried out by corporations and government agencies. They include such acts as illegal, punitive and provocative moves against rival political organizations, such as was exposed during the RCMP's attempts to discredit and disorganize Québec nationalist groups through wiretapping, harassment and acting as *agents provocateurs* in the 1970s. Crimes of domination also include economic crimes of corporations such as price-fixing, evading occupational health and safety laws and environmental protection laws; as well as what Quinney calls "acts of social injury" such as discriminatory hiring practices against women and minorities.

A second category of crimes is "crimes of accommodation," which includes personal crimes (murder, rape and other types of assault) and predatory crimes (theft or embezzlement). Such crimes are usually committed by those without significant social power who largely accept the social order as it is, without feeling any great commitment to it. In contrast, "crimes of resistance" are acts that express rejection of the capitalist social order. These acts can range from non-violent demonstrations and breaking censorship laws, to acts of industrial sabotage and terrorism.

Quinney's analysis of the capitalist state was an advance on an earlier Marxist theory known as "instrumentalism." This theory argued that the major centres of government, the judicial system, civil service and the armed forces, were directly manned by individuals drawn from the capitalist class, who then wielded power simply in the interests of their class. This simplistic model could not account for such obvious developments as the legitimation of trade unions, the rise of government restrictions on business practices in the interests of regional imbalances, environmental considerations or the protection of workers' health and safety.

The instrumental theory of the state was replaced by the structuralist model, which introduced two major ideas. First, while the state operates in terms of the functional needs of capitalism as both an economic and a political system, these requirements are not necessarily in harmony but are usually in tension with each other. The economic system continuously generates inequalities, unemployment, and other social problems that threaten the legitimacy and political stability of the capitalist society as a whole.

Second, the structuralist Marxists argue that the class system is a very complex one which includes divisions within the capitalist class. Thus capitalists associated with exporting industries do not have the same interests as those producing for domestic markets; those associated with heavy industries have concerns that differ from those in consumer goods, and so on. Rarely will a single policy satisfy all capitalist groups, so they struggle among themselves. This leaves political parties and state agencies some leeway to respond to pressures from other class groups and to develop their own solutions to managing the various problems arising from capitalist economic contradictions.

However, for many non-Marxists the structural approach fails as a model of social reality because it presents society as one in which social conflicts and tensions are all-pervasive, and such conflicts are primarily centred around economic class divisions. Yet most people do not experience society, at least in Canada, to be in a state of perpetual class warfare. One response to this problem has been the adoption of the ideas of the Italian Marxist, Gramsci, especially his notion of "hegemony." During his several years in Canada, Ian Taylor, one of the early critical criminologists, was active in refining the critical approach he helped to initiate and applying a Gramscian perspective on crime in Canada.

A CANADIAN POLITICAL ECONOMY OF CRIME

Given his research interests and his political goals, Taylor links his analysis of crime to the political economy of relations between the state and civil society. Taylor sees the pattern of crime as a direct result of the system of political, economic and social domination. Economic changes result in changes in crime; *objectively* in the kinds and quantity of crime that is occurring, *subjectively* in the attention paid by the public and the media to crime, and *officially* in the labourpower assigned to deal with crime and the reporting of particular kinds of crimes.

Throughout his work, Taylor has consistently argued that changing or shifting rates of crime are a consequence of an economic crisis occurring in Canada, Britain and the United States. All three nations are characterized by Taylor as "advanced capitalist societies." This means that they are liberal-democratic in political structure, monopoly capitalist in economic structure, and "hegemonic" in social structure.

A liberal-democratic state is one in which the state apparatus itself, the government and its agencies, acts to mediate among conflicting groups in society by assigning to subordinate classes some measure, albeit modest, of political involvement and some measure, albeit modest, of economic security. That means that a liberal-democratic state organizes its political structure around political parties and organizes its political "agenda" around social, health and welfare services. Neither the level of political participation nor the distribution of services challenges the domination of the economic elite, but are both sufficient to mobilize loyalty to the state and to diffuse radical opposition.

Economically, Taylor argues, Canada, Britain and the United States are dominated by powerful multinational capitalist enterprises. These enterprises are bound neither organizationally, politically nor economically to any one country. They are free to shift their operations wherever market forces direct. While these enterprises may dominate the economy, as long as economic conditions are favourable there is enough prosperity to go around to allow small and medium-scale enterprises to operate as well. Thus, economic domination may be real, but it is not obvious, given the large number of individual and small enterprises.

The term "hegemony" refers to the processes whereby subordinate classes assign both legitimacy and loyalty to the particular form of domination in place in their society. Hegemony therefore constitutes a pattern of social relationships among groups and a social and political structure that serves to maintain that pattern. As Taylor (1983: 8) describes it, one crucial element in the process that generated this social structure was: "The extension of the electoral franchise to the mass of propertyless workers [as] ... a means of winning their consent not simply to the parliamentary system nor to any particular party, but quite specifically to the underlying form of capitalist economy."

Other political elements include the provision of public education, worker's compensation, unemployment insurance and provincial public health care programs. The economic "cost," at least for the dominant classes, has been the monetary loss through higher taxes to support these programs, as well as some subordination of the free market to the "ideological prioritization of the political realm" (Taylor, 1983: 9). This cost was well worth paying, especially since tax laws have placed the real financial burden on the middle class and as long as there was adequate performance by the capitalist economy.

This last point is crucial for Taylor, who argues that the economic crises of the 1970s and early '80s put great strain on the stability of the advanced capitalist societies. These recurrent economic crises led to political crises, which in turn led, in the case of Britain and the United States, to hegemonic crises. Where Canada differs from Britain or the United States is that the economic and political crises have *not* led to a hegemonic crisis.

The economic crises are easy enough to illustrate. The dramatic recession of the early 1980s, for example, led to rapid inflation, widespread unemployment and severe hardship for the poor, for single parents and for farmers, a situation that seems to be recurring as this is being written in the 1990s. Politically, too, Canada has passed through a series of crises, beginning with the election of the Parti Québécois in 1976, the Québec referendum on sovereignty-association in 1980, the failure to develop a national energy policy in 1982, the constitutional crisis ending with Québec's exclusion from the process of patriation of the constitution, the fierce free trade debate during the national election of 1988, and the subsequent inability to ratify the Meech Lake Accord to bring Québec into the constitution.

These economic and political crises have not led to a hegemonic crisis, Taylor contends, because Canadian workers have typically desired a "bourgeois" and "stable" state (1983: 9-12). In addition, Canadians typically look to the state to take decisive action to improve the economy. For these reasons, there has been, Taylor argues (1983: 15), "no fundamental collapse in the belief of the mass of the people in ... the existing form of state and social order."[1]

Despite his claim that Canada does not face a hegemonic crisis, Taylor asserts that the state and the police have consistently acted as if it does. Canadian authorities, Taylor suggests, have routinely repressed dissident groups such as left-wing, socialist groups and Québécois "separatists." The most obvious and dramatic example was the use of the War Measures Act in 1970 to send troops into Montréal during the "October Crisis," but there has since been a whole catalogue of revelations about RCMP and police "dirty tricks" including illegal break-ins, the opening of mail, arson and the use of *agents provocateurs*. Indeed, Taylor argues that despite the popular image of Canada as a "liberal" state, the Canadian government has typically used or condoned a high level of repression against "dissident groups," of which the massive deployment of military troops and armament against the Mohawk demonstrators in Kanesetake and Kahnewake in 1990 is the most recent example, as of this writing.

Another issue raised by Taylor is the tendency for Canada's police forces to shift their priorities from those of the local community to those of the state. One result has been that the police have little sympathy for community members and little contact with community groups. This is evident in police suspicion of minority groups and their tendency to overreact when dealing with minority-group members. The most spectacular example was the arrest of 289 people in Toronto in 1981 during raids on steambaths frequented by homosexuals. Other serious examples include the shooting of Blacks by police officers in Montréal and Toronto, such as the shooting of Anthony Griffen in the parking lot of a Montréal police station when he tried to escape police custody.

Taylor examines a number of other issues related to crime in Canada, such as the role of prisons in maintaining public order, legislation on sexual assault, the high crime rate among native people, and gun control. His conclusion on all these issues is to argue against the "conspiratorial" view of the state as a tool of the capitalist class, characteristic of the earlier, instrumentalist, critical criminology of the 1970s. As Taylor (1983: 64) puts it, "the state is not a monolithic expression of 'capital' or 'patriarchy' and ... there are spaces for significant reformist activity."

THE "NEW" CRITICAL CRIMINOLOGY

Critics of critical criminology have argued that theorists like Richard Quinney and Ian Taylor fail to explain precisely how the capitalist economy and state determines the kinds and amounts of deviance existing in capitalist societies. The capitalist societies of Western Europe and North America differ greatly in crime rates, legal systems, policing and penal practices and philosophies. Legal codes and the framework of assumptions or legal culture underlying them have pre-capitalist origins in English common law, canon law, Roman law and various feudal codes. These pre-capitalist foundations affected the development of laws and social control during the rise of capitalism. Consequently, identifying the specifically *capitalist* elements of the law, state and crime control is extremely difficult.

Further, the relationship between capitalism and crime is problematic. Historical and anthropological evidence shows that predatory and personal crimes such as robbery, murder and rape are found in a great many different societies. Crimes of domination and repression such as corruption and violation of constitutional rights are at least as prominent in the supposedly post-capitalist societies of the Soviet Union and Eastern Europe as in capitalist societies. Quinney's concept of crimes of resistance assumes clear political motivation and consciousness are involved. Yet class consciousness is not a clear and pronounced feature of ordinary social life in most advanced industrial countries (Mann, 1973), so why should this be the case in relation to acts such as sabotage and terrorism? Studies of industrial sabotage and pilferage do not demonstrate the existence of a subversive, oppositional or class consciousness beyond a primitive assertion of a claim to greater rewards than the existing wage scale (Ditton, 1977; Henry, 1978). Studies of social movements of protest suggest that joiners' motives and perceptions have a very complex relationship to the nature and goals of the movement they join.

While the goal of an overall Marxist theory of crime and social control remains unrealized, critical criminologists have made some important contributions to historical and structural issues, particularly in connection with law creation and law enforcement. Perhaps the most impressive example of this new historical and structural awareness is found in *Discipline and Punish*, written by the French philosopher-social scientist Michel Foucault (1979). This work identifies a modern Western industrial system or approach to social control that underlays all our major institutions, including the family, the school, the factory, the hospital and the prison. This system has its origin in the eighteenth-century transition from social control through punishment by torture and execution as a public spectacle to more discreet, less blatantly brutal techniques of social control based on disciplined self-control. For Foucault, this transition involves a complex, interconnected set of cultural, institutional and political changes so inextricably intertwined with the rise of capitalism that he refuses to follow the Marxist assertion of a clear cause-and-effect relationship between economy, class and the state. Rather, he looks at the shift from punishment to discipline as it is expressed in the history of ideas; in adaptations of preindustrial organizations such as the monastery, the court administrations, and armies as the state changes from feudal to absolutist form; in the rise of factories and labour markets; and in the emergence of new occupations dedicated to developing and applying new concepts of social control in areas of health, education and penology.

On a more modest scale, critical criminologists have also introduced new interpretations which add to our understanding of deviance. For example, Ian Taylor looks at the phenomenon of "moral panics" promoted by moral entrepreneurs who aim to reform law and morality (Taylor, 1982). Labelling theorists such as Becker (1963) and Gusfield (1963) had treated such phenomena as achieving largely symbolic outcomes, in that an activity such as marijuana smoking or selling alcoholic beverages becomes stigmatized but not actually suppressed or controlled. Taylor argues that moral panics are also important because they *mystify* the social conditions that give rise to social problems in the first place, and misdirect our attention away from the basic social contradictions. He explores the publicity and media attention surrounding muggings in England in the early 1970s, which produced calls for stiffer penalties and more intense policing. This moral panic defined the mugging problem as one of individual lawlessness requiring more law and order to solve. In the process, the economic changes underlying the disintegration of the old, established, working-class communities and their economic foundations, and the higher youth unemployment, which promoted higher delinquency, were ignored. Taylor argues that moral entrepreneurship and moral panics, as well as the changes in morality and laws that they sometimes cause, all emerge from changing social conditions, which have to be analysed by sociologists of deviance. The labelling theorists tended to focus on the link between moral enterprise and legal changes, to the exclusion of the broader historical and structural context.

Finally, critical criminology has expanded the analysis of "white-collar crime" to focus on the ability of the powerful to evade, deflect or weaken the impact of laws on their own activities. Traditional analyses of crime accounted for the prominence of lower-class, immigrant and racial-minority groups among those arrested and committed in terms of the cultural, psychological and social environmental circumstances of these groups. Critical criminologists account for the class profile of arrests and internments in terms of the intentional and functional biases of law and social control.

Thus "street crimes" are the object of constant media attention and police publicity. A state of sustained "moral anxiety" surrounds break-ins, muggings and bank heists, which shapes our perception of crime and criminals. But, "suite crimes" arising from the actions of corporations, professionals and government agencies result in deaths, injury, impoverishment and environmental degradation on a far grander scale than any injuries produced by ordinary criminals. But, because of the abilities of corporate, professional and governmental elites to operate in secrecy; because of the prestige of the institutions and occupations involved; because of the often complex and technical nature of the wrongdoing, our conception of crime does not extend to the wrongdoing of the powerful (Goff and Reasons, 1978). Even where spectacular disasters occur and can be traced to dubious business practices and governmental laxness, as in the case of the Ocean Ranger disaster, where an oil rig sank off the coast of Newfoundland with a loss of the entire crew of 84, industry and government move quickly "to institute mechanisms to normalize the situation, to gain control of the aftermath of the disaster" (House, 1985: 209). As a result, corporate negligence and government laxness in setting and enforcing standards faded in the context of the ensuing intercorporate legal wrangling and commissions of inquiry hearings. In keeping with the perspective of contemporary Marxism, the lack of "visibility" of corporate crime is seen as arising from a complex combination of circumstances: the great majority of corporate activities that produce real hardship are outside the Criminal Code because of the technical character of the law itself (Glasbeek, 1989); the ideological and cultural influences on our definitions of crime (Goff and

Reasons, 1978); the legal and administrative procedures protecting the accused, which make prosecution often extremely difficult (Casey, 1985); provincial and federal government failure to enforce Criminal Code provisions against corporate offenders (House, 1985); and the complex and impersonal nature of corporate activities (Jackall, 1980).

THE FEMINIST PERSPECTIVE

Like other sociological perspectives, the feminist perspective is composed of a wide variety of different points of view and diverse and sometimes conflicting theories. Nevertheless, there are a number of common themes and concerns that can be identified in the work of feminists. Sydie (1987: 360) summarizes some of these themes among feminist sociologists as follows:

> Feminist sociology emphasizes the experiences of women, the uncovering of hidden realities, because there can be no sociological generalizations about human beings as long as a large number of such beings are systematically excluded or ignored.

Above all, feminists emphasize that our notions of what it means to be male or female and our dealings with one another as male or female are consequences of the social arrangements and social processes prevalent in our society. No one is ever "just" male or female, because gender is neither biological nor "natural." To be a female in our society is to act out a role that is defined for us by others and by the expectations we carry around with us. To be a female is also to participate in a set of social relations that define for us our status vis-_-vis others. It goes without saying that this is true as well for males, but with this difference: the "feminine" role allotted to women in our society is one that tends to place them in, at best, a subservient role to men, one in which they are sometimes or often degraded or victimized. Feminists, too, then, have an emancipatory goal. If gender relations always reflect the pattern of social relations in a society, then changing gender relations requires changing those social relations as well.

Like the critical criminologists, feminists produce a critique both of society as it is presently organized and of the disciplines of sociology and criminology themselves. When directed at criminology, the feminist critique asserts that both the sociology of deviance and criminology have failed to pay sufficient attention either to the activities of women as "criminals" or to the experiences of women as the victims of crime.

Some feminists suggest that the lack of attention paid to women as criminals is a result of a "constitutional" bias among male criminologists, who see women as constitutionally incapable of certain forms of crime, such as violent crimes, yet at the same time constitutionally inclined towards other forms of deviance, such as prostitution or sexual deviance (Smart, 1977). In this respect, the study of female deviance progressed little from the time of Lombroso (see Chapter Two) until the emergence of a feminist criminology in the late 1970s. Female crime seemed to need no special explanation or research, since it was the outcome of innate "feminine" characteristics or tendencies.

In their review of feminist criminology, Downes and Rock (1988) suggest that several non-constitutional theories to explain the relative absence of female crime have appeared over the years. They summarize the two major ones as follows (Downes and Rock, 1988: 283):

> Subcultural theories have assumed that females pursue less criminogenic and more attainable goals than men, namely marriage and family life, and are therefore insulated from the social sources of delinquency, the main exception being the strain to sexual deviance. Control theories specify with some precision the far more intensive and extensive informal social controls that are brought to bear on girls rather than boys, which constitute powerful inhibitors against criminality.

Feminists themselves have not developed an alternative explanation of lower rates of female crime, but some have argued that as women have become more emancipated and the controls against women have decreased, more women are likely to commit crimes and to be labelled as criminals. Hatch and Faith (1991), have found, however, that at least in Canada, this has not been the case; while the number of female offenders has been increasing, the rate of increase is lower than that for male offenders. This means that the ratio of female to male offenders is decreasing.

In recent years, a number of studies have appeared which examine female crime or the female criminal (Adler, 1975; Campbell, 1984; Carlen, 1985; Lindsay and Walpole, 1978; Schur, 1984). While these studies open up what has been to date a neglected area of research, there is little they contribute to a specifically feminist approach to crime or deviance. Noting that women, too, can be deviant tells us little about how crime is experienced by women, especially how women are targeted or victimized by crime. It is in this latter area that feminists have made substantial contributions towards the study of deviance and have de-romanticized the view of the criminal characteristic of both labelling theorists and critical criminologists. When it comes to rape, wife-beating or pornography, the "underdog" is not the deviant but the victim, and if we are to be on someone's side, as Howard Becker insisted, then feminists argue it should be on the side of the victim. Taking sides is a political act, and feminists have been at the forefront of attempts to alter policy or legislation in regard to crimes against women. One area in which there has been much publicized progress in reforming the law is in the area of sexual assault. Canada now has one of the strongest laws on the books against rape and other forms of sexual assault. Yet many questions remain about how effective the new laws really are and whether they meet the real needs of women in Canadian society.

Rape

Most people today consider rape to be a violent, brutal crime and recognize its persistence to be a serious social problem (Goode, 1990). Yet this was not always the case. Just a few years ago, rape was rarely viewed as a serious crime, either by the courts or by the police. Instead, it was the victim of rape who was stigmatized in society. The dramatic changes in attitudes, laws and actions concerning rape in the last few years are largely the result of efforts made by feminists.

Sociologists, too, paid little attention to rape before feminists began to raise it as a crucial issue for a feminist sociology. Previously, research on rape was largely limited to the attempt to understand the actions and motivations of the rapist, a task sociologists tended to leave to psychologists. Those few sociologists who did look at rape, such as Menachem Amir (1971), viewed it as a crime largely precipitated by the victim; a point of view that adopted unquestioned and culturally biased notions both of rape and of its victims.

This absence of interest in rape points out some of the theoretical deficiencies of existing sociological perspectives on deviance. Functionalist theories have always seemed most plausible when applied to "vice," organized forms of deviance which violate accepted social norms or mores but which also provide illicit services, such as prostitution, gambling, political corruption or organized crime. The discrepancy between accepted, "official" norms and actual social practices fits well into the functionalist distinction between manifest and latent functions. But the functionalist explanation is not nearly as convincing when dealing with other forms of deviance, such as violent crimes. Few people would find a claim that rape somehow benefits society either plausible or acceptable.

As for the labelling approach, this perspective is most plausible when applied to "victimless" deviance such as mental illness, homosexuality or recreational drug use (Schur, 1965). These are forms of behaviour about which there is serious disagreement in society, with many people arguing that they are not or should not be considered deviant. In such cases one can argue that the "deviance" resides in the definitions being applied, and is not intrinsic to the behaviour. But, again, what of rape? Is rape deviant merely because people in our society define it as deviant? Or is rape, as many feminists assert, a fundamental violation of women, a violent and extreme version of the ordinary subordination of women by men found in our society (Tomaselli, 1986)? Rape, many feminists insist, *is* inherently deviant.

Critical theory, too, was blind to rape. The instrumentalist focus on class relations as the "cause" of crime, characteristic of early critical theory, closed the critical theorist off from considering other forms of conflict and other ways in which power can be displayed, used and abused. Critical theory therefore ignored the inequalities found in gender relations, ethnic conflict, elder abuse and so on (Downes and Rock, 1988).

But it is not sufficient to say that rape was ignored *because* it did not easily fit into the existing dominant perspectives on deviance. We must also recognize that these perspectives were largely produced by men and reflected their interests and concerns. To male sociologists and criminologists, rape was just another crime; one of interest only if it were theoretically significant. Since men do not feel personally threatened by rape, since it has no personal resonance which carries over from their personal experience to their research agendas, it took the development of the feminist perspective to raise the issue of rape as a significant, distinctive and urgent problem for sociological theory and research.

Feminists have paid particular attention to rape for a number of reasons. First and foremost, rape is a terrifying, violent and humiliating experience that many women undergo and that almost all women fear. Changing the laws related to rape, providing help and other services to women who have been raped, and finding ways to prevent rape are therefore some of the most important practical tasks facing the women's movement. In addition, some feminists assert that rape symbolizes and reflects the pattern of male/female relations found in our society. While few men may be rapists, most men tend to take advantage—wittingly or unwittingly—of the domination over women accorded to them in our society. Fear and dependence, feminists assert, mark women's social relations with men, whether it be at work, on a date or in the home, and women can never be equal to men in society as long as that fear and dependence persist. Finally, rape has been a major issue for feminists because it is one on which many women agree and which is of urgent and personal concern to them. Rape has served as an issue that can sensitize women—and men—to the concerns and goals of the women's movement.

Yet a sociological consideration of rape uncovers the same degree of socio-cultural contradictions and ambiguities with regard to rape as we have found to be the case for alcohol and drug use, suicide and juvenile delinquency. Rape, it has been argued, arouses far more "horror, anger and controversy than any other crime of violence" (Tomaselli, 1986: 11). Yet, as Clark and Lewis (1977: 24) note, some cases of rape are "dismissed with a knowing wink as a natural consequence of the sexual game." How are we to account for such diametrically opposed attitudes towards rape being current at the same time? Obviously, there is extensive disagreement and debate over whether rape is a sexual act, an act of violence, an expression of men's domination over women or some combination of all three. There is disagreement as well over whether rape is caused by the diseased mind of the "mad rapist" (Douglas and Waksler, 1982), whether it is an exaggeration of "normal" sexual relations (Hills, 1980) or whether rape is somehow precipitated by the victim herself (Amir, 1971).

We cannot look to the law to clarify the issues for us. The law is itself an expression of socio-cultural definitions and assumptions rather than some "objective" alternative to them. For this reason, laws concerning rape are specific to every country and are sharply limited in their definition of rape, whether they view rape as a serious crime, how they punish the rapist, and how they treat the victim. For example, in many parts of the United States a husband cannot be charged with raping his wife. Legally, then, sexual assault by a husband in those jurisdictions is never "rape." Obviously, such a legal definition implies a whole set of socio-cultural assumptions and understandings about what rape is, the nature of husbands' "rights" of sexual access to their wives and so on. For this reason, the law can serve as no more than a starting point from which to uncover the socio-cultural understandings about rape found in our society (Boyle, 1991).

Still, the law and the workings of the criminal justice system do provide us with a starting point from which to uncover those broader socio-cultural definitions and assumptions concerning rape and the structural conditions that promote them.

Rape as Crime

Current Canadian laws on sexual assault came into effect in 1983 to remedy some of the biases and abuses built into previous laws on rape. Rape had been defined exclusively as "forced" penetration of the penis into the vagina "by a man on a women who is not his wife" (Pettifer and Torge, 1987: 21). The current law differentiates among "simple sexual assault," "sexual assault with a weapon" and "aggravated sexual assault." "Simple sexual assault" covers a wide spectrum of behaviour in which some degree of force is used. This includes behaviour that was previously characterized as "indecent assault," as well as rapes in which no weapon is used. Over 90 percent of all sexual assaults are characterized as simple sexual assaults (Johnson, 1988: 27). "Sexual assault with a weapon" implies the use or threat to use a weapon or to otherwise cause bodily harm. About 5 percent of sexual assaults fall into this category, with a very small number of additional cases of "aggravated sexual assault," in which the life of the victim is endangered or the victim is maimed or disfigured. The new law also allows for a husband to be charged with sexual assault on his wife, and for men to be classed as the victims of sexual assault.

While many people have hailed the new legislation as taking significant steps towards improvements, there are still many unresolved issues of concern to women (Boyle, 1991). As one example, Pettifer and Torge (1987) point to the section on "belief of consent" as a problem in the new law. This section states that if the accused had an "honest belief" that the victim consented to the act, then the accused should be acquitted. This means, as Pettifer and Torge note, that if no weapon was used during the assault, which is the case in 90 percent of sexual assaults, "the burden is then on the victim to prove that she submitted out of fear." This legal loophole has been criticized on the grounds that it does not appear when considering any other crime (Box, 1983). Would a jury acquit a bank robber who pleaded in his defence "I didn't know the bank didn't want to be robbed?" Obviously not. Still, there are some important differences between bank robbery and rape. A case in which a man rapes a women at gun-point is also rather straightforward. Here, the jury would point to the gun as proof that there was no honest belief of consent. But few cases of sexual assault, as we have seen, actually fall into this category. Instead, date rapes, or assaults by friends, relatives or acquaintances make up the bulk of the cases. Unlike the impersonal relations between bank and customers, sexual relations among people are so intimate a matter, and so prone to misinterpretation even by the parties involved, that outsiders must have some rigorous criteria to make decisions concerning them. For better or worse, some decision concerning "intent" must be made, just as it is made in the case of murder. But in the case of murder we do not simply take the defendant's word on "intent," nor do we stigmatize the victim for "leading" the killer on. The problem does not necessarily reside in the law itself, but in the failure of the legal system in the past to treat women who have been raped in a fair, unbiased and equal manner.

A recent case in Québec illustrates this ongoing bias. A 69-year-old "alcoholic" was acquitted by a judge of a charge of raping a 65-year-old wheelchair-bound woman in 1991 on the grounds that he was "too drunk to know what he was doing" (Buckie, 1991). Such a defence is not acceptable in the case of other crimes, however. Again, bank robbers would not be acquitted if they were drunk when committing the robbery. The judge justified his decision by arguing that the prosecutor could not prove intent *because* the defendant was drunk, and therefore the rights of the defendant have priority over "the protection of society." Since such a decision is unlikely in the case of another crime, such as robbery, this tells us that to this judge, at least, rape is less serious and poses less of a threat to "society" than do other crimes. Note as well that the impersonal phrase "threat to society" is used to cover what must have been a horrible and traumatic assault on a physically helpless woman.

Reporting Rape

Rape, in the form of sexual assault, is a crime in Canada, defined and treated as such by the criminal justice system. Yet, as the example just given above illustrates, to limit ourselves to the strictly legal aspects of rape tells us little about how the criminal justice system actually works, how and when it defines some behaviour as sexual assault or why so many women are reluctant to report that they have been raped or otherwise assaulted. It tells us even less about our society, the conditions that lead to rape or the role rape plays in the lives of the men who commit rape or of the women who are their victims. Rape refers to a wide variety of social behaviours that reflect socio-cultural definitions of "men," "women" and the relationships between them. Understanding rape requires that we understand those social relationships.

We begin with the frequent assertion that the majority of rapes are not reported to the police or other authorities. Some estimates suggest that as few as 10 percent of rapes are reported, and one major survey found that 62 percent of sexual assault victims did not report the assaults to the police (Boyle, 1991). While there are other crimes that are not always reported, that such a very low percentage of rapes are reported suggests that rape is not simply a straightforward criminal matter. In contrast, imagine a bank manager deciding not to report a robbery to the police.

Sometimes the failure to report a crime is based on fear of retaliation by the criminal. Statistics show that less than half the victims of violence report the incident to the police, with 21 percent of those not reporting giving as their reason fear of revenge (Sacco and Johnson, 1990).[2] In the case of rape such fears are often quite reasonable and realistic. After all, the rapist has already committed a violent assault on the victim. Since most men accused of rape are not convicted, the victim is often right to expect that the courts will not protect her by locking up the rapist.

Another reason that so few rapes are reported is that many rapes are committed by someone who is well known to the victim. In this case, the rape is not some isolated act but is a part of an ongoing set of social relationships, which may continue after the rape has occurred. Take the case of "date rape," one of the most common forms of sexual assault. The victim and her rapist are likely to be part of the same social network, to have friends and acquaintances in common, to see one another on some type of regular basis. An accusation of rape would create a whole set of difficulties for the victim. She might simply not be believed and would then lose her friends; she might be unable to continue with her work or other social activities; she might be stigmatized by those who believe she was somewhat or wholly responsible for the rape, or just because her accusation "ruined" the other person's life. To the degree that she had some sort of personal relationship with the rapist before the rape she, too, may blame herself. Perhaps she was not definite enough or forceful enough in resisting sexual advances, perhaps she unwittingly led him on. In such situations a woman often feels a sense of guilt or confusion that leaves her unable to act or that can be manipulated by her attacker. When the rapist is a co-worker or a supervisor at work, the situation becomes even more complex. Imagine, then, how complex the feelings and issues involved become when the rapist is a woman's husband. Even though Canadian law allows a woman to charge her husband with rape, many women may feel they would be the object of ridicule for doing so or that they would hurt their children or other family members. Since Boyle (1991: 100) reports that the Canadian Urban Victimization Survey found that 41 percent of victims of reported sexual assault knew their assailants, we can suspect that a far greater percentage of those who did not report their attacks knew their assailants.

Blaming the Victim

Added to these personal concerns and issues is the general cultural tendency prevalent in our society to blame the victim in the case of rape. As competent, knowledgeable members of this society, women know that it is they who are likely to be blamed when they are raped. Pettifer and Torge (1987: 25) identify the following beliefs about rape victims that lead to such victims being blamed for their rape:

1. It is not really possible to rape a non-consenting woman.

2. Women ask to be raped (and probably enjoy it).

3. Only "loose" women get raped; nice girls don't get raped.

4. Women commonly report rape that has not occurred.

It should not be necessary to assert that these beliefs are false; unfortunately, that is not the case. These beliefs persist despite ongoing efforts to educate the public about the reality of rape. Whatever the laws may be, as long as even a few police officers, judges and members of juries hold to these beliefs, the criminal justice system does not operate to protect women and punish rapists. And, as long as women know that these beliefs are prevalent, they will be reluctant to report rape or to lay charges.

Many women who do report rape to the police report being shocked by the attitude the police often display. They may seem to be indifferent or callous; to interrogate the woman as if the victim were the real criminal; to seem eager to humiliate the woman; and to show more regard for the rights of the rapist than for those of the victim. Hills (1980: 59) has described the experience many women undergo when dealing with the police after a rape as a "degradation ceremony." Some women assume that this indicates sympathy on the part of the police towards the rapist, perhaps some secret masculine "rapport," or a tendency to blame the victim for her own circumstances. Douglas and Waksler (1982: 254) suggest a different interpretation, arguing that, based on their past experience, the police may know that, whatever the real merits of a case, they have little chance of obtaining a conviction under most circumstances. Their decision not to follow up on a case or their attempt to convince or pressure the victim to drop charges is, from their point of view, a practical response to the legal and occupational constraints imposed on them.

Does this justify the indifference of the police? If Douglas and Waksler are right, it is irrelevant whether the police share the common-sense biases and myths concerning rape that are prevalent in our culture. It is enough that they must take these notions and myths into account for their effectiveness in dealing with rape to be jeopardized. This means that, regardless of whether any individual police officer, lawyer or judge is biased or not, the system as a whole works in such a way as to deny women their rights and their self-respect.

Socio-Cultural Assumptions About Rape

This socio-cultural tendency to blame the victim of rape rather than the rapist is part of a much broader set of cultural assumptions. Most contemporary sociological theories of rape look to a combination of these cultural assumptions with a set of structural factors to explain the role rape plays in society. Cultural attitudes towards the rapist and the victim are seen to serve as justifications or as ideological expressions of the structural relations between men and women in our society. Still, while there are many different versions and interpretations of such structural factors, the view that ours is a "sexist culture" is widely accepted as one of the causes of rape.

The term "sexist" does not mean that our society is "obsessed" with sex, but that our culture stereotypes men and women as fundamentally different from each other. It means as well that when they are assigned to men and women, these stereotypes become their fate. To the degree that men and women are treated differently in society, that "fate" takes the form of gender inequality.

While the public often blames rape on the actions of a mentally deranged "mad rapist" (Douglas and Waksler, 1982), it has also been assumed in Western culture that all men—at least all "real" men—are sexually aggressive. Hills (1980), for example, describes what he calls the "masculine mystique." Men are taught a masculine ideal that values "strength, power, independence, forcefulness, domination and toughness" (Hills, 1980: 63), qualities that are valued in dealing both with women and with other men. In addition, Hills suggests that men have a tendency to "compartmentalize" sex, that is, to consider sex a separate, "natural" matter, different from love or caring. This means that men will be willing to take advantage of almost any opportunity that presents itself for sexual relations. If this is so, then men may believe themselves to have a "natural" propensity to commit rape when placed in a situation that causes them to "lose control." For example, should a women arouse a male's "natural" sexual aggressiveness by the clothing she wears, by flirting or by "teasing" the man, she has no one to blame but herself if the man then loses control. When these elements of the masculine mystique are combined with cultural stereotypes about women, this pattern of culturally approved male behaviours, Hills argues, is a principal cause of rape.

While some men may see themselves as "naturally" aggressive sexually, men are far more likely to blame the victim. Stereotypes about women may emphasize their "glamorous" or "helpless" qualities, but women are supposed to be "naturally" passive sexually and to have been socialized to be careful when dealing with men. A woman who is sexually active or one who fails to be properly discreet sexually, i.e., a women who is inappropriately feminine, again is believed to have no one to blame but herself if she is raped. Put differently, the question typically asked when a rape occurs is not why the man committed rape, but why it was *this particular woman* who was raped. Was she leading the man on, did she secretly want to be raped, did she consent and then regret her actions once it was "too late"? As long as rape is seen as primarily a sexual act, then the onus seems to be placed on the woman to explain why it was *she* rather than another who was attacked.

The tendency to blame the victim in the case of rape persists even in sociological explanations of rape. Indeed, the notion of the victim having "precipitated" her rape is found in some of the major sociological accounts of rape. Nelson and Amir (1975: 48), for example, assert that, "subconsciously, many of those who hitch-hike may be reacting to the thrill gained from deliberately challenging a potential dangerous situation." Women who are raped when hitch-hiking, then, supposedly "precipitated" their own rape.

Feminist Views of Rape

Little real progress was made in understanding rape until feminists began to insist that rape be considered an act of violence rather than a sexual act. As long as rape was seen as primarily sexual, the question was always raised of how the woman somehow "aroused" her attacker. Once rape is understood as an act of violence, it makes no more sense to blame the victim who is raped than to blame the person who is mugged for being attacked, the bank for being robbed or the public figure for being assassinated.

Understanding that rape is an act of violence also changes how we classify rape vis-à-vis other forms of deviance. Rape becomes only one of many forms of violence directed at women in society; not only other forms of sexual assault, but also wife-beating, pornography and even sexual harassment. Some feminists go even farther and argue that rape is the outcome of the general pattern of social relations between men and women in our society.

This last point illustrates how a feminist account of rape differs from the cultural accounts that are prevalent today. Feminists do not deny that ours is a sexist society, and they will make use of cultural notions as data in explaining rape. But feminists usually see the structural features of society which determine the nature of social, sexual, economic and other relations between men and women as the source of these cultural notions and as the "true" cause of rape.

We noted earlier that there are many different feminist theories and viewpoints, and this is true as well in the case of rape. Boyd and Sheehy (1989) identify a number of different feminist approaches to understanding and dealing with rape. "Liberal" feminists focus on the inadequacies of current laws on rape and seek to reform the law in order to minimize sexual discrimination. "Marxist" and "socialist" feminists examine rape in the context of capitalist social relations, especially property relations. They argue that the law does not so much discriminate against individual women as define women collectively as the sexual property of men. Law reform will have no effect as long as the fundamental property relations found in Canadian society persist. "Radical" feminists emphasize the patriarchal nature of Canadian society and the ways in which rape serves to maintain the subordination of women and the domination of men. "Result equality" feminists look to inadequacies in how laws on rape are applied and seek ways to ensure the more effective application of the law. Finally, "integrative" feminists seek to ensure that women's experiences and women's points of view are taken into account by legislatures, the courts and the legal profession when formulating laws on rape and applying them.

Boyd and Sheehy (1989: 265) do not see this diversity of viewpoints, goals and strategies as a disadvantage but as a sign of strength. They argue that each version of feminist theory directs attention to an important issue and, together, they contribute to a complete theory of rape.

Perhaps the best-known Canadian account of rape is the socialist feminist work of Clark and Lewis (1977). Their work is particularly significant because they provide a thorough and succinct overview of the issues related to rape and do so from a consistent and coherent point of view. In their book, Clark and Lewis move decisively away from a cultural explanation of rape towards a structural account, one that merges the feminist analysis of patriarchy with the critical theorists' analysis of capitalism.

Clark and Lewis begin by viewing Canadian society as dominated by patriarchal values and a capitalist social and economic structure. In such a society, women are seen as the property of men, and a means through which male offspring can be produced and wealth transmitted to them. Rape, then, is not viewed by the legal system as a crime against women but as an assault on men's property, particularly on men's right to exclusive sexual access to their wives, and their reproductive control over women. This explains "the reluctance of the police and prosecutors to proceed with charges where the women involved were neither virgins under the care of their fathers nor monogamous wives 'owned' by their husbands" (Boyd and Sheehy, 1989: 263).

Like the early, instrumentalist versions of critical theory, assuming that capitalism "causes" rape suggests that other, non-capitalist societies are free of rape. While there is no evidence that rape is universal, there is plenty of evidence that rape occurs now and has occurred historically in a wide variety of different societies that are not characterized by a capitalist economic system (Porter, 1986). As for the claim that Canada is a patriarchal society in which women are the sexual and reproductive property of men, the term "patriarchal" is used in so many different senses that it is difficult to determine what, if any, meaning should any longer be assigned to the term. If Canada *is* patriarchal in the sense that men are dominant, would that not work to diminish rather than augment the incidence of rape? As Porter (1986: 221) points out, in a patriarchal society in which rape was considered a crime against the men who own the women as sexual property, rape was less frequent because "heads of households had strong incentives to prosecute those who violated their mothers, wives or daughters." If anything, Porter suggests, it is because gender relations have become "destabilized" that rape has increased and become "politicized" (Porter, 1986: 223). Pauline Bart (1991), too, recently presented a succinct explanation of why she feels women in Western society are *not* treated as property. As Bart (1991:) put it: "Property is valued. Crimes against property are taken seriously. We should be so lucky!"

Perhaps the most serious problem with analyses of rape such as that of Clark and Lewis is that they assume a "functional" link between rape and the basic capitalistic structure of Canadian society. This means that essentially nothing can be done about rape unless one fundamentally transforms the society as a whole. Anything less must fail until that functional link is abolished. "Good law," Bart (1991: 102, citing Heald) notes, is not seen as leading to a "good society." Most feminists themselves rejected the logic underlying this argument when they suggested ways in which the laws concerning rape could be reformed, many of which were incorporated in the new legislation on sexual assault passed in 1983.

Nevertheless, whatever the deficiencies of Clark and Lewis's analysis, their work was a major influence on other feminists concerned with understanding rape. More importantly, their book was not only an analysis of rape, it was a call to action, an agenda for legal reform and social change, which was largely accepted by feminists and non-feminists alike. Indeed, the women's movement has made major strides and has been able to influence legislation on sexual assault, abortion and other major issues because many feminists have rejected the functionalist implications of their own analyses and have fought to change and reform Canada's legal system and Canadian society.

The claim that rape is an act of violence rather than a sexual act marked an important stride forward in understanding rape and in changing people's attitudes towards rape. Nevertheless, it presents too restricted a view of both rape and the rapist. Why assume that sexual desire and violence are mutually exclusive, or that all rapes are invariably one rather than the other? Is there only one reason why people fight, kill, steal, drink alcohol, gamble or engage in any other deviant act? Pauline Bart (1991: 269) has made the important point that distinguishing between sex, violence and power "makes no sense" when they are as interrelated as they are in Western society. As she puts it (Bart, 1991: 270), "strategically, some feminists interested in working with the criminal justice system say rape is not about sex only because that helps in getting rape treated as a crime and not a good time."

Feminists have taught us to look beyond the stereotypes and myths in our treatment of women who are raped. We should be doing the same when looking at rape itself and at the rapist. There are different types of rape just as there are different reasons why men rape.

Types of Rape

Steven Box (1983) identifies five types of rape: "sadistic," "anger," "domination," "seduction" and "exploitation" rapes. The "sadistic rape" is an act of extreme violence directed at a woman and intended to maximize her pain and mutilate her body. This type of rape may be the least common, but it is the most savage and perpetuates the myth that rape is the act of a "mad rapist." Whereas the "sadistic rape" is designed to destroy the body of the woman, particularly her genitalia, the "anger rape" is a brutal attack designed to degrade and humiliate the victim.

Many cases of women being raped by strangers fall into this category of rape. Neither the "sadistic rape" nor the "anger rape" is a sexual act *per se*, but there does seem to be a sexual element tied into the violence of the rapist. It is the violent attack upon the woman's body, rather than any sexual act performed, that seems to provide sexual pleasure to the rapist.

The "domination rape" is an act whereby the rapist strives to prove his sexual superiority and control over the victim. This form of rape has as its goal "sexual conquest" rather than violence, although violence will be used if a woman does not submit to threats alone. The rapist will typically believe that women either deserve or want to be raped and may justify his acts to himself by believing that his victims secretly "enjoyed" being raped.

"Seduction rape" (Box uses the term "seduction-turned-into-rape") is often referred to as "date rape." Box (1983: 128) describes this form of rape as follows:

> The assault arises out of an "acceptable" seductive situation, but where the victim decides or has previously decided that physical intimacy will stop short of coitus. The male, for a variety of reasons, but mainly a mixture of self-defined sexual urge and the need to dominate adversaries, pursues and pressurizes, cajoles and bullies, and ultimately "persuades."

As Box points out, the rapist rarely uses force, but there is no question that the victim did not voluntarily consent to coitus. The victim's "consent" was obtained through fear or intimidation, through manipulation or guilt, or in any other way that the rapist can take advantage of. This is probably the most common form of rape, but it is one women are unlikely to report to authorities or even to tell to friends. Instead, a woman is likely to blame herself for letting the situation "get out of hand" or for agreeing to the date in the first place.

An "exploitation rape" is one in which a man placed in a dominant position over women, such as a supervisor at work, a teacher in college, an official dealing with a woman's case or a famous or influential associate, will take advantage of his position to demand sexual "favours." In these cases no violence will be used, but the woman's "consent" is a consequence of her economic or social vulnerability and dependence. It is no more a genuine consent to sexual relations than is true in the case of "seduction rape."

"Exploitation rape" is particularly crucial in understanding rape, because many people do not consider it to be rape at all. The woman, after all, whatever her reasons, "consented" to sexual relations. But "exploitation rape" has nothing to do with consent; it is a consequence of the structural subordination of women, the fact that many women are economically or socially dependent upon men. This makes it a particular concern of feminists. "Sadistic rapes," "anger rapes," "domination rapes," even "seduction rapes," can be dealt with to some degree by changes in the law designed to protect women and to punish the offenders. But "exploitation rape," with its implied "consent," requires a fundamental change in the relations between men and women; perhaps even a change in the structure of society. Only by eliminating the structural subordination of women to men can exploitation be eliminated.

Box's neat typology, of course, distorts the reality of rape, as he himself admits. An instance of rape can rarely be fit into one and only one of these categories. Elements of sadism, the desire to dominate and some form of exploitation are often combined in many instances of rape. A "seduction rape" may involve the rapist exploiting his ability to damage the reputation of his victim, or a fear on her part that if she does not acquiesce her date will become violent.

Perhaps it might be more useful to think of violence, sexuality and exploitation as present to some degree in all cases of rape. Different types of rape then can be categorized along a set of continuums in which sadism, anger, domination, seduction and outright exploitation differ only in degree.

ASSESSING CRITICAL AND FEMINIST CRIMINOLOGIES

Assessing the critical and feminist perspectives poses a number of difficulties and special challenges that do not arise when looking at other sociological perspectives. One is that the theoretical and empirical adequacy of these perspectives is often beside the point, despite the excess of theoretical debates. Many critical criminologists and feminists often seem less concerned to understand society "correctly" than to do something about it, as Pauline Bart (1991) so bluntly stated above. These are activist perspectives, attempts to change the circumstances within which men and women live out their lives in society. In the same way, feminist sociologists are concerned to change the discipline of sociology so that it takes notice of women and women's concerns. In this respect the feminist perspective has been successful. Feminists have ensured that the issues of concern to women and their perspectives on these issues cannot be ignored.

In addition, critical criminologies of all types continue to evolve. Influenced in part by feminist analyses of rape and pornography, as well as by increasingly sophisticated notions of class and of political economy, the newer critical criminology sees crime less as an *expression* of capitalist social relations than as a sign of the *failure* of capitalist social relations. Crime, it is now argued, is a real problem, one that typically victimizes women, the poor, ethnic and racial minorities and marginal groups such as homosexuals or political activists. Crime is no longer necessarily seen as a form of "struggle" or "resistance" to capitalism, but as yet another form of exploitation of the disadvantaged. Crime in this sense points to the failure of the capitalist state in its liberal-democratic form to live up to its promise of serving the interests of all groups in society. As a form of "left realism" (Lea and Young, 1984), this new form of critical criminology seeks legal and structural solutions to the problem of crime.

One area in which this "left realism" has developed a special interest is the issue of "minimal policing" (Kinsey, Lea and Young, 1986). Minimal policing assumes the development of a new relationship between the police and the local community, one that is directed towards the needs of the community rather than the priorities of the state. Such a form of policing implies (Kinsey, Lea and Young, 1986: 189): "maximum public initiation of police action and maximum access to the police, and minimal police-initiated action and minimum use of coercion." Similar proposals for "community-based policing" have been made in Canada (Murphy and Main, 1985). As in the case of feminism, adherents of left realism are concerned to generate a political agenda fitted to the local political reality. Whether they will be successful, only time will show.

One final point concerning the future direction of critical theories of deviance. The structuralist version of critical theory has been criticized for containing an implicit *functionalist* theory of society. As you may recall, the structuralist model argues that the state operates in terms of the functional needs of capitalism as both an economic and a political system. This means that individuals act on the basis of "objective" interests that benefit the state or their class without necessarily being aware of those interests. People's actions, in other words, are independent of people's own experiences and their own decisions. Recent theoretical work, however, is directed at developing a new critical theory that is not functionalist in its assumptions. Hindess (1986: 114), for example, argues that:

> Actors do indeed reach decisions and act on them ... [as] a consequence of their decisions. Decisions themselves are reached through processes that are internal to the actor in question, that is, they are not reducible to the expression of the actor's position within a system of social relations.

At the same time, Hindess does not limit the notion of the actor to the individual, but includes the notion of the corporate actor. In this respect (Hindess, 1986: 115), "capitalist enterprises, state agencies, political parties and church organizations are examples of social actors."

Looking at how such corporate actors make decisions and act on them avoids the individualism of labelling theory and the functionalism of structuralism.

This point of view has at least two consequences for the study of deviance. One is, as Hindess (1986: 123) puts it, that "the general forms of law and property relations characteristic of the modern West are sustained not by some necessity inherent in capitalism as a mode of production but because they are situated in complex networks of intersecting practices and conditions." One way to do this is to see the law as a set of resources used by groups and corporate actors to achieve their goals.

The second consequence for the critical analysis of deviance has to do with the political implications of theory. "The familiar distinction on the left between reform and revolution," Hindess (1986: 125) argues, "cannot be sustained." Instead, "if there is no fundamental structure producing necessary effects, then changes in some social conditions cannot be dismissed as mere reforms" (Hindess, 1986: 125).

We have not presented "left realism" or Hindess's work as the be-all and end-all of critical sociology, but as examples of how the critical approach continues to evolve and change. This evolution indicates that the critical approach will continue to provide new insights on deviance and crime for the foreseeable future.

NOTES

1. We may wonder whether this "fundamental belief" is not more strained now than it was when Taylor wrote in the early 1980s. The failure of the Meech Lake Accord, the election of an NDP government in Ontario, the Senate "revolt" over the GST, the emergence of the Bloc Québécois in Parliament, and what was in effect an armed insurrection by Mohawk natives in Québec; all seem to be signs that some of Canadians' belief in the stability and desirability of their state and the existing social order is being questioned.

2. All together, 54 percent of those who failed to report violent incidents felt that the police would be unable to do anything, 63 percent that it was "too personal," and 65 percent that the incident was "too minor" (Sacco and Johnson, 1990).

CHAPTER

8 Ethnomethodological and Phenomenological Approaches to Deviance

In the last chapter we examined some of the new "critical" approaches to deviance that have developed since the early 1970s. Critical theories emphasize the role played by power and group conflict both in creating deviance and in enforcing laws. Some critical theorists go still farther and try to identify how the patterns of deviance found in a society are linked to the economic and political organization of that society. Critical theories continue to influence much of the contemporary discussion of deviance, especially as new forms, such as feminist theory, revitalize it, and this perspective remains particularly significant in Canadian sociology.

A second major perspective on deviance that developed during the 1970s, the ethnomethodological perspective, emerged out of a very different set of assumptions and concerns. The ethnomethodologists accept much of the labelling perspective's view of deviance, but they have consistently argued for an even more relativist and "social constructionist" approach to understanding deviance than that found in labelling theory.

The term "ethnomethodology" literally means the systematic study ("-ology") of the methods ("-method-") used by people ("ethno-") as they simultaneously act, make sense of their actions, and communicate this sense to others in everyday life. Ethnomethodology itself grew out of yet another sociological perspective, phenomenology, which continues to be a separate approach in sociology. The two perspectives are very similar in some ways, dramatically different in others. Before continuing, we will deal briefly with the characteristics of both the phenomenological and ethnomethodological perspectives, how they differ from other, more traditional, sociological perspectives, and some of the differences between the two of them (Rogers, 1983; Heritage, 1984; Sharrock and Anderson, 1986).

SOCIAL CONSTRUCTION AND SOCIAL ORDER

What has made deviance such a persistent topic of interest for sociologists from the time of Émile Durkheim and the social pathologists until today? The answer is not that most sociologists find the odd, the offbeat or the marginal interesting *per se*, for, with the exception of some of the Chicago sociologists and some labelling theorists, few sociologists seem to study, describe or analyze deviance for its own sake. Rather, most sociologists are interested in the intimate connection of deviance to the "problem" of social order. As we discussed in Chapter One, sociologists look to deviance in order to answer fundamental questions about the nature of social order: its source, how it may be disrupted, and how it is restored.

All of the sociological perspectives we have discussed so far—except for labelling theory—see social order as structural, cultural and/or institutional in origin. To the functionalists, for example, social order persists by socializing the individual, motivating him or her through internalized norms, values and beliefs, or by enforcing compliance through rules and laws. Such institutional, structural or cultural approaches to social order can be seen as "top-down" explanations for human behaviour: they see individuals moved to conform or to deviate because they are pushed by social and cultural forces beyond their control.

Since a "top-down" approach assumes the origin of social order to be structural, institutional or cultural in nature, most sociologists, beginning with Durkheim, have considered the individual social actor to be largely irrelevant. The individual's needs, personality, desires or motives are not considered the *source* of their actions. For example, you as a human being have fundamental needs, wishes or hopes that are central to you as a living being, but these are not substantially different from those of a Babylonian peasant farmer living 2500 years ago. The fact that you learn to read, write, add and subtract—indeed, that you are currently attending university or college—whereas a Babylonian peasant did not, is not a consequence of *your* needs, but of the development of a modern, technological society and its need for an educated, knowledgeable and productive work force.

Let us remain with the example of education somewhat longer. When we look at a classroom of college students during class time, much of the behaviour that goes on during the class has little to do with the particular individuals taking the course. Even if a totally different set of students was taking the course, little would change because the course is designed to meet institutional "needs," rules or standards rather than personal idiosyncrasies. It would still be held at the same time, in the same room, with the same course content; students would still sit facing the teacher, by and large pay attention, most of the time, to what the teacher is saying, take notes, raise their hands when they wished to ask a question and so on. Explaining what is "happening" in class, then, need make little or no reference to the actual individuals who are enrolled in the course, their personal wishes, characters or motives. A graduate seminar in sociology may be different from a college class of Biology 101, but again, it is not the particular students enrolled in either who are the *source* of this difference.

A social constructionist approach takes a radically different view of the relationship between the individual and society. Rather than seeing social order as the outcome of institutional or structural controls over individuals, the social constructionist sees social order as the outcome of individuals interacting, working together, negotiating their differences and coming to share common experiences, meanings, goals or values. As every teacher knows, the social order of the classroom can be easily disrupted, sometimes by nothing more than a student coming in very noisily and very late. When such a disruption occurs the teacher—and the students—will often work together at re-establishing order. The teacher may, for example, make a joke to "laugh away" the violation of institutional rules by the student, defining it as not serious enough to require action, thereby allowing the class to go on as before. To the social constructionist, social order is created and maintained because, and to the degree that, we all work to establish it and to shore it up.

Phenomenology and ethnomethodology, along with symbolic interactionism and labelling theory, make use of a social constructionist approach to social order. Where functionalists study how social relations, rules and norms stabilize social organizations and institutions, these alternative theories analyse how individuals create and organize social settings that are meaningful and reasonable for them. In particular, interactionists, phenomenologists and ethnomethodologists focus on how individuals actually *interpret* and make *use* of norms, rules, and values in face-to-face interaction and communication. They try to develop a sociological interpretation of social order and deviance from the "bottom up" by observing and interpreting the experiences, actions and meanings held by the social actors themselves. For this reason such social constructionist approaches are often referred to as *interpretive* sociology (Wilson, 1971).

Douglas and Waksler (1982: 141) suggest that phenomenological sociology essentially deals with two questions: "How do individuals make sense of their world? What is the relation between the meanings they construct and the situations they face?" Phenomenological sociologists try to understand a person's experience of social relations and social processes, and look at the inner world of subjective meaning and feeling accompanying social actions and situations.

Phenomenology began as a method developed by philosopher Edmund Husserl as a means of studying the nature and contents of experience. Husserl noted that in everyday life we tend to assume that our experiences simply mirror the objects and reality around us; that we experience dogs, cats, birds, trees, people and colours as we do because they are out there for us to experience. But if you think about it for a while you will realize that our experience is not simply a mirror of reality. We also experience "objects" that are not "out there" at all: ideas, feelings, concepts, numbers, symbols, metaphors and so on, which are not physical objects to be directly experienced. Additionally, even when physical objects are "out there," our cultural preconceptions, expectations, biases or interests will affect how and what we experience. To you a dog may be a pet, to someone else living elsewhere it may be tonight's meal. To the farmer, rain is experienced as a very different "thing" than it is by a tourist on a one-week vacation, hoping for sun.

Husserl (1931) developed phenomenology as a philosophical method designed to overcome the everyday confusion between experience and objects. Phenomenologists engage in a series of "reductions" or mental experiments in which they "bracket" or ignore the reality of the objects they experience and focus instead on the experience itself. By doing so, they claim they can uncover the characteristics common to all experience, whether of objects, ideas, sensations or feelings. Phenomenology in this sense is a strictly philosophical method with little direct relevance for sociology.

It was an Austrian sociologist, Alfred Schutz, who developed a phenomenological approach to sociology. Schutz (1961) did so by reversing Husserl's method. Phenomenological sociologists are interested in precisely those cultural preconceptions, assumptions, biases and beliefs of everyday life that the phenomenological philosopher seeks to "bracket" or ignore. To the sociologist these are important forms of data; rather than bracketing everyday life assumptions, the phenomenological sociologist studies the details of everyday life experience.

Experience, however, even everyday life experience, is an enormously broad and varied phenomenon. This has given the phenomenological approach little focus or consistency in the past and has inhibited the widespread acceptance or use of this approach. In contrast, by turning away from experience towards the specific "methods" used by people to order their experiences, ethnomethodology is better suited to the development of a specific "school" of thought. The search for "folk methods" emphasizes the patterns to be found in human behaviour, patterns non-ethnomethodological sociologists often refer to as "norms" or "rules" when explaining social behaviour. Most sociologists and anthropologists simply take for granted that cultural and institutional sets of "normative" expectations and rules internalized by individuals make sense of the world for them, serve to motivate their actions, and channel their behaviour. Remember how Kingsley Davis saw the ideology of "romantic love" as motivating and directing individuals towards marriage and raising a family (Chapter Four). Ethnomethodologists, in contrast, seek out the actual practical activities used by people in using norms and rules to make sense of their world. Still, there is enough common ground with other forms of sociology to make the ethnomethodological approach more attractive to most sociologists than the phenomenological.

Ethnomethodologists argue that ethnomethods are needed if people are to relate the particular situation in which they find themselves at any given moment to the abstract cultural or institutional norms they have learned to be a part of their society. Harold Garfinkel, the founder of ethnomethodology, cites Schutz as virtually the only sociologist attempting to describe many of the unnoticed ways we have of interacting with others to create and maintain a sense of purpose and orderliness (Rogers, 1983, 81-82). Schutz argued that a primary task for sociology is the study of the common-sense ways human experience is organized into stable, coherent systems of meaning, which permit social communication and interaction to proceed smoothly. Norms *per se* specify expectations, but they do not tell people *how* to act to fulfil or meet those expectations. People therefore develop methods that enable them either to act out norms or to justify to themselves or to others why they did not. People will then refer to the norms to account for or explain their action (or inaction) *after* they have acted.

Like phenomenologists, ethnomethodologists are also concerned to try to uncover a person's understanding of social relations and processes. However, ethnomethodologists are not interested in describing the inner world of subjective meaning and experience. They look instead to the individuals' own "accounts," what they say about social relations and how they say it, and look as well to the links between these accounts and the individuals' actions. Garfinkel and the other ethnomethodologists seek to uncover meaning not in individuals' experiences but in their talk and action.

To the ethnomethodologists, both labelling and critical theories remain grounded in an approach in which deviance is something to be accounted for, whether through the actions of social control agents or through the agency of class interests. In this respect, non-ethnomethodological sociologists are simply producing "accounts" of deviance like anyone else; they are not questioning the bases—the background expectations, assumptions and taken-for-granted understandings—out of which these accounts are produced.

When looking at deviance, then, the ethnomethodologists have a dramatically different approach from that of other sociologists. Instead of asking such questions as: "Why do people come to violate rules?" or "What happens to people who violate rules?" the ethnomethodologists ask what they consider a more basic question: "What do people mean when they say they are acting out or following a rule?" (Wieder and Wright, 1982). Until this question is answered, the ethnomethodologists assert, we do not know what deviance is, for we do not know what we mean by social order. Ethnomethodologists refer to such questions as "constitutive" because they are questions about how meaning is constituted or constructed in everyday life.

We can now briefly summarize some of the differences among symbolic interactionism, phenomenology and ethnomethodology. Consider the phenomenon of jokes as an example. The symbolic interactionist might look to the meaning a joke would have in the particular situation in which particular people happen to be interacting (Gross, 1979). Also, the joke conveys a message apart from its literal meaning, and the interactionist might be interested in how the joke is used to express or discuss issues that may be taboo or uncomfortable in "serious" conversation (Emerson, 1969). The phenomenologist will ask very different and more fundamental questions: "What is a joke?" "Why is a joke funny?" Zijderveld (1983), for example, argues that a joke is funny because it plays with meanings, unexpectedly altering or inverting the conventional meanings of everyday life. The ethnomethodologist's approach is different again, looking for the ways or methods in which people indicate to one another that what is being said now is a joke. For example, Sacks (1974) studied the "sequential organization" of telling a joke in conversation. He suggests that a joke is preceded by a "preface" such as "Hey, I heard a great joke last night," or "That reminds me of a joke." Such a preface allows the joke-teller to inform the hearers that a joke is about to be told.

THE CRITIQUE OF LABELLING THEORY

While phenomenological sociology and ethnomethodology share some common features with labelling theory, they are also critical of some features of it. Labelling theory is applauded for making a positive contribution to the analysis of deviance and interaction, yet it is criticized for not following out the implications of its own argument far enough nor following rigorously enough the implications of its critique of functionalism. Labelling theory is seen as useful in breaking with dominant conceptions of society as rational systems and in reaffirming the

Chicago view of society as a "mosaic" of culturally diverse competing groups (Becker, 1977: 63-73). Labelling theory also directed attention to the relativity of deviance, that what is deviant to one group is accepted in another, and consequently that there is no framework of shared cultural values as assumed by functionalism. Therefore, a central issue for labelling theory is the social process of developing and enforcing rules in a setting of group conflict, stratification and challenge to the rules. Crime statistics, suicide and other "objective indicators" of deviance or social problems are reflections of the ability of some groups to impose their definitions of rules and rule-breaking on others. Such definitions require periodic defence in the face of social change, or they will be replaced by new definitions that result from social movements led by moral entrepreneurs.

For phenomenological sociologists, the labelling perspective focuses too exclusively on the labelling activities of such rule-enforcers as teachers, police officers, psychiatrists, social workers, judges and so on. What is left out of the analyses are the experiences of those who are labelled as rule-breakers. While all of us are influenced by the opinions of others, we are not simply "looking-glass selves" (Cooley, 1964) who mirror the expectations of others. We may adopt the views of those who label us, or we may reject them. We may invert the values of those who label us, valuing what they despise, or we may just revel in our notoriety. We may simply not care what the rest of the world thinks of us, as long as we are at peace with ourselves. Being labelled is only one of the factors through which we come to think of ourselves as certain kinds of people or come to act in certain ways. For example, as Douglas and Waksler (1982: 142) put it, the phenomenologist looking at homosexuals might ask such questions as "What does 'gay' mean to those in the gay world? How do they arrive at and use those meanings?"

For ethnomethodologists, labelling theory "glosses over" (i.e., abbreviates or gives insufficient attention to) the specific processes through which labels are generated and used. What labelling theory requires, according to ethnomethodologists, is much greater and more detailed attention to the interactive and communicational techniques used to make sense of deviance (Pollner, 1974; 1978), to accomplish deviant identity (Garfinkel, 1967), and the ways agents of social control communicate so that their handling of deviants and deviant acts seems "reasonable" to all concerned (Sudnow, 1965).

Both approaches argue that most sociologists take for granted basic elements of social reality that should instead be the main focus of their research. This argument is clearest in criticisms of the ways sociological studies of deviance have followed Durkheim and made use of official statistics of crime, delinquency, mental illness and so on. Most sociologists recognize that such statistics are likely to underrepresent the number of deviant activities that actually occur. For example, not all burglaries are reported to the police, and an unknown number of suicides may use techniques such as driving accidents, drowning or fatally combining alcoholic drinks with drugs. In each of these cases, the death might be considered accidental, unless there is evidence such as a suicide note or a past history of depression or suicidal tendencies that could support another interpretation of the fatality. Most sociologists admit that many forms of deviance are underreported, but they assume that, as a whole,the undetected cases are very similar to the recorded ones. In other words, there is no bias in the recording of deviance that could result in the recorded cases being very different from the undetected ones.

As noted in Chapter Three, much of the debate over the use and usefulness of official statistics on deviance has centred on the topic of suicide. Jack Douglas (1967), for example, has argued that the variations in suicide rates presented by Durkheim—different rates between Protestants and Catholics, rural and urban areas, professional and other occupations—reflect, at least in part, a result of the differences in the ways these different communities view suicide. So, in Catholic communities where there is great moral disapproval of suicide, individuals are more likely to hide their suicidal tendencies, not to leave suicide notes, and choose ambiguous means for killing themselves. All of this means that actual suicides may be far higher than officially recorded. In such communities, too, families are likely to conceal evidence of suicide, and may get physicians and priests to help in this concealment.

Similarly, rural communities are characterized by closer relationships than is the case in urban communities. Again, we would expect that rural people would choose ways of committing suicide that could be interpreted as accidents, and that their families would try to conceal the evidence of suicide and would get doctors and priests to "reorganize" the evidence so that it could be seen as a "respectable death." By contrast, urban areas have more isolated individuals, many of whom are strangers to their neighbours. In these areas, many people have little reason to conceal their suicidal intentions and actions. Those who discover the body and make the arrangements for medical examination and disposal are less likely to be pressured not to identify the death as suicide.

Douglas argues that we cannot take official suicide statistics at face value because they emerge from the suicidal person's concerns for preserving a "front" or identity even in death, and from the various concerns and activities by the people around the individual as they respond to the death. Since the statistics are the result of some very complex social dynamics, looking at the statistical patterns as the key to understanding suicide overlooks the way these statistics have been generated through the interpretation of each death. Douglas maintains that what should be of concern to sociologists is to discover the definitions and procedures used for identifying causes of death and for interpreting death in some socially relevant way.

Harold Garfinkel pushed Douglas's ideas further in his study of the activities in a Los Angeles suicide prevention centre. When an apparent suicide occurred, police, psychiatrists and other involved professionals looked for anything that could be used to build up "a professionally defensible" and "recognizably rational account" (Garfinkel, 1967) of the circumstances causing the individual to take his or her own life. In this search anything can be relevant—the body, its trappings and setting, the contents of a bathroom medicine cabinet or a refrigerator, photographs, rumours and hearsay reports by the deceased's neighbours, family and friends and so on. All of these items, however trivial or dubious, are woven into a reasonable story or "account" that makes the suicidal act understandable as a final, inevitable conclusion to the life that the deceased is now "seen" to have lived.

It is the gathering, interpretation and organization of the elements that contribute to making sense of the death as suicide that ethnomethodologists want to describe. These kinds of activities are, for ethnomethodologists, basic to the way we live, for they allow us to organize our experiences in ways that fit the experiences of others around us. Everyone else also organizes their experiences through the same activities or "ethnomethods," and this permits everyday life to proceed in an orderly and meaningful way. Most sociologists, in their search for patterns of social relationships, social structures and cultural values, overlook the foundations on which such patterns are based. These orderly social patterns—relationships, structures, values—are, for ethnomethodologists, "accomplishments," the result of interpretive "work" by participating individuals who classify, codify and communicate their understanding of every social situation by using a vast number of procedures, while being scarcely aware of doing so.

THE ANALYSIS OF SEXUAL IDENTITY AND GENDER

Ethnomethodologists have also looked at sexual identity as a social arrangement in which individuals have to do interpretive "work." Sexual identity requires the awareness, presentation and interpretation of gender cues. In the course of socialization, we acquire the social skills necessary to present to others our own gender identity, and to interpret other people's signs, cues and activities as indications of their gender identities. Such signs and cues include dress, body displays and management, patterns of speech and bodily adornments such as jewellery, purses and bags.

The enormous amount of interpretive and communicative "work" involved in accomplishing a sexual identity was the focus of Garfinkel's study of Agnes, a transsexual. Agnes was born male with normal male genitalia, and was treated as a boy by family and friends until the age of 17. When Garfinkel first met Agnes, she was 19 and had been referred to the Department of Psychiatry at the University of California, Los Angeles, for counselling in preparation for a sex-change operation. By this time, Garfinkel (1967: 119) tells us, Agnes "had long, fine dark-blonde hair, a young face with pretty features, a peaches-and-cream complexion, no facial hair, subtly plucked eyebrows, and no make-up except for lipstick." She also had developed breasts, having 38-25-38 measurements. For Garfinkel, Agnes represented a golden opportunity to discover the social processes involved in living in a gendered world on the assumption "that something can be learned about what is taken for granted in the 'normal' case by studying what happens where there are `violations.'" (Kessler and McKenna, 1985: 114).

Agnes's "violations" from the "normal" were not only physical. She presented herself to the hospital and psychiatric staff as a woman, one who "happens" to have a penis. She had a boyfriend who she claimed had no idea that she had a penis, and it was for this reason that she was seeking an immediate sex-change operation.

Agnes faced two basic problems in accomplishing the change from masculine to feminine gender identity. She needed to pass successfully as a woman among people who knew nothing of her masculine past. This seemed to her to require that she know how to be "female," to have her "woman's act" together. Secondly, she had to persuade those who did know of her masculine past that she had really been a woman all along. Garfinkel felt that Agnes, in coping with these two problems, had to become a "sensitive ethnographer of gender." Her account of the problems she faced, then, should provide rich insight into the techniques we all use in being and presenting ourselves to others as a male or a female.

Being a man or a woman, Garfinkel argues, requires a vast array of techniques and skills, an array that Agnes had only partly pulled together when Garfinkel met her. By the time Agnes had come to UCLA she had learned the art of presenting her feminine identity in terms of her dress, make-up, grooming and other external physical signs, such as jewellery, purse and so on. Less easily mastered were the techniques of feminine comportment—femininity represented by ways of talking, walking, sitting and moving. While those who are born into womanhood have a large number of personal experiences that provide for increasing mastery and decreasing self-consciousness in these matters, Agnes's past lacked these useful resources and was also a direct source of inappropriate techniques—stereotypes—of feminine presentation.

Agnes managed these problems by using two techniques that Garfinkel called "secret apprenticeship" and "anticipatory following." In the former she used social situations as opportunities to learn clearly identified feminine skills. For example, she asked her boyfriend's mother to teach her how to cook a number of Dutch dishes, but Agnes was learning cooking skills in general under this arrangement. In group settings she tended to be passive, which allowed her to observe appropriate feminine behaviour in various social settings. Ironically, she learned that passivity, and letting another person dominate conversation, were characteristics of women valued by men!

Agnes's greatest concern before her operation was to conceal her male body. This led to careful management of situations requiring changing or removal of clothes, such as changing into a swimming costume or medical examinations, and generally being extremely careful to avoid any situations where a risk of physical exposure was possible. For example, while Agnes could drive, she did not own a car for fear of being involved in an accident and being exposed while unconscious.

For Agnes, the main solution to the problem of convincing her family and intimate friends of her "real" feminine identity was the sex-change operation itself. At the same time, this depended on persuading the UCLA psychiatrists that her wish to become physically female was not an arbitrary, erratic whim, but was based on her lifelong sense of herself as a woman. This required her to explain away her undeniably masculine genitalia, to convince the doctors and psychiatrists that her penis "had always been an accidental appendage stuck on by a cruel trick of fate" (Garfinkel, 1967: 129). In explaining away her physique, she also reconstructed her past in relation to her body. As Garfinkel (1967: 129) summarizes in his analysis of her psychiatric examinations, "The penis in Agnes' accounts had never been erect; she was never curious about it; it was never scrutinized by her or by others; it never entered into games with other children; it never moved 'voluntarily'; it was never a source of pleasurable feelings."

While Garfinkel's analysis of Agnes focused on the "techniques of womanhood" she had learned or was learning, he also noted some of the interpretive "work" required of those others associated with the transition to the new gender. For the psychiatrists, Agnes had to be identified apart from other gender types such as homosexuals or transvestites (those who dress in clothes of the opposite sex). Agnes's feelings of femininity had to be examined closely to ensure that they were "genuine," of long duration and were not "artificially" stimulated by the ingestion of hormonal drugs such as estrogen. The investigative work of these psychiatrists, then, was very similar to that of the Suicide Prevention Centre professionals when attempting to decide that a death was the result of suicide, or of the police when deciding how to proceed with a youthful offender on the street. For the UCLA psychiatrists, it was necessary to "read" Agnes's statements, and to interpret them in such a way that a final decision on the acceptability of the sex-change operation could be made.

Agnes's family and friends also had to decide how to relate to the transition from one gender to another. Agnes's family initially reacted with bewilderment and hostility to her early claims to a female identity. Agnes's claims for her feminine identity challenged basic assumptions in her social circle of intimates. However, once the sex-change operation was completed, Agnes's family expressed "relieved acceptance and treatment of her as a 'real female after all'" (Garfinkel, 1967: 128).

Garfinkel argues that sexual status, like many other taken-for-granted features of society, works in two mutually reinforcing ways. People accept a gendered world with two sexes as its foundation, that is, the division into males and females as "normal" and "natural," whereas more than two sexes would be fantastical, abnormal and unnatural. Second, the normal or natural arrangement is also understood to be a "good thing," that is, a morally appropriate arrangement, therefore to be defended from disruption, interference or breakdown. As Garfinkel (1967: 22) puts it, for "normally gendered persons the perceived environments of sexed persons are populated with natural males, natural females, and persons who stand in moral contrast with them, i.e. incompetent, criminal, sick and sinful." However, ethnomethodology is not concerned with those in "moral contrast" to the normal, natural, morally approved but taken-for-granted social arrangements. What is of interest is the social construction of normality and people's techniques in making and keeping normal appearances.

Two other ethnomethodologists, Suzanne Kessler and Wendy McKenna (1985), have followed Garfinkel's approach to gender in arguing that a two-gendered world is what "we" assume as normal and natural. They demonstrate that this two-gendered world is not normal and natural for all societies, by examining the anthropological literature on *berdache*—the adoption of opposite-sex identities among American Indians and some other hunting and gathering societies—which creates a third gender identity. Travellers' reports and studies by early anthropologists display a great deal of confusion about the institution of *berdache*, reflecting, as Kessler and McKenna argue, the disruption of our normal assumptions that construct a two-gendered world. Using these studies, interviews with transsexuals like Agnes, and tests of gender perception among students viewing drawings of various combinations of physical identifiers of gender, these researchers reinforce Garfinkel's argument that gender is a social construct requiring mastery of a large number of methods of talk, of posture and movement, of dress and grooming and of appropriate accessories, as well as of appropriate life histories. Nevertheless, they criticize Garfinkel for placing so much emphasis on the gender work done by Agnes; they argue that all participants in social settings work with gender displays to affirm their own sexual identities and those of the others in the situation.

This discussion of gender work requires amplification, however. Gender is a complex phenomenon in our society, whose meaning, relevance and use varies from situation to situation and from individual to individual. In some ways, both Garfinkel and Kessler and Mckenna place too much emphasis on gender work, yet at the same time they miss out on some crucial features of how we work at gender and sexual identity.

For most of us, most of the time, gender is not something we work *at*, because much of the work has been done for us. Being male or female is not something that gradually happens to us or that we build up in the course of working with or interacting with others. We are defined as male or female from the moment of birth—indeed, given modern prenatal technology and care such as the use of ultrasound scans, many parents know months before birth whether their child will be male or female. In the hospital, the new baby is wrapped in a pink blanket if a girl, a blue blanket if a boy. "Appropriate" gifts are given to the child by relatives and friends, and the baby often arrives home to a room already decorated and wallpapered for its gender. The "maleness" or "femaleness" of the child is never absent as a background feature of the child's primary socialization. Often it is a foreground feature, as when girls are taught to be "little ladies" and boys are taught what it takes to be a "man." Once school begins, these lessons are reinforced and extended as children learn the broader cultural definitions of female and male behaviour. Most of the work, then, is already done for us by others, and by the cultural and social institutions around us, which define what it means to be a male and what it means to be a female.

In contrast, Agnes had to think about *how* to act "like" a woman in almost every situation in which she found herself. How many women of 19 have to think about this? An adult woman usually does not have to think about whether her behaviour is or is not "what women do" because she *is* a woman. Therefore what she does is what women do. On the other hand, a woman may have to think about whether her behaviour is "feminine," which is quite a different matter. Femininity is a set of culturally valued ideals and standards. So a cocktail waitress may be expected to consciously work at being or appearing "feminine," while a woman seeking a management position during a job interview may have to consciously work at avoiding being "too feminine."

Yet if there is "work" being done in terms of gender, that work is most crucial and troublesome when it comes to sexual identity and sexual relations. We rarely have to work at our gender identity, but we do build up, often slowly, tentatively and with much anxiety, our sexuality. Unlike gender in general, then, where the roles already exist, predefined for us and ready to be filled, sexuality involves a set of relationships built up through interactions with others. Indeed, in our society sexual identity, sexuality and sexual relations are intimately connected. As Weeks (1986:13) notes, "the term [sex] refers both to an act and to a category of person, to a practice and to a gender." This symmetry of sex as identity and sex as action, then, imposes a tyranny over our sense of self as a sexual person and over our conception of who is or is not an appropriate sexual partner. This symmetry is reinforced by conventional morality, with violations often severely stigmatized. Sexual deviance challenges and undercuts this symmetry, putting into question the very sense of self most people prefer to take for granted.

Garfinkel's interest in Agnes was specifically in what her case had to tell us about "normal" gender, and this is an interesting and important issue. But the case of Agnes raises many more issues than this. What of those who, like Agnes, choose a life that is neither conventional nor "normal," in which they decide for themselves what their gender or sexuality or identity will be? This latter question is as crucial as the former. But taking this question seriously undercuts and puts into question many of the assumptions on which our notions of sexuality itself have been based. The example of homosexuality illustrates this point.

THE ANALYSIS OF HOMOSEXUALITY

Just as rape illustrates one limitation of the labelling perspective—the limits of relativism—the topic of homosexuality illustrates yet another limitation—the limits of "societal reaction." Because it emphasizes those interactional and labelling processes that *precede* emergent motivation and identity, the labelling model focuses on how "others," i.e., the agents of social control, respond to deviance, and the impact this response has on the identity, motivations and life circumstances of the "deviant." As a result, the labelling perspective predisposes the researcher to focus on the operation of "stigma" in the life of the homosexual, and how the homosexual's life is organized around this experience of stigma (Plummer, 1975).

Bell, Weinberg and Hammersmith (1981: 90) summarize the labelling argument as follows, "Boys who have been labeled sexually different, [e.g., 'sissy' or 'queer'] would be more likely than other boys ultimately to develop a sexual orientation consistent with that label, even if they did not originally have any proclivity toward homosexuality." Homosexuality, in other words, is viewed as a moral career in which stigma is the decisive contingency as well as the organizing principle around which the career is organized.

Sexuality, labelling theorists assert, is not innate; it is a sense of one's self as a social object. Individuals interpret or assign meanings to behaviour and traits. This allows the infinite variety of human social

and behavioural characteristics to be neatly classified in only a few dis-
crete categories. So, a boy may be described as "effeminate" and come to
see himself as "different" from others (Salamon, 1988: 131):

> the label "homosexual" may be created and/or become of major con-
> cern to an individual through others' reactions to them. Thus, the
> father/mother/peer group who accuse the male child of being a
> "sissy," or a wimp who, similarly, upon discovering the child during
> an episode of sexual exploration [e.g. playing "Doctor" with another
> of one's gender, masturbating, etc.] may furnish hostile and
> graphic accounts of the "meaning" of such acts. From an interac-
> tionist perspective, the role of "significant others" is crucial.

This sort of labelling process works, Plummer (1981a; 1981b) argues,
because labels are not merely names, they are sets of cultural expectations
and resources; they tell the individual that he or she really *is* a homosexual, as well as how to go about being and behaving as a homosexual.

Yet, as the work of Plummer (1981c) shows, few labelling theorists
leave it at that, because labelling by itself is so obviously inadequate for
understanding homosexuality or homosexuals. The point is not that the
labelling perspective is "wrong," but that it is limited. Because it directs
attention away from the experiences of homosexuals and lesbians themselves, the labelling approach fails to identify a number of issues that
are crucial for understanding homosexuality. For example, being a homosexual is not like being a prostitute or a bank robber, gays insist, because homosexuality refers not to what they *do* but what they *are*.

Certainly the issue of stigma and the application of labels and social
control to homosexuals is an important topic and one to which we must
devote substantial attention. Even today, when homosexuality is more
widely asserted and more accepted than at any other point in the history of Judeo-Christian civilization (Salamon, 1988), almost all homosexuals know, as Goode (1984: 178) puts it, that they would "face
condemnation by at least some 'straights' in their lives were they to re-
veal their orientation to everyone they knew." Yet not all heterosexuals
condemn homosexuals, and not all homosexuals care whether they are
condemned or not. Homosexuality is not just a sexual "orientation," it is
part of a lifestyle, and it is essential to pay attention to homosexuals'
own experiences and feelings as well as how they go about organizing
their own status and identity.

SOCIAL AND "SCIENTIFIC" STIGMA

In Western industrial societies dominated by a Judeo-Christian religious culture, homosexuality has been intensely stigmatized as an abhorrent violation of religiously prescribed and "naturally" endowed
moral principles. Until the late eighteenth century, various European
countries proscribed "sodomy" (contact of the penis with anus or mouth)

with severe penalties such as flogging, castration or burning at the stake. While these extreme punishments were largely abandoned by the nineteenth century, homosexuality was still considered a crime in most Western countries until very recently, and is still—at the time of this writing—punishable by life imprisonment in the Republic of Ireland. Twenty-six state governments of the United States have retained harsh statutes on the law books, although the laws are often not enforced. Police harassment of known gathering places for homosexuals is well entrenched in most Western countries, regardless of the sodomy laws. The arrest of 266 people by police, following raids on gay baths in Toronto in 1981 (Salamon, 1988: 116), and the well-publicized break-up of a homosexual party by police in Montréal in 1990 are two cases in point.

In the past century, the stigma of homosexuality has partially shifted away from moral condemnation towards the labelling of such sexual preference as "pathological" by medical and psychological researchers. The analysis of sexuality by medical, psychological and social scientists has been slow to develop and has often been based on hidden value judgements. In the late nineteenth century, Kraft-Ebbing, Freud, Havelock Ellis and others attempted to develop a science of sexual behaviour. These attempts to break away from moral and religious condemnation translated the stigma attached to sexual activity to a medical stigma, arguing that homosexuality, and other sexual deviations from sex for procreation within marriage, arose from pathological constitutions or disturbed family relationships and the psychological experiences associated with them. In 1965, one of the leading sociologists of deviance (Edwin Schur) argued that while many laws against homosexuality were too punitive, some should be retained in order to minimize the extent of homosexuality. Only in 1974 did the American Psychiatric Association abandon its classification of homosexuality as a sexual pathology associated with mental illness.

Apart from the weight of our cultural heritage, other factors render homosexuality and lesbianism a difficult and elusive subject for scientific analysis. The study of sexual behaviour has, as has been noted, only become a legitimate area of scientific study very recently. All aspects of sexual behaviour are highly intimate, emotionally charged, and have to be studied indirectly through interviews and questionnaires without checks on the possible gaps between verbal reports and actual behaviour. The continuing stigmatization of sexual deviation by many groups also results in the existence of an unknown number of covert homosexuals, who may well make up the majority of this population and yet are unavailable for study. Sagarin (1973: 8) suggests that estimates of the membership of all homophile organizations in the United States combined may well take in about one in two thousand self-identifying homosexuals. Members of such organizations are probably very different from those who practise and express homosexuality covertly, in much the same way as "joiners" of clubs and voluntary associations tend to have higher education and jobs, and have more systematized beliefs, values and attitudes about the issues that bring them to join like-minded others in formal associations. While sociologists have long made the distinction between overt and covert homosexuality (Leznoff and Westley, 1956), few systematic comparisons of these groups have been made. Indeed, the obstacles to studying the covert population have made any attempts to overcome them subject to major objections on the grounds of infringement of fundamental individual civil rights.

Labelling theorists and other sociologists have found homosexuality to be an ideal test case for demonstrating that deviance is not a characteristic inherent in an act but a quality emerging from the societal or group responses to selectively interpreted activities. Two kinds of evidence are used to support this position. First, the activity is found in a variety of social contexts without generating stigmatizing interpretations and social control reactions. Second, even where stigmas and other social sanctions exist, the interpretations upon which they are based and through which they are meaningful and legitimate are culturally and historically relative. Thus with respect to the first argument, expression of homosexual attraction and attachments were accepted as part of the normal male life cycle in a variety of ancient civilizations such as Classical Greece and the ancient Middle East, and in several tribal societies such as the Arande in Australia, and the Siwan in North Africa (Ford and Beach, 1951). Further, special social roles have existed for homosexual males, such as temple prostitutes in the ancient Middle East, and shamans in the nomadic peoples of Soviet Central Asia. Such historical and cultural variations in the sociocultural definition of appropriate sexual expression and sex roles suggests to the labelling theorists that it is the "erotophobic heritage of Judeo-Christianity" (Sagarin, 1973: 3) that has to be explained, not the existence and nature of homosexuality as such.

The identification of homosexuality as a "social problem" in modern societies has proceeded by way of the medical and psychological characterization of homosexuality as a symptom of or an actual pathological condition requiring medical or psychiatric intervention. Yet no clear distinction between homosexuality and heterosexuality has been found. Kinsey (Kinsey et al., 1948), the first modern sex researcher, found only 4 percent of his sample of white males were exclusively homosexual, while 37 percent had at least one homosexual experience and 50 percent had experienced homoerotic attraction. Psychiatric studies have only analysed homosexuals who have sought counselling, a group who are likely to differ from those who do not seek such aid. Individuals from the former group are likely to have disturbed family backgrounds and troubled personal and emotional problems. To identify special family patterns that might be associated with homosexuality one would have to study individuals who do not seek psychological help. Research on a large sample of such individuals, both homosexual and heterosexual, found no link between family patterns and sexual preference (Bell, Weinberg and Hammersmith,1981). Nor have biological studies found any hormonal patterns or genetic characteristics peculiar to homosexuals. Lacking clear social, psychological and biological evidence pointing to "constitutional" and clear-cut causes of homosexuality, labelling theorists argue that our social arrangements stigmatize same-sex preference on the basis of social conventions rooted in cultural and institutional traditions.

Such cultural traditions have been changing slowly since the late 1940s. The publication of the Kinsey Report in 1948 reflected a greater openness to public discussion of sexuality and the slow growth of permissiveness towards sexual behaviour. The institutional and social structural foundations of traditional social controls—small, relatively homogeneous residential communities, the importance of organized religion, relatively fixed social status—gave way to an urbanized, secularized, highly geographically and socially mobile society of strangers integrated by abstract bureaucratic rules. However, as we shall see, openness about sexual expression also permits moralizing countermovements.

HOMOSEXUAL IDENTITY AND EXPERIENCE

Stigma, however, is not the end of the matter; it is only the beginning. Because of the stigmatization of homosexual and lesbian behaviour, the social organization of gays is split between covert practitioners who keep their sexual orientations private and "pass" as heterosexuals, and those overt practitioners who express their sexual orientations publicly and defy stigmatization (Leznoff and Westley, 1956). Phenomenological sociologists are interested in several aspects of this split between covert and overt organization of the sexually deviant. First, the process of coming to terms with one's stigmatized sexual orientations in adolescence and early adulthood occurs at the point where conventional morality is most entrenched (Kohlberg, 1973). The normal adolescent uncertainties about sexual expression are compounded by a growing discomfort arising from the gulf between one's sexual leanings and the majority's heterosexual conventions. A little later this sense of the tension between one's basic sexual identity and social demands is reinforced by career demands and the expectations of family and many peers that marriage and family life will follow with adulthood. In the course of coping with these conventions and expectations, the homosexual or lesbian is creating an adult self that may well be one split between public conventionality and private deviance. This self-definition process is often amorphous, diffuse, not clearly time-bound, but flows out of the often trivial everyday experiences that demonstrate the differences between straights and gays, and that generate feelings of insecurity and "otherness" in interactions with straights (Warren and Johnson, 1972).

Second, in the course of developing a gay identity and discovering the existence of other gays and gay communities, phenomenological sociologists argue that the redefinition of self continues throughout much of adult life, so that the "deviant" or "moral career" of gays is far more diffuse, takes longer and has fewer clearly decisive points than the models of "moral careers" derived from studying the mentally ill or the criminal. The latter have been the population studied by labelling theorists, whose model suggests a decisive break with the straight world and a highly (if informally) organized succession of steps and stages ensuing from an original act of delinquency that was apprehended by an agent of social control. However, first-hand accounts by homosexuals and lesbians suggest that the encounter with gay communities is not a simple discovery of a place without stigma. The gay communities themselves have a variety of roles and role stereotypes into which newcomers do not necessarily fit very easily (Warren and Johnson, 1972). Studies of gays have uncovered individuals who feel that stereotyped roles are imposed too rigidly upon newcomers, and that it takes several years of association with other gays to develop an identity within the gay network that feels comfortable and "natural." The extent of fluidity and experimentation implied by the first-hand reports suggests much longer and more complex processes of "career development" than are considered by labelling theory (Warren and Johnson, 1972; Warren and Ponse, 1977; Messinger and Warren, 1984).

Finally, phenomenological sociologists argue that the split between a hidden gay identity and a publicly presented straight "front" involves a different experience of impression management than occurs in straight individuals. Impression management refers to the techniques used by individuals to control interaction in any given situation and to control as well the identity or "self" that they present to others (Goffman, 1959). Given the stigma attached to homosexuality and lesbianism, gays may have to develop impression management techniques far more consciously than is the case for most people. It may also generate ambivalence towards the hidden "self." The constant need to hide one's "true" sexual identity may continuously create intense anxiety and self-hatred, ultimately draining all other social roles of any significance or value. Alternatively, the "felt necessity of wearing masks in settings other than the gay community leads many secret gays to conceive of the gay community as the only milieu in which they can express their real existential selves" (Warren and Ponse, 1977: 687).

AIDS AND GAY IDENTITY

The complexity of gay identity and experience has been compounded by the impact of AIDS on public stereotypes and tolerance. During the 1960s and early 1970s a variety of social movements pressed for greater tolerance of various stigmatized groups such as blacks, women, the handicapped and so on. As well, the countercultural movement of that era emphasized open eroticism as part of its "program" to move to a more tolerant and expressive culture. All this occurred (in Canada and the United States, at least) in the context of a broader, long-term liberalization of sexual attitudes and behaviour, which was reflected in the rise of sexual technique manuals, the rapid spread and diversification of birth-control methods, and the increased circulation of erotic-pornographic magazines and, later, video movies. In Canada, this culminated in then-Prime Minister Pierre Trudeau's famous comment that the state has "no business in the nation's bedrooms," and the 1969 decriminalization of private homosexual acts between consenting adults.

The result of these trends was an increased visibility of gays, reflected in the rise of visible gay residential areas in the largest cities, gay services such as clinics, bath houses and theatres, and gay cultural and communication organizations such as newspapers and magazines. This increased visibility precipitated both increased "official" tolerance as reflected in legislation and court judgments against discrimination suffered by gays, the decriminalization of homosexuality, and the rise of conservative social movements attempting to counter what they viewed as the dissolution of family and morality (Salamon, 1988).

These processes led to unprecedented public debates over the values expressing sexual orientation and identity. This "politicized" debate led many gays to "come out of the closet" and expose their hitherto hidden sexual identity.

The appearance of AIDS has strengthened the political and moralistic groups attacking gays and created further difficulties and complexities in the experience of being gay. AIDS first emerged in the popular mass media as "the gay plague," a viral infection resulting from promiscuity and unconventional sexual practices. Consequently, homosexuality is once again being stigmatized as dangerous and polluting, and demands to medicalize and to criminalize such behaviour have revived. However, gays have experienced two decades of relative tolerance and empowerment (particularly in the largest cities, where gays are concentrated enough that they can organize an effective defence). Further, as the major victims of AIDS, gays have good reason to act together to demand medical research and health services focused on this disease and its sufferers. In the face of greater openness and opportunities to be heard as well as very real practical problems associated with AIDS and moral enterprise, gays have abandoned extremely radical visions of social change, and become more pragmatic, more focused on specific issues and immediate needs.

The gay liberation movement's retreat from cultural and expressive transformation to down-to-earth issues such as needle-exchange programs, hospices for terminally ill AIDS sufferers, etc., has also affected the identity and experience of gays. The popular media emphasis on the "gay plague" and its origins in promiscuous homosexuality led to an acrimonious debate within gay communities about their sexual practices and "lifestyles." Both the mass media and groups within the gay community have attempted to adopt a "liberal" response to the emergence of AIDS: that long-term, monogamous, same-sex ties are acceptable, even respectable, but promiscuous behaviour is now unacceptable given the risk of AIDS transmission. As with heterosexual communities, a more conventional model of sexual relationships is now in vogue or at least given lip service, since the continued spread of sexually transmitted diseases such as herpes and clamydia suggests that extensive pre- and post-marital sexual encounters still exist. Consequently, there is a return to the pre-1960s covert organization of sexual encounters, and the experience of gay sexuality is fraught with considerable doubt and self-blame. Many gays, as well as many straights now in their late 30s and 40s, came of age during a period of increasing tolerance and institutional defence of sexual openness, and have since experienced a waning of support for and practise of sexual openness. At the same time, the rise of AIDS and its severe impact on gays forces on them a continuation of a continuous overt and active "politics of sexual expression," to ensure that the disease is treated as a medical problem rather than an excuse to restigmatize or to intensify the stigma that continues to haunt homosexuality. Insofar as some level of acceptability has emerged for homosexuals, it has been expressed by distinguishing between intolerable promiscuity and tolerable, stable, monogamous relationships.

CONCLUSION

We noted earlier that the example of homosexuality illustrates some significant limitations in the labelling perspective on deviance. We can go further and argue that the example of homosexuality also illustrates some limitations in the sociology of deviance itself.

One theme running throughout this book has been the progressive "de-moralization" of the sociology of deviance. By asserting that deviance is "normal," albeit in a very limited sense, Émile Durkheim fundamentally broke with the moralism of the positivists and the social pathologists. This de-moralization or "moral neutrality" (Lofland, 1969) was further developed by the Chicago School with their celebration of ethnic and subcultural diversity, and by the functionalists in their search for the functions of deviance. The labelling theorists made a further contribution by defining deviance, not in the actions of the "deviants," but in the reactions of the agents of social control. Finally, the ethnomethodologists and phenomenologists have turned to the experiences of the "deviants" themselves, letting us know how they experience their acts, their ideas of right and wrong, and their calculations of morality and practicality.

Despite this progress, some, such as Lofland (1969), have argued that however much the sociologist may attempt to be free of moralizing presuppositions and to be value-free, morality and moral judgements pervade the discipline. Take our selection of subjects to be studied, for example. Few people think twice about the choice of suicide or rape as examples of "deviance," but what of the choice of homosexuality? By choosing to treat this topic as an instance of social deviance, however evenhanded and objective we try to make this treatment, are we not accepting and thereby perpetuating the notion that homosexuality is somehow deviant (Lofland, 1969)? Do we not still feel that we have to account for homosexuality, to explain how someone comes to be a homosexual? Homosexuals might well ask, "Why are *we* being included in a book on deviance?"

What the example of homosexuality makes clear is that we as sociologists must be both clear and careful about the categories we use to identify "types" of deviance and deviants. Such categories, whether derived from the law or from popular opinion, embody a set of assumptions that sociologists should treat as data, not as facts. Even then, we must still be cautious when using any category to refer to sets of real people. The term "homosexual" implies a unity to behaviour, identity or circumstances that is simply absent in the case of the many varied and diverse people we call homosexuals. Just as importantly, it is clear that for many homosexuals today social stigma does not determine their fate. Homosexuals and lesbians have organized to protect their rights as citizens and human beings. They are unwilling either to passively accept "straight" society's view of them or to merely respond to cases of discrimination or oppression.

The sociology of deviance has not yet been completely successful in incorporating these new attitudes and new ways of looking at the relationship between "deviants" and "conformists." Phenomenological and ethnomethodological sociologists have made a contribution by directing us towards the experiences of the "deviants" themselves, but fail to consider how and why conventional society treats certain designated groups and individuals as deviant.

Indeed, it is not clear that phenomenological and ethnomethodological interpretations contain a theory of deviance at all. Ethnomethodology emphasizes the ways deviance exposes aspects of social life common to everyone, universal processes of "making sense together." For phenomenologists, the focus is on the experiences that separate the deviant from the conformist; the intense anxieties about personal identity and relationships to others that may heighten consciousness of social interaction of which conformists are blithely unaware. Both traditions emphasize detailed descriptions of ongoing interaction as the basic research strategy; a strategy that leads to an exclusive concern with the present rather than the historical, and with micro social organization rather than with analysis of organizations, institutions and social movements.

While phenomenological investigations may lead to the sharp differences between groups with different identities, relationships and experiences, ethnomethodology focuses on the hard work everyone engages in to create a (admittedly fragile and precarious) set of mutually understandable and reasonable procedures for getting on with daily living. Daily living takes place in a world of "normal" activities that are morally approved and that are viewed as "natural" and "reasonable." Problems in this world, such as persons believed to be one sex wanting to change to the other, intensify the activities around such persons so that the transition is smoothly accomplished without extensive damage to a wide array of accepted routines. Agnes wanted to be a normal and natural woman; her family wanted her to be a normal and clearly gendered man; the psychiatrists wanted to be sure that her gender desires were real and reasoable. However, one might argue that our two-gendered world makes life sufficiently difficult for homosexuals and lesbians, that "deviant communities" emerge where different gender constructs operate. For ethnomethodologists such deviant communities are of little interest in themselves, except insofar as they more clearly show the techniques used to create gender divisions of whatever kind. Whatever the nature of a community and its social order, it is the techniques permitting that order to persist beyond the conscious perception of its members that is of interest to ethnomethodologists. The study of deviant, abnormal or "exotic" cases is undertaken to learn how what is taken for granted underlies and makes possible a social order. Such cases may provide an opportunity to see how "folk methods" work, giving us an insight into the universal properties of interaction. What makes one social situation different from another, however, or what changes take place over time, are not issues in which the ethnomethodological tradition has been interested.

How do we go about overcoming these limitations? The sociology of deviance should reintegrate its different perspectives and reconceive both the deviant and the conformist as social and cultural subjects who are located within a distinct social structure and whose experiences may be their own, but are nonetheless *meaningful* only because they are shared with others. As we hope to show in the next chapter, the future development of the sociology of deviance lies, not in perpetuating distinct and conflicting perspectives, but in generating an integrated and unified understanding of the complex relationship between deviance and conformity.

CHAPTER
9 Conceiving Deviance

To the student or ordinary person, sociology often appears to have a bewildering variety of theories, perspectives, concepts and definitions. As we have seen, the sociology of deviance is no exception to this; if anything, it may well be the most diverse and contentious area of study of all. In Chapter One we suggested that this abundance of sociological interpretation tells us something about the nature of social reality and the broad and diverse subject matter with which sociologists deal. Unlike other social sciences, whose subject matter is relatively clearly defined and circumscribed, sociologists deal with all types of modern and premodern societies, with a multitude of different forms of social organizations and social institutions, and with an enormous variety of interpersonal situations and experiences. Moreover, the concepts or models used by sociologists to describe one type of society, organization or situation will very often not be applicable to another. Many of the concepts and interpretations useful for understanding tribal societies, for example, simply do not apply to industrial societies, while the social arrangements to be found in bureaucratic organizations are very different from those that characterize intimate personal relationships or informal social groups. What would be considered appropriate social behaviour at work is not the same as appropriate social behaviour at church, at a party or in a family. All of these highly varied social phenomena require specific concepts capable of describing their distinctive characteristics. The only way to get all this diversity under control is to use a very abstract and high level of generalization, but that forces us to ignore all of the differences we will have discovered, and it is these differences and the reasons for them that are often the most significant issues needing to be explained.

In addition, differences in perspective will also emerge when different people have different reasons for examining the same phenomena. For example, one sociologist may examine a work setting in order to understand how such settings can be made more rational and efficient, while another may be interested in understanding the interpersonal relationships that develop among the workers. Again, specific concepts will be developed to highlight what has to be explained. As a consequence, the special characters of different kinds of social phenomena are reflected in different sets of questions and issues, which are then interpreted within different theoretical frameworks. Attempts to generalize from one set of phenomena will often lead to a very different and contradictory theory than will result from generalizations based on a different set of phenomena. These factors apply to sociology as a whole, and go far to explain why the discipline is continuously dogged by debates between the adherents of different theories.

If, as has been suggested, deviance embraces a range of acts from "public nosepicking to treason" (Bordua 1967: 149), then the diversity of subject matter and focus characteristic of sociology in general is also to be found in the sociology of deviance. Along with this diversity of focus on different aspects of social reality comes a diversity of concepts and theories.

To the Chicago sociologists, for example, the city itself was a new phenomenon that needed to be studied in detail and understood. They focused on the relationships between social groups in cities: their conflicts, their competition for scarce and valued resources and their interdependence. In order to uncover such relationships, these sociologists observed the many daily encounters among members of different groups on the city streets, at work, at leisure and so on. This provided rich descriptions of people's lives but little systematic theorizing except at a very low level of generality, as in symbolic interactionism, which focuses on the meanings and goals of individuals, or at such a high level of generality, as in ecological theory, that the meanings and goals of individuals are not taken into account.

In contrast, functionalist and anomie theorists were concerned with the way society as a whole fitted together through the operation of mutually supporting values and institutions. Since this pattern of "social integration" was never perfect, its imperfections placed "strains" on the actions and experiences of individuals as they attempted to follow socially prescribed goals. After identifying an area of strain, functionalist and anomie sociologists were then interested in the various patterns of individual and group responses to inconsistent social pressures.

Labelling theorists were concerned to show that what the functionalists saw as impersonal societal values and social system pressures were in fact the creation of social movements of moral entrepreneurs, which deliberately acted to change values and rules concerning what is or is not deviant. Labelling theory also focused on the ways definitions and interpretations of deviance flowed from face-to-face interaction and communication, especially within agencies of social control and between these agencies and the broader population. Both of these concerns of labelling theory were directed against the tendency of functionalism and anomie theory to assume that a uniform set of cultural values existed through all sections of a society, without diversity, conflict or change.

Ethnomethodology argued for an even closer look at the interactional techniques that were necessary to produce and maintain mutually understandable rules and definitions during interaction. Phenomenologists, for their part, argued for much greater attention to the subjective experiences accompanying social interaction, while radical, critical and feminist theorists argued for a more extended look at the various dimensions of power and oppression involved in the social definition and control of deviance. Clearly, all of these theories are looking at different aspects of social reality and if, in the long run, it is possible to develop an overall theory of deviance, it will be necessary to combine some or all of them.

However, after working through our survey of the diverse range of theories and concerns in the sociology of deviance, the student may still wonder why different kinds of deviance seem to be of concern at different times, and why different kinds of interpretations of deviance emerge, only to be pushed to the background by the development of other interpretations at a later date. Although it is something of a simplification, there is not simply a diversity of coexisting interpretations of deviance, but a sequence to their appearance and prominence. The Chicago School had its heyday in the 1920s and early 1930s. Functionalism developed as a foundation for sociological theory in the United States from the 1930s to the 1950s. Anomie theories, developed from Merton's pioneering application of Durkheim's theory to the United States in the 1930s, was highly influential during the 1940s and 1950s. Labelling theory, the successor to Chicago sociology, developed in the late 1950s and 1960s. Ethnomethodology experienced a brief meteoric rise from the mid-1960s to the 1970s, settling down to a minor current in sociology thereafter. Phenomenology, like ethnomethodology, has become an independent, albeit minor, sociological tradition since the 1960s. Finally, radical, critical and feminist sociologies have become important sociological traditions since the early 1970s.

This sequence of theories is an indication that, unlike theories in the natural sciences, sociological theories are not primarily disproved or made obsolete by new discoveries, but fade in and out of use according to the kinds of social phenomena sociologists are concerned to understand at any particular point in time. Sociologists' concerns are never purely intellectual puzzles but are also related, to some degree at least, to the kinds of social problems and issues of concern in the larger society. To understand, then, the diversity and range of sociological interpretations of deviance, is to understand something of the society at the time the particular interpretations emerge and become important in sociology.

Émile Durkheim's sociology centred on the crucial and overriding phenomenon of his age: the emergence of modern industrial society. This issue had been the major preoccupation of European social scientists from the time of Karl Marx. Marx had established the terms of reference with which this issue was to be discussed: the classification of modern society as capitalist society, identifying its social and economic foundation in the mode of production and forms of class conflict, describing the problems it generates for the individual and for social groups, and providing the solution to these problems. Marx's theory attempted to account for the changes that had characterized European society up to that time and to predict the changes that were yet to come.

In contrast to Marx, the social pathologists, who were primarily conservative and traditionalist, argued that change itself was the major social problem of the age, leading to the breakdown of social order and the emergence of all manner of crime and vice. They sought to strengthen traditional institutions in order to put an end to the social problems of modernity.

Durkheim was determined to show that his version of sociology would provide a superior explanation of modernity than had Marx's, or those of the social pathologists or competing versions of sociology. Like Marx and the social pathologists, Durkheim agreed that modernity had produced social problems, but he argued that these problems were a consequence of neither economic factors nor the breakdown of traditional institutions. To Durkheim, social problems resulted from an imbalance in the relationship between the individual and society; for example, "anomie," the failure of society to regulate the individual's wants and desires. Durkheim chose to do his research on suicide, in part, because he believed that suicide rates exhibited the consequences of these forms of imbalance in a particularly clear fashion.

SOCIAL THEORY AND SOCIAL CHANGE IN THE UNITED STATES

Durkheim's sociology did not travel well to North America, because the issues with which he was concerned were irrelevant to most Canadian and American sociologists. Their interest was less in the breakdown of a past social order than it was in the creation of a new society. The shape of this new society began to be apparent in the 1920s, as the United States was experiencing economic growth without massive immigration for the first time in its history. Towns and cities were growing, and the society was rapidly becoming more urbanized. Distances between communities were being reduced and individual mobility increased by the spread of the automobile and other systems of modern transportation.

Indeed, a modern mass society was developing with the spread of tabloid newspapers, the movies and, by the late twenties, the radio. The children of southern and eastern European immigrants who had flocked to America before 1920 were increasingly assimilated into American culture and moving up the occupational and income ladders. These immigrant communities still bore many of their cultural trappings, but were overwhelmingly urban, located in the largest and most dynamic industrial centres, where labour demand was highest and most consistent. Such areas were also the major centres of urban settlement for American Blacks, displaced in increasing numbers at this time by the rapid mechanization of southern agriculture.

Consequently, the northern and eastern American cities were a social mosaic of many different ethnic groups at various stages of assimilation into American society, having different degrees of economic success; and a large visible minority of recently rural American Blacks, concentrated into clearly separated residential areas and occupying the lowest rungs on the occupational and income ladder. In addition there were, of course, pockets of upper- and middle-class groups, descended from even older immigrant groups. All these groups resided in a society marked by rapid technological change and steady economic growth. Technological and economic change produced experiential and cultural gaps between older and younger generations; technological change combined with economic growth promoted income and occupational mobility; and economic growth and mobility, in turn, promoted rising expectations and aspirations. These conditions were novel and undocumented, and we can understand why the Chicago School saw their task as the detailed description of life in the cities, with special focus on the competition, conflict and accommodation between the different social groupings in the city. Putting these detailed descriptions together, they believed, would result in a clear picture of life in the (then) modern USA.

With the growth of towns, the penetration of all parts of the country by road transportation, movies and newspapers, and the end of large waves of immigration, religious and ethnic differences became less prominent and inequalities based on employment, occupation, income and education increased in importance in the United States. These economic inequalities were made even sharper by the Great Crash of 1929 and the long economic depression that followed in the 1930s. Social problems associated with ethnic rivalries and relations were replaced by problems of unemployment, poverty and labour-management conflict. Merton's (1938) analysis of the "value strain" arising from the gap between the values of economic success and the obstacles to that success arising from social conditions was a reflection (admittedly, a highly abstract one) of the intensely felt economic and political insecurity of the times.

Merton's essay was important in several respects. It shared with other works by Merton clarity of style and cogent and logical argument and, despite its abstraction, it seemed to capture essential characteristics of American society. These qualities made it a model of sociological analysis in general, and of functional analysis in particular. The essay showed that functionalism seemed able to analyse social diversity, deviance and conflict as convincingly as the Chicago School, and to connect such characteristics to the nature of "mainstream" American values. The analysis of anomie, then, seemed more in step with the new, culturally more homogeneous but economically divided urban industrial society that America had become.

After the Second World War, America changed yet again. Converting the domestic economy to peacetime production and helping to reconstruct the war-shattered economies of Europe led to a lengthy period of prosperity. One major effect of this economic prosperity was that home ownership became far more common than ever before. Vast tracts of rural land near cities were developed as suburbs, and the population settled down to raise families and devote time and earnings to furnishing their homes with an unprecedented array of consumer goods. Road transport and the automobile played an even greater role than before in making decentralized suburban development, shopping malls, school busing and lengthy journeys to work major features of postwar life. The new forms of industrialism and larger size of firms demanded better educated and more skilled workers, technicians and managers. This industrialism and the baby boom that accompanied it required an expanded and more accessible education system, a system that became a major growth industry and that itself demanded large numbers of educated workers.

In the context of these changes in the 1940s and the 1950s, both professional sociologists and lay social observers expressed concern over the rise of new and apparently connected social problems. The new prosperity and higher standards of living were producing a society increasingly centred on consumption. Powerful organizations associated with the mass media and the advertising industry were shaping these consumption patterns, and a new cultural homogeneity was emerging. High social mobility accompanied by persistent anxiety over job performance were reinforcing homogeneity. The increasing time taken to travel to work and the anxieties involved in job success placed increasing responsibility on women to organize children's lives and to cope with the stresses of their husbands'. The result was a "mother-centred" family, reinforced even further by the white-collar, technical jobs held by men. Such jobs were difficult for children to understand, so that their ideas of their fathers became vague compared to earlier times, when most work activities embodied more easily understandable manual strengths and skills. Consequently, male children had fewer role models available to them through the family, and depended on the schools for adequate role imaging and career motivation. Thus, children's and youths' encounters with the educational system came to be seen as a crucial determinant in the development of adolescent adjustment or deviance.

The sociologists of juvenile delinquency in the 1940s and 1950s retained a sense of American society as one with a fairly clear, economically based system of stratification. This class image faded with the emergence of Black political protest and the anti-war and countercultural movements of the 1960s. Many sociologists were liberals and therefore highly sympathetic to the criticisms of social arrangements put forth by Black activists, peace groups and countercultural spokesmen. The last, after all, echoed many of the sociologists' own critical interpretations of America written during the 1950s, which characterized that society as overwhelmingly materialistic, conformist and obsessed with economic achievement to the exclusion of less tangible aspects of the quality of life. A reinvigorated and more assertive liberalism was also reflected in the shift from analysis of *deviance* as a problem to the analysis of *social control* as a problem in the sociology of deviance.

This shift occurred in several stages, each expressed through different post-functionalist interpretations of deviance. In the "expansive" stages of early 1960s liberalism, labelling theorists exposed the unnecessarily harsh treatment of "exotic" deviants, such as drug users, and blameless deviants, such as the mentally ill. The treatment of such "deviants" was shown to flow from arbitrary, albeit perhaps sincerely and intensely felt, moral convictions, conventions and traditions. The implications of these studies were that American society should relax, should not be so "uptight" about some traditional concerns (such as drugs and pre-marital sex), and should take a more critical look at the pressures a competitive and materialistic society places upon its members, pressures reflected in mental illness, alcoholism, delinquency and drug abuse.

In the 1970s, several sociological interpretations of deviance developed as critical alternatives to both functionalism and labelling theory. Each vied with the other as a replacement for the theory or theories criticized. Radical, critical or political-economic interpretations reflected the influences of the political and countercultural movements of the sixties in attacking the scientific claims of earlier sociologies, and argued for the importance of political or personal sympathies as a basis for insightful and realistic social analysis. There was interest in hitherto neglected or downplayed social science traditions such as Marxism and the Frankfurt School, and the greater emphasis in these traditions on combining partisanship and scholarship. Sociologists of deviance working in these traditions emphasize historical shifts in definitions of deviance and associated attempts at the social control of deviance. Such shifts are interpreted as reflecting the ideologies and interests rooted in the economic and political organization of classes, and the struggles of dominant classes to maintain their dominance against subordinate classes seeking to change the current social arrangements of domination. Sociological works adopting these interpretations have succeeded in analysing large-scale, historical shifts in social control, but have not successfully explained many aspects of contemporary deviance such as current conflicts over sexual morality, drug use and the apparent rise of domestic violence. Consequently, the critical and political economic approaches have been unable to shake off criticisms from feminists and phenomenologists, who justifiably argue that major areas of deviance require other kinds of analysis. Clearly sociology has, until recently, primarily explored and interpreted a "man's world," with scant attention to gender-based inequalities and experiences. In addition, alongside feminism, phenomenologists have insisted that human experience is a legitimate dimension of social investigation, and one that has been too long neglected by sociologists. Again, the rise of feminism and phenomenology as significant bodies of theory in sociology mirrored the emergence of feminism and subjectivism in the countercultural ferment of the late 1960s, and their persistence as political movements and cultural currents to the present.

SOURCES OF COMPETITION AND FRAGMENTATION IN SOCIOLOGICAL THEORY

At this point, the student may suspect that while changing reality may account for some of the changes in theories of deviance, it does not account for the continuing competition between several theories and the continuing lack of integration of the field. This competition and fragmentation reflects differences in perceptions, experiences and intellectual commitments within the profession of sociology itself. In many respects these differences have intensified over recent times and make up the immediate intellectual and institutional environment within which scientific, cultural and intellectual pursuits take place. This immediate context has shaped the development of sociology as a whole and the sociology of deviance within it.

The number of sociologists, their journals, professional organizations and locations of work have increased vastly over the course of this century. At the beginning of the twentieth century, sociologists were part of the affluent and established minority of upper- and upper-middle-class Americans who went to university. Consequently they were homogeneous in ethnic, class and cultural terms. Many of them came from small towns characterized by social, political and religious conservatism. All were believers in the nineteenth-century vision of the nature of science and the need to apply scientific methods to social analysis and social problems. This image of science was straightforward: science was based on careful observation, unimpeded by value judgements or *a priori* theorizing. There was also considerable consensus about the nature of social problems; the major ones being the social disorganization of the big cities, the pitiable conditions of the urban poor, and the need to assimilate and "Americanize" recent immigrants.

By the 1930s a new generation of sociologists emerged, drawn increasingly from the larger cities, more cosmopolitan in their awareness of European sociology. The two most prominent of these, Talcott Parsons and his pupil Robert Merton, argued for a more systematic conception of the discipline, one not merely imitating the social sciences and their methods, but one that attempted to think through its aims and to establish basic concepts that would direct observation rather than follow it. Coming from urban backgrounds, rather than seeing social disorganization, they accepted the diversity of urban groups and living patterns, as well as the tensions and conflicts that accompanied this urban multiculturalism. Their cosmopolitanism permitted them to view current American social problems with a certain detachment, by comparing them with the social phenomena of other times and places, and viewing such problems as material for testing the interpretive powers of their theories rather than as immediate practical concerns.

This generation of sociologists set the tone for sociology for the 1940s and 1950s. However, the postwar expansion of higher education, and demands for great numbers of university-educated people to work in government and business bureaucracies changed the character of sociologists as an intellectual group. Again, their numbers increased; this time enormously, and the increase was accompanied by a great diversification in social backgrounds, experiences and career locations. Conditions within universities also changed with the rise of mass higher education and the postwar "baby boom."

Standardization of the curriculum, increasing numbers of students and a general bureaucratization of the university system now required more systematic labour on the part of the professoriate. There was increased pressure for university teachers to continue to do research and to publish throughout their careers. The result was a massive turn towards small-scale and narrowly defined empirical research and a rise in specialization. Theory and research tended to split apart, and research methods themselves became a major preoccupation of the profession. The diversity of personal backgrounds, values, ideologies and interests broke down the momentary coherence Parsons and Merton had provided to American sociology.

These fragmenting conditions within the ranks of professional sociologists have continued unchecked since the 1950s, even though the expansion of higher education has ended. In addition, new factors have contributed to reinforce intellectual divisions within sociology. The 1960s contributed a broad willingness to question the legitimacy of authority everywhere, including the authority of established interpretations in the social sciences. The inherited intellectual traditions were increasingly attacked as empirically false and ideologically biased. Alternative sources of theory and interpretation were looked to, such as Marxism, phenomenology and literary criticism. These developments have led to a multiplication of the philosophical, political and ideological bases of sociological theorizing, a broadening of the range of phenomena that are defined as important to study, and an intensification of theoretical debates in all areas of sociological analysis. Social reality, it is realized, has become more complex, but there is as yet no breakthrough in developing a synthesis of the many partial interpretations that have been developed to analyse different aspects of this complexity.

CANADIAN SOCIOLOGY AND THE SOCIOLOGY OF DEVIANCE

Canadian sociology has had a different development, one that has been influenced both by the intellectual traditions in Canadian universities and by aspects of Canadian society itself. These circumstances are also reflected in Canadian sociological interpretations of deviance.

Prior to the 1970s, Canada had not yet developed an indigenous sociological approach and was dominated by British and American theoretical and intellectual trends. Why was there no indigenous sociology in Canada? One reason may be the frequently remarked-upon failure of Canadians during that era to question their society. Canadians, as we are often told (see Chapter One), have traditionally tended to be subservient to authority and somewhat smug about the superiority of their society over that of the "violent," "crude" and "materialistic" United States. While Canada has had a long history of political movements and political action, which have generated new political parties such as the CCF and Social Credit parties in the 1930s and the Bloc Québécois and the Reform Party today, there was little in the way of distinctively Canadian intellectual analysis of local social problems prior to the 1970s.

The emergence of an indigenous approach to sociology in the 1970s reflected several factors. Sociology in Canada was insignificant until the wave of university expansion of the 1960s. Prior to that point, only McGill and the University of Toronto had sociology offerings in their courses of study. The McGill department of sociology was influenced by the Chicago School of the 1930s and 1940s, particularly as a result of the prominent Chicago sociologist Everett Hughes, who taught there for a time. Hughes retained a concern with inter-ethnic diversity and tensions, but he was less interested in patterns of urban crime, delinquency and deviance. He was more interested in the development of an urban and industrial anthropology that explored and made sense of the patterns of daily lives in families, communities, factories and offices, and the web of meanings through which members of these institutions made sense of their lives. The original concern of the Chicago School with the dynamics of ethnic and multicultural tensions, conflicts, accommodations and adjustments was also less prominent in the Québec society of that era, characterized more by the "two solitudes" than by either conflict or accommodation.

At the University of Toronto, sociology existed as part of the Department of Political Economy, in a university whose faculty was much influenced by British academic traditions unsympathetic to sociology. In this environment, sociology developed as social history, largely concerned to analyse the historical development of Canadian society. American sociology was viewed as too concerned with the present day, lacking in historical perspective, and especially as too narrowly focused on social problems.

The marginal existence of Canadian sociology meant that, when sociology spread with the expansion of university education in the 1960s, "American-style" courses, using American research material and texts, dominated. This coincided with the rise of youth protest and countercultural movements largely imitative of American models. However, these movements also emerged at a time when Canadian nationalism was on the rise, especially expressed in concerns over American investment in our economy and in American domination of the mass media. The result was that a strong nationalist, anti-American sentiment coloured much of the protest, including protests over the Americanization of faculty and curriculum in the universities. As in the United States, these protest movements affected sociology. However, while in the United States the populist, "underdog ideology" of labelling theory formed the basis for the development of later sociologies of deviance, in Canada "American Sociology" was criticized by adopting and reworking a distinctly Canadian social theory, namely, the staples theory of Canadian economic development.

This theory interpreted Canadian economic development in terms of its colonial ties to Britain, and then its subordination to the United States through investment in major areas of the economy. Staples analysis was attractive because it interpreted Canadian history as one of dependency on stronger external forces, made sense of the domination of overseas investment in Canadian industry, and made clearer the reasons for the prominence and persistence of primary industries such as fishing, farming and logging. Much of the last two decades of Canadian sociology has been spent on the critical elaboration of this approach, often using ideas drawn from Marxism. Such concerns emphasize class inequalities and conflicts, industrial relations, patterns of international economic interdependence, regional inequalities and the role of the provincial and federal governments in developing and applying policies that perpetuate high foreign investments, a strong, resource-based economy and the consequent regional and class inequalities.

Ironically, the appropriateness of structural, political-economic interpretations to Canada's resource-based economic development and to the clear regional and class inequalities resulting from this development pattern has resulted in critical, radical and political economic sociologies becoming "mainstream" interpretations in Canada. Interpretations of deviance flowing from these analyses emphasize class relations as the foundations of social control and societal definition and reaction to deviance. Definitions of deviance are seen as elements of the political ideology of the ruling class, while reactions to deviance are viewed as a result of economic and political interests in maintaining the present social order. In theoretical terms, the sociology of deviance in Canada shares much with the radical "New Deviance" or "Critical Criminology" approaches found in Britain. It is possible that Canada's history of government economic and political intervention and the heritage of the two charter elites make class analysis and focus on the role of the state a more reasonable basis for sociological analysis than in the seemingly fluid and ethnically fragmented United States. However, despite its leanings towards radical and political economic analysis of deviance, it is difficult to identify a distinctive Canadian approach to deviance, possibly because Canada is, after all, now not really so different from other advanced industrial, multicultural societies.

PROSPECTS FOR AN INTEGRATED PERSPECTIVE ON DEVIANCE

Is an integrated sociological approach to deviance likely to emerge in the near future? Possibly, but we would not bet on it. Unlike the phenomena studied by natural scientists, social phenomena constantly undergo change. Take the place of the Québécois and the Native peoples in Canadian society as an example. Since we began this book, Canada has gone through the debacle of the Meech Lake Accord and the Oka "crisis," and now faces the prospect of a referendum on Québec sovereignty in the near future. Natives, who in the past were largely ignored in constitutional discussions, now insist that they be full partners in all constitutional debates; while the Québécois, who in the past were the most passionate participants in such debates, now stand distant and apart from the discussions. It seems that many Québécois now want out of Canada, just as many Native people now want, finally and equally, to be in. What seemed to be a relatively stable nation with a bright future ahead of it three years ago may well be on the verge of breaking up. What that would lead to down the road is anybody's guess. Perhaps none of this will come to pass, and by the time you read this book these issues will have been resolved, but the point is that change, often dramatic and unpredictable change, is the condition under which we live our lives.

Just as our subject matter changes, so, too, do the tools we use to understand it, such as the concepts and perspectives we use. New forms of crime and deviance, such as computer crime, are always emerging. New moral entrepreneurs come on the scene again and again, each with their ideas of what we all should or should not do. Consider such issues as whether women should be allowed to sell their services as surrogate mothers; whether physicians should tell their patients they have AIDS; or whether staring, by a male, at women in a swimming pool is sexual harassment. Existing perspectives on deviance not only fail to deal with such issues, they often cannot even formulate what *is* at issue in such cases.

New perspectives on deviance, then, will continue to appear, and an integrated approach—even if one were possible—would be outdated as soon as it appeared. Rather than a weakness, however, it is possible that this is one of sociology's strengths. By remaining open to the nuances of social life, we retain the ability to identify the new and attempt to understand changing social circumstances.

That is why we continue to study past perspectives on deviance, such as those of Durkheim or the functionalists. Each of these approaches still has much to teach us, not only about what mistakes to avoid, but also about how to try to order and make sense of the flow of social events. As we have seen, each of the perspectives made valuable contributions to our understanding of deviance and each has provided some insights that could be used and built upon by later sociologists. An awareness of the successes and failures of past perspectives also teaches us to avoid the intellectual arrogance of being sure that we have all the answers. As long as there are still questions to ask and answers to find, the sociology of deviance will remain one of the most exciting and energetic areas of sociological research.

BIBLIOGRAPHY

Adler, Freda
1975 *Sisters in Crime: The Rise of the New Female Criminal.* New York: McGraw-Hill.

Akers, Ronald L.
1985 *Deviant Behavior: A Social Learning Approach.* Belmont, CA: Wadsworth.

Alexander, Bruce K. and Patricia. F. Hadaway
1982 "Opiate Addiction: The Case for an Adaptive Orientation." *Psychological Bulletin* 92: 367-81.

Amir, Menachem
1971 *Patterns in Forcible Rape.* Chicago: University of Chicago Press.

Baechler, Jean
1979 *Suicides.* New York: Basic Books.

Bales, Robert F.
1962 "Attitudes Toward Drinking in the Irish Culture." pp. 15787 in D.J. Pittman and C.R. Snyder (eds.), *Society, Culture, and Drinking Patterns.* New York: John Wiley and Sons.

Baron, Stephen W.
1989 "The Canadian West Coast Punk Subculture: A Field Study." *Canadian Journal of Sociology* 14: 289-316.

Bart, Pauline
1991 "Review of 'Theories of Rape' by Lee Ellis." *Contemporary Sociology* 20: 268-70.

Becker, Howard
1963 *Outsiders.* New York: The Free Press.

1964 *The Other Side: Perspectives on Deviance.* New York: The Free Press.

1973 "Labelling Theory Reconsidered." pp. 177-208 in *Outsiders.* New York: The Free Press.

1977 *Sociological Work: Method and Substance.* New Brunswick, NJ: Transaction Books.

Becker, Howard, Blanche Geer, Everret Hughes and Anselm Strauss
1961 *Boys in White: Student Culture in Medical School.* Chicago: University of Chicago Press.

Bell, A.P., M.S. Weinberg and S.K. Hammersmith
1981 *Sexual Preference: Its Development in Men and Women.* Bloomington: Indiana University Press.

Berstein, Basil

1971 *Class, Codes and Control.* London: Routledge and Kegan Paul.

1975 *Towards a Theory of Educational Transmission: Class, Codes and Control Vol. 3.* London: Routledge and Kegan Paul.

Birdwhistell, Ray

1970 *Kinesics and Context: Essays on Body Motion Communication.* Philadelphia: University of Pennsylvania Press.

Birenbaum, Arnold and Henry Lesieur

1982 "Social Values and Expectations." pp. 97-122 in M. Rosenberg et al. (eds.), *The Sociology of Deviance.* New York: St. Martin's Press.

Blumer, Herbert

1969 *Symbolic Interactionism.* Englewood Cliffs, NJ: Prentice Hall.

Bordua, David

1961 "A Critique Of Sociological Interpretations Of Gang Delinquency." *Annals of the American Academy of Political and Social Science* 338: 120-36.

1967 "Recent Trends: Deviant Behaviour and Social Control." *Annals of the American Academy of Political and Social Science 369: 149-63.*

Bourdieu, Pierre

1977 *Outline of a Theory of Practice.* Cambridge: Cambridge University Press.

Bourdieu, Pierre and Jean-Claude Passeron

1977 *Reproduction in Education, Society and Culture.* Beverly Hills: Sage.

Box, Steven

1983 *Power, Crime, and Mystification.* London: Tavistock.

Boyd, Neil

1986 *The Social Dimension of Law.* Scarborough: Prentice-Hall.

1988 "Legal and Illegal Drug Use." pp. 152-84 in V.F. Sacco (ed.), *Deviance: Conformity and Control in Canadian Society.* Scarborough: Prentice-Hall.

Boyd, Susan B. and Elizabeth A. Sheehy

1989 "Overview." pp. 255-70 in T. Caputo et al. (eds.), *Law and Society: A Critical Perspective.* Toronto: Harcourt Brace Jovanovich.

Boyle, Christin

1991 "Sexual Assault: A Case Study of Legal Policy Options." pp. 99-109 in M.A. Jackson and C.T. Griffiths (eds.), *Canadian Criminology: Perspectives on Crime and Criminality.* Toronto: Harcourt Brace Jovanovich.

Buckie, Catherine

1991 "Alcoholic Too Drunk To be Guilty." *Montreal Gazette* (May 1), A1-A2.

Buckner, H. Taylor

1971 *Deviance, Reality, and Change.* New York: Random House.

Campbell, Anne
1984   *The Girls in the Gang*. Oxford: Basil Blackwell.

Canada, Department of National Health and Welfare
1988   *Health Protection and Drug Laws*. Ottawa: Minister of Supply and Services.

Caputo, Tullio, Mark Kennedy, Charles E. Reasons and Augustine Brannigan (eds.)
1989   *Law and Society: A Critical Perspective*. Toronto: Harcourt Brace Jovanovich.

Caputo, Tullio and R. Linden
1987   "Early Theories of Criminology." pp. 104-20 in R. Linden (ed.), *Criminology: A Canadian Perspective*. Toronto: Holt, Rinehart and Winston.

Carlen, P.
1985   *Criminal Women*. Cambridge: Cambridge University Press.

Casey, John
1985   "Corporate Crime and the State: Canada in the 1980s." pp. 100-11 in T. Fleming (ed.), *The New Criminologies in Canada: State, Crime and Control*. Toronto: Oxford University Press.

Chambliss, William
1973   "The Saints and the Roughnecks." *Society* 11: 24-31.

1978   "Toward a Political Economy of Crime." pp. 191-211 in C.E. Reasons and R.M. Rich (eds.), *The Sociology of Law: A Conflict Perspective*. Toronto: Butterworths.

Charon, Joel M.
1985   *Symbolic Interactionism: An Introduction, an Interpretation, an Integration*. Englewood Cliffs, NJ: Prentice Hall.

Charron, Marie-France
1981   *Le Suicide Au Québec*. Québec: Ministère des Affaires Sociales.

Chaudron, C.D. and D.A. Wilkinson
1988   *Theories on Alcoholism*. Toronto: Addiction Research Foundation.

Cicourel, Aaron V.
1968   *The Social Organization of Juvenile Justice*. New York: John Wiley.

Cicourel, Aaron V. and John I. Kitsuse
1963   *The Educational Decision-Makers*. Indianapolis: Bobbs-Merrill.

Clark, Lorenne M.G. and Debra Lewis
1977   *Rape: The Price of Coercive Sexuality*. Toronto: The Women's Press.

Clinard, Marshall B.
1964   *Anomie and Deviant Behaviour: A Discussion and Critique*. New York: The Free Press.

Clinard, Marshall B. and Robert F. Meier
1979   *Sociology of Deviant Behavior*. Chicago: Holt, Rinehart and Winston.

Cloward, Richard A. and Lloyd E. Ohlin
1960   *Delinquency and Opportunity*. Glencoe, IL: The Free Press.

Cohen, Albert K.
1955   *Delinquent Boys: The Culture of the Gang*. Glencoe, IL.: The Free Press.

Cohen, Albert K. and James F. Short
1958   "Research on Delinquent Subcultures." *Journal of Social Issues* 14: 20-36.

Cohen, Stanley
1972   *Folk Devils and Moral Panics*. Harmondsworth, Middlesex: Penguin.

Coleman, James
1961   *The Adolescent Society*. New York: The Free Press.

Comack, A. Elizabeth
1985   "The Origins of Canadian Drug Legislation: Labelling Versus Class Analysis." pp. 65-86 in T. Fleming (ed.), *The New Criminologies in Canada: State, Crime, and Control*. Toronto: Oxford University Press.

Conrad, Peter and Joseph W. Schneider
1980   *Deviance and Medicalization: From Badness to Sickness*. St. Louis: C.V. Mosby.

Cook, S.J.
1969   "Canadian Narcotics Legislation, 1908-1923: A Conflict Model Interpretation." *Canadian Review of Sociology and Anthropology* 6: 36-46.

Cooley, Charles Horton
1964   *Human Nature and the Social Order*. New York: Shocken.

Coser, Lewis
1978   *Masters of Sociological Thought*. New York: Harcourt Brace Jovanovich.

Currie, Elliot P.
1968   "Crimes without Criminals: Witchcraft and Its Control in Renaissance Europe." *Law and Society Review* 3: 7-32.

Cusson, Maurice
1983   *Why Delinquency?* Toronto: University of Toronto Press.

Darwin, Charles
1871   *The Descent of Man*. London: John Murray.

Davis, Kingsley
([1937]1980)   "The Sociology of Prostitution." pp. 8-21 in S.H. Traub and C.B. Little (eds.), *Theories of Deviance*. Itasca, IL: F.E. Peacock.

Dean, Dwight G.
1961   "Alienation: Its Meaning and Measurement." *American Sociological Review* 26: 753-58.

Dentler, Robert A. and Kai T. Erikson
1959   "The Functions of Deviance in Groups." *Social Problems* 7: 98-107.

Denzin, Norman K.
1971   "Rules of Conduct and the Study of Deviant Behavior: Some Notes on the Social Relationship." pp. 120-59 in J.D. Douglas (ed.), *Deviance and Respectability*. New York: Basic Books.

1989   *Interpretive Interactionism*. Newbury Park, CA: Sage Publications.

Dickson, D.T.
1968   "Bureaucracy and Morality: An Organizational Perspective on a Moral Crusade." *Social Problems* 16: 143-56.

Ditton, Jason
1977   "Perks, Pilferage and the Fiddle: The Historical Structure of Invisible Wages." *Theory and Society* 4: 39-71.

Douglas, Jack D.
1967   *The Social Meanings of Suicide*. Princeton: Princeton University Press.

Douglas, Jack D. and Frances Waksler
1982   *The Sociology of Deviance*. Boston: Little, Brown.

Downes, David and Paul Rock
1988   *Understanding Deviance*. Oxford: Oxford University Press.

Durkheim, Émile
1951   *Suicide*. New York: The Free Press.

1982   *The Rules of Sociological Method and Selected Texts on Sociology and its Method*. New York: The Free Press.

Eliade, Mircea
1971   *Shamanism*. Princeton: Princeton University Press.

Ellis, Desmond
1987   *The Wrong Stuff: An Introduction to the Sociological Study of Deviance*. Don Mills: Collier Macmillan.

Ellis, Lee
1989   *Theories of Rape: Inquiries into the Causes of Sexual Aggression*. New York: Hemisphere Publishing Corp.

Emerson, Joan P.
1969   "Negotiating the Serious Import of Humor." *Sociometry* 32: 169-81.

Emerson, Robert M.
1969   *Judging Delinquents: Context and Process in Juvenile Court*. Chicago: Aldine.

Ericson, Richard V.
1981   *Making Crime: A Study of Detective Work*. Toronto: Butterworths.

1982   *Reproducing Order: A Study of Police Patrol Work*. Toronto: University of Toronto Press.

Erikson, Kai T.
1965 *Wayward Puritans: A Study in the Sociology of Deviance*. New York: John Wiley.

Fingarette, Herbert
1989 *Heavy Drinking*. Berkeley: University of California Press.

Fleming, Berkley and Tom Goff
1983 "Sociological Perspectives" pp. 23-69 in M. Rosenberg et al. (eds.), *Introduction to Sociology*. Toronto: Methuen Publications.

Fleming, Thomas
1985 *The New Criminologies in Canada: State, Crime, and Control*. Toronto: Oxford University Press.

Fleming, Thomas and L.A. Visano
1983 *Deviant Designations: Crime, Law and Deviance in Canada*. Toronto: Butterworths.

Ford, Clelland S. and Frank A. Beach
1951 *Patterns of Sexual Behavior*. New York: Harper and Row.

Foucault, Michel
1973 *Madness and Civilization: A History of Insanity in the Age of Reason*. New York: Random House Vintage.

1976 *Mental Illness and Psychology*. New York: Harper and Row Torchbooks.

1979 *Discipline and Punish: The Birth Of The Prison*. New York: Random House.

Friedenberg, Edgar Z.
1983 "Culture in Canadian Context." pp. 117-39 in M. Rosenberg et al. (eds.), *Introduction to Sociology*. Toronto: Methuen.

Gallagher, Bernard J., III
1987 *The Sociology of Mental Illness*. Englewood Cliffs, NJ: Prentice Hall.

Garfinkel, Harold
1967 *Studies in Ethnomethodology*. Englewood Cliffs, NJ: Prentice Hall.

Gellner, Ernest
1975 "Ethnomethodology: The Re-Enchantment Industry or The Californian Way of Subjectivity." *Philosophy of the Social Sciences* 5: 431-50.

Gibbs, Jack P.
1972 "Issues in Defining Deviant Behavior." pp. 39-68 in R. Scott and J. Douglas (eds.), *Theoretical Perspectives on Deviance*. New York: Basic Books.

Gibbs, Jack P. and Walter T. Martin
1964 *Status Integration and Suicide: A Sociological Study*. Eugene, OR: University of Oregon Press.

Giddens, Anthony

1971   "Introduction." pp. xix-xli in T. Masaryk, *Suicide and the Meaning of Civilization*. Chicago: The University of Chicago Press.

1977   *Studies in Social and Political Theory*. New York: Basic Books.

Glasbeek, H.J.

1989   "Why Corporate Deviance is Not Treated as a Crime: The Need to Make Profits a Dirty Word." pp. 126-45 in T. Caputo, M. Kennedy, C. Reasons and A. Brannigan (eds.), *Law and Society: A Critical Perspective*. Toronto: Harcourt Brace Jovanovich.

Goff, Colin and Charles H. Reasons

1978   *Corporate Crime in Canada*. Scarborough: Prentice-Hall.

Goffman, Erving

1959   *The Presentation of Self In Everyday Life*. Garden City, NY: Doubleday.

1961   *Asylums*. Garden City, NY: Doubleday.

1963   *Stigma*. Englewood Cliffs, NJ: Prentice Hall.

1967   "Mental Symptoms and Public Order" in *Interaction Ritual: Essays on Face-to-Face Behavior*. Garden City, NY: Doubleday Anchor.

1971   "The Insanity of Place" in *Relations in Public: Microstudies of the Public Order*. New York: Basic Books.

Goode, Erich

1973   *The Drug Phenomenon: Social Aspects of Drug Taking*. Indianapolis: Bobbs-Merrill.

1978   *Deviant Behavior*. Englewood Cliffs, NJ: Prentice Hall.

1984   *Deviant Behavior* 2nd ed. Englewood Cliffs, NJ: Prentice Hall.

1990   *Deviant Behavior* 3rd ed. Englewood Cliffs, NJ: Prentice Hall.

Gottfredson, Michael R. and Travis Hirschi

1990   *A General Theory of Crime*. Stanford: Stanford University Press.

Gould, Stephen Jay

1981   *The Mismeasure of Man*. New York: W.W. Norton.

Gouldner, Alvin W.

1973   "Foreword." pp. ix-xiv in I. Taylor, P. Walton and J. Young, *The New Criminology: For a Social Theory of Deviance*. London: Routledge and Kegan Paul.

Gove, Walter

1980   *The Labelling of Deviance: Evaluating a Perspective*. Beverly Hills, CA: Sage.

Green, Melvyn

1986   "A History of Canadian Narcotics Control: The Formative Years." pp. 24-40 in N. Boyd (ed.), *The Social Dimensions of Law*. Scarborough: Prentice-Hall.

Gross, Edward

1979 "Laughter and Symbolic Interaction." *Symbolic Interaction* 2: 1, 111-12.

Grusky, Oscar and Melvin Pollner

1981 *The Sociology of Mental Illness: Basic Studies*. New York: Holt, Rinehart and Winston.

Gusfield, Joseph R.

1963 *Symbolic Crusade: Status Politics and the American Temperance Movement*. Urbana: University of Illinois Press.

1984 *The Culture of Public Problems: Drinking-Driving and the Symbolic Order*. Chicago: University of Chicago Press.

Gussow, Zachary and George S. Tracy

1975 "Status, Ideology, and Adaptation to Stigmatized Illness: A Study of Leprosy." pp. 112-21 in F. Scarpitti and P. McFarlane (eds.), *Deviance: Action, Reaction, Interaction*. Reading, MA: Addison-Wesley.

Haas, Jack and William Shaffir

1974 *Decency and Deviance*. Toronto: McClelland and Stewart.

Hagan, John

1977 *The Disreputable Pleasures*. Toronto: McGraw-Hill

1991 *The Disreputable Pleasures* 3rd ed. Toronto: McGraw-Hill.

Harris, Michael

1990 *Justice Denied: The Law Versus Donald Marshall*. Toronto: HarperCollins.

Hatch, Alison J. and Karlene Faith

1991 "The Female Offender in Canada: A Statistical Profile." pp. 70-78 in R. Silverman, J. Teevan and V. Sacco (eds.), *Crime In Canadian Society* 4th ed. Toronto: Butterworths.

Heath, Anthony B.

1987 "Anthropology and Alcohol Studies: Current Issues." *Annual Review of Anthropology* 16: 99-120.

Hebdidge, Dick

1979 *Subcultures*. London: Tavistock.

Henry, Andrew F. and James F. Short

1954 *Suicide and Homicide*. New York: The Free Press.

Henry, Stuart

1978 *The Hidden Economy: Context and Control of Borderline Crime*. London: Martin Robertson.

Hepworth, Mike

1980 "Deviance and Control in Everyday Life: The Contribution of Erving Goffman." pp. 80-99 in J. Ditton (ed.), *The View From Goffman*. New York: St. Martin's Press.

Heritage, John
1984 *Garfinkel and Ethnomethodology*. Cambridge: Polity Press.

Hills, Stuart L.
1980 *Demystifing Social Deviance*. New York: McGraw-Hill.

Hinch, Ron
1985 "Marxist Criminology in the 1970s: Clarifying the Clutter." pp. 27-42 in T. Fleming (ed.), *The New Criminologies in Canada: State, Crime, and Control*. Toronto: Oxford University Press.

1987 "Cultural Deviance and Conflict Theories." pp. 177-98 in R. Linden (ed.), *Criminology: A Canadian Perspective*. Toronto: Holt, Rinehart and Winston.

Hindess, Barry
1986 "Actors and Social Relations." pp. 113-26 in M. Wardell and S. Turner (eds.), *Sociological Theory in Transition*. Boston: Allen and Unwin.

Hodgins, Sheilagh
1987 "Biological Factors Implicated in the Development of Criminal Behaviours." pp. 121-37 in R. Linden (ed.), *Criminology: A Canadian Perspective*. Toronto: Holt, Rinehart and Winston.

House, J. Douglas
1985 *The Challenge of Oil: National Quest for Controlled Development*. St. John's: Memorial University

Hughes, Everret C.
1958 *Men and Their Work*. New York: The Free Press.

Hunter, Linda and Judith Posner
1987 "Culture as Popular Culture." pp. 79-107 in M. Rosenberg et al. (eds.), *Introduction to Sociology*. 2nd ed. Toronto: Methuen.

Husserl, Edmund
1931 *Ideas*. London: Macmillan.

Inciardi, James A.
1986 *The War on Drugs: Heroin, Cocaine, Crime, and Public Policy*. Palo Alto: Mayfield Publishing Company.

Jackall, Robert
1980 "Crime in the Suites." *Contemporary Sociology* 9: 354-58.

Jackson, Margaret A.
1991 "Search for the Cause of Crime: Biological and Psychological Perspectives." pp. 173-95 in M.A. Jackson and C.T. Griffiths (eds.), *Canadian Criminology: Perspectives on Crime and Criminality*. Toronto: Harcourt Brace Jovanovich.

Jackson, Margaret A. and Curt T. Griffiths
1991 *Canadian Criminology: Perspectives on Crime and Criminality*. Toronto: Harcourt Brace Jovanovich.

Johnson, Holly
1988   "Violent Crime." *Canadian Social Trends* 9 (Summer): 24-29.

Kessler, Suzanne and Wendy McKenna
1985   *Gender: An Ethnomethodological Approach*. Chicago: University of Chicago Press.

Kinsey, Alfred C., Wardell B. Pomeroy and Clyde E. Martin
1948   *Sexual Behavior in the Human Male*. Philadelphia: W. B. Saunders.

Kinsey, Richard, John Lea and Jock Young
1986   *Losing The Fight Against Crime*. Oxford: Basil Blackwell.

Kitsuse, John I.
1964   "Societal Reactions to Deviant Behavior: Problems of Theory and Method." pp. 87-102 in H. Becker (ed.), *The Other Side: Perspectives on Deviance*. New York: The Free Press.

1980   "The New Conception of Deviance and Its Critics." pp. 273-84 in W. Gove (ed.), *The Labelling of Deviance: Evaluating a Perspective*. Beverly Hills, CA: Sage.

Kitsuse, John I. and Aaron V. Cicourel
1963   "A Note on the Use of Official Statistics." *Social Problems* 11: 131-39

Kitsuse, John I. and David C. Dietrick
1964   "Delinquent Boys, A Critique." *American Sociological Review* 59: 208-15.

Kohlberg, Lawrence
1973   "Stage and Sequence: The Cognitive Developmental Approach." pp. 347-400 in D. Goslin (ed.), *Handbook of Socialization Theory and Research*. Chicago: Rand McNally.

Law Reform Commission of Canada
1974   *The Meaning of Guilt: Criminal Law—Strict Liability. Working Paper No. 2*. Ottawa: Information Canada.

Lea, John and Jock Young
1984   *What is to be Done About Law and Order?* Harmondsworth: Penguin.

Lemert, Edwin
1951   *Social Pathology*. New York: McGraw-Hill.

1967   *Human Deviance, Social Problems and Social Control*. Englewood Cliffs, NJ: Prentice Hall.

1982   "Issues in the Study of Deviance." pp. 233-57 in M. Rosenberg et al. (eds.), *The Sociology of Deviance*. New York: St. Martin's Press.

Letkemann, Peter
1973   *Crime as Work*. Englewood Cliffs, NJ: Prentice Hall.

Leznoff, Maurice and William A. Westley
1956   "The Homosexual Community." *Social Problems* 3: 257-63.

Liazos, Alexander
1972 "The Poverty of the Sociology of Deviance: Nuts, Sluts, and Preverts." *Social Problems* 20: 103-20.

Linden, Rick
1987 *Criminology: A Canadian Perspective*. Toronto: Holt, Rinehart and Winston.

Lindesmith, Alfred R.
1947 *Opiate Addiction*. Bloomington, IN: Principia Press.

1965 *The Addict and the Law*. Bloomington, IN: Indiana University Press.

Lindesmith, Alfred R. and John H. Gagnon
1964 "Anomie and Drug Addiction." pp. 158-88 in M. Clinard (ed.), *Anomie and Deviant Behaviour: A Discussion and Critique*. New York: The Free Press.

Lindsay, Peter H. and Peggy Ann Walpole,
1978 "Crimes of Violence and the Female Offender." pp. 40-50 in M. Gammon (ed.), *Violence in Canada*. Toronto: Methuen.

Lipset, Seymour Martin
1991 *Continental Divide: The Values and Institutions of the United States and Canada*. New York: Routledge.

Lofland, John
1969 *Deviance and Identity*. Englewood Cliffs, NJ: Prentice Hall.

MacAndrew, Craig and Robert Edgerton
1969 *Drunken Comportment*. Chicago: Aldine.

Mann, Michael
1973 *Consciousness and Action Among the Western Working Class*. London: Macmillan.

Matza, David
1964 *Delinquency and Drift*. New York: John Wiley.

1969 *Becoming Deviant*. Englewood Cliffs, NJ: Prentice Hall.

McKie, Craig
1987 "Canada"s Prison Population." *Canadian Social Trends* 6: 2-7.

1990 "Lifestyle Risks: Smoking and Drinking in Canada." pp. 86-92 in C. McKie and K. Thompson (eds.), *Canadian Social Trends*. Toronto: Thompson Educational Publishing.

Mead, George Herbert
1934 *Mind, Self, and Society*. Chicago: University of Chicago Press.

Mendelson, Jack and Nancy H. Mello
1985 *Alcohol: Use and Abuse in America*. Boston: Little, Brown.

Menzies, Robert J.

1991 "Mental Disorder and Crime in Canada." pp. 197-238 in M.A. Jackson and C.T. Griffiths (eds.), *Canadian Criminology: Perspectives on Crime and Criminality*. Toronto: Harcourt Brace Jovanovich.

Merton, Robert K.

1938 "Social Structure and Anomie." *American Sociological Review* 3: 672-82.

1964 "Anomie, Anomia, and Social Interaction: Contexts of Deviant Behavior." pp. 213-42 in M. Clinard (ed.), *Anomie and Deviant Behaviour: A Discussion and Critique*. New York: The Free Press.

1968 *Social Theory and Social Structure*. New York: The Free Press.

Messinger, Sheldon and Carol A.B. Warren

1984 "The Homosexual Self and the Organization of Experience: The Case of Kate White." pp. 196-221 in J.A. Kotarba and A. Fontana (eds.), *The Existential Self in Social Relations*. Chicago: University of Chicago Press.

Miller, Walter B.

1958 "Lower Class Culture As A Generating Milieu Of Gang Delinquency." *Journal of Social Issues* 14: 5-19.

1974 "American Youth Gangs: Past And Present," pp. 210-39 in Abraham S. Blumberg (ed.), *Current Perspectives on Criminal Behavior*. New York: Alfred A. Knopf.

Mills, C. Wright

1967 "The Professional Ideology of Social Pathologists." pp. 525-52 in *Power, Politics and People*. New York: Oxford.

Murphy, Emily F.

1922 *The Black Candle*. Toronto: Thomas Allen.

Murphy, Chris and Graham Main

1985 *Community Based Policing: A Review of the Critical Issues*. Ottawa: Ministry of the Solicitor General.

National Task Force on Suicide

1987 *Suicide in Canada*. Ottawa: Health and Welfare Canada.

Nelson, S. and Menachem Amir

1975 "The Hitch-Hiker Victim of Rape." pp. 47-64 in I. Drapkin and E. Vlano (eds.), *Victimology*. Lexington: D. C. Heath Lexington Books.

Palmer, Bryan

1976 "Most Uncommon Common Men: Craft and Culture in Historical Perspective." *Labour/Le Travailleur*, 1: 5-31.

Palson, Charles and Rebecca Palson

1975 "Swinging in Wedlock." pp. 47-59 in F. Scarpitti and P. McFarlane (eds.), *Deviance: Action, Reaction, Interaction*. Reading, MA: Addison-Wesley.

Pantich, Leo (ed.)
1977   *The Canadian State: Political Economy and Political Power*. Toronto: University of Toronto Press.

Park, Robert E.
1950   *Race and Culture: Essays in the Sociology of Contemporary Man*. New York: The Free Press.

Parsons, Talcott
1937   *The Structure of Social Action*. New York: The Free Press.

1951   *The Social System*. New York: The Free Press.

Pettifer, Shirley and Janet Torge
1987   *A Book About Sexual Assault*. Montréal: Montréal Health Press.

Piliavin, Irving and Scott Briar
1964   "Police Encounters with Juveniles." *American Journal of Sociology* 70: 206-14.Pittman, David J.

Pittman, David J.
1967   *Alcoholism*. New York: Harper and Row.

Pittman, David J. and C.R. Snyder
1962   *Society, Culture, and Drinking Patterns*. New York: John Wiley. pp. 157-87.

Plummer, Kenneth
1975   *Sexual Stigma: An Interactionist Account*. London: Routledge and Kegan Paul

1979   "Misunderstanding Labelling Perspectives." pp. 85-121 in D. Downes and P. Rock (eds.), *Deviant Interpretations: Problems in Criminological Theory*. Oxford: Martin Robinson.

1981a "Building a Sociology of Homosexuality." pp. 17-29 in K. Plummer (ed.), *The Making of the Modern Homosexual*. London: Hutchinson.

1981b "Homosexual Categories: Some Research Problems in the Labelling Perspective of Homosexuality." pp. 53-75 in K. Plummer (ed.), *The Making of the Modern Homosexual*. London: Hutchinson.

1981c *The Making of the Modern Homosexual*. London: Hutchinson.

Pollner, Melvin
1974   "Sociological and Common-Sense Models of the Labelling Process." pp. 27-40 in R. Turner (ed.), *Ethnomethodology*. Harmondsworth: Penguin.

1978   "Constitutive and Mundane Versions of Labeling Theory." *Human Studies* 1: 269-88.

Polsky, Ned
1969   *Hustlers, Beats, and Others*. Garden City, NY: Doubleday Anchor.

Pope, Whitney

1976   *Durkheim's Suicide.* Chicago: University of Chicago Press.

Porter, John

1965   *The Vertical Mosaic.* Toronto: University of Toronto Press.

Porter, Roy

1986   "Rape—Does It Have a Historical Meaning." pp. 216-26 in S. Tomaselli and R. Porter (eds.), *Rape.* Oxford: Basil Blackwell.

Prus, Robert and Styllianoss Irini

1980   *Hookers, Rounders and Desk Clerks: The Social Organization of the Hotel Community.* Toronto: Gage.

Prus, Robert and C.R.D. Sharper

1979   *Road Hustler: The Career Contingencies of Professional Card and Dice Hustlers.* Toronto: Gage.

Quarantelli, E.L. and Dennis Wenger

1975   "A Voice From the Thirteenth Century: The Characteristics and Conditions for the Emergence of a Ouija Board Cult." pp. 143-57 in F. Scarpitti and P. McFarlane (eds.), *Deviance: Action, Reaction, Interaction.* Reading, MA: Addison-Wesley.

Quinney, Richard

1974   *Critique of Legal Order: Crime Control in Capitalist Society.* Boston: Little, Brown.

1975   "Crime Control in Capitalist Society: A Critical Philosophy of the Legal Order." pp. 181-201 in I. Taylor, P. Walton and J. Young (eds.), *Critical Criminology.* London: Routledge and Kegan Paul.

1977   *Class, State, and Crime: On The Theory and Practice of Criminal Justice.* New York: David McKay.

Radcliffe-Brown, A.R.

1935   "Structure and Function in Primitive Society." *American Anthropologist,* 37: 58-72.

Rains, Prudence

1971   *Becoming An Unwed Mother.* Chicago: Aldine.

1975   "Imputations of Deviance: A Retrospective Essay on the Labeling Perspective." *Social Problems* 23: 1-11.

1982   "Deviant Careers." pp. 21-41 in M. Rosenberg et al. (eds.), *The Sociology of Deviance.* New York: St. Martin's Press.

Reasons, Charles E.

1982   "Organizational Crime." pp. 150-70 in M. Rosenberg et al. (eds.), *The Sociology of Deviance.* New York: St. Martin's Press.

Reasons, Charles E. and Robert M. Rich

1978   *The Sociology of Law: A Conflict Perspective.* Toronto: Butterworths.

Rock, Paul
1973   *Deviant Behaviour*. London: Hutchinson University Library.
1979   *The Making of Symbolic Interactionism*. Totowa, NJ: Rowman and Littlefield.

Rogers, Mary F.
1983   *Sociology, Ethnomethodology, and Experience: A Phenomenological Critique*. Cambridge: Cambridge University Press.

Rosenberg, Bernard and Harry Silverstein
1969   *The Varieties of Delinquent Experience*. Waltham, MA: Blaisdell Publishers.

Rosenberg, M. Michael, Robert A. Stebbins and Allan Turowetz
1982   *The Sociology of Deviance*. New York: St. Martin's
Press.

Rosenhan, David L.
1973   "On Being Sane in Insane Places." *Science* 179: 250-58.
1975   "The Contextual Nature of Psychiatric Diagnosis." *Journal of Abnormal Psychiatry* 84: 462-74.

Rubington, Earl and Martin Weinberg
1968   *Deviance: The Interactionist Perspective*. New York: Macmillan.

Rushton, J. Phillipe
1989   "Evolutionary Biology and Heritable Traits (With Reference to Oriental-White-Black Differences)". Paper presented at the Annual Meeting of the American Association for the Advancement of Science, San Francisco.

Sacco, Vincent F.
1988   *Deviance: Conformity and Control in Canadian Society*. Scarborough: Prentice-Hall.

Sacco, Vincent and Holly Johnson
1990   "Violent Victimization." *Canadian Social Trends* 17: 10-13.

Sacks, Harvey
1974   "An Analysis of the Course of a Joke's Telling in Conversation." pp. 337-353 in R. Bauman and J. Sherzer (eds.), *Explorations in the Ethnography of Speaking*. Cambridge: Cambridge University Press.

Sacks, Oliver
1987   *The Man Who Mistook His Wife for a Hat*. New York: Harper and Row.

Sagarin, Edward
1973   "The Good Guys, the Bad Guys, and the Gay Guys." *Contemporary Sociology* 2: 3-12.

Salamon, E.D.

1988   "Homosexuality: Sexual Stigma." pp. 105-151 in V.F. Sacco (ed.), *Deviance: Conformity and Control in Canadian Society.* Scarborough: Prentice-Hall.

Scarpitti, Frank R. and Paul T. McFarlane

1975   *Deviance: Action, Reaction, Interaction.* Reading, MA: Addison-Wesley.

Scheff, Thomas J.

1966   *Being Mentally Ill: A Sociological Theory.* New York: Aldine.

1975   *Labelling Madness.* Englewood Cliffs, NJ: Prentice Hall.

1984   *Being Mentally Ill: A Sociological Theory.* 2nd ed. New York: Aldine.

Schur, Edwin M.

1965   *Crimes Without Victims: Deviant Behavior and Public Policy: Abortion, Homosexuality, and Drug Addiction.* Englewood Cliffs, NJ: Prentice Hall.

1980   "Comments." pp. 393-404 in W. Gove (ed.), *The Labelling of Deviance* 2nd ed. Beverly Hills: Sage.

1984   *Labelling Women Deviant.* New York: Random House.

Schutz, Alfred

1961   *Collected Papers I.* The Hague: Martinus Nijhoff.

Scull, Andrew T.

1977   *De-Carceration: Community Treatment and the Deviant—A Radical View.* Englewood Cliffs, NJ: Prentice Hall.

Sharrock, Wes and Bob Anderson

1986   *The Ethnomethodologists.* London: Tavistock.

Shaw, C.R. and H.D. McKay

1931   *Social Factors in Juvenile Delinquency.* Washington, DC: U.S. Government Printing Office.

1942   *Juvenile Delinquency and Urban Areas.* Chicago: University of Chicago Press.

Sheldon, William H.

1949   *Varieties of Delinquent Youth: An Introduction to Constitutional Psychiatry.* New York: Harper and Row.

Shore, Marlene

1987   *The Science of Social Redemption: McGill, the Chicago School, and the Origins of Social Research in Canada.* Toronto: University of Toronto Press.

Short, James F. and Fred L. Strodtbeck

1965   *Group Process and Gang Delinquency.* Chicago: University of Chicago Press.

Smart, Carol

1977 *Women, Crime and Criminology: A Feminist Critique.* London: Routledge and Kegan Paul.

Smart, Reginald G. and Alan C. Ogborne

1986 *Northern Spirits: Drinking in Canada Then and Now.* Toronto: Addiction Research Foundation.

Spector, Malcolm and John I. Kitsuse

1977 *Constructing Social Problems.* Menlo Park, CA: Cummings.

Srole, Leo

1956 "Social Integration and Certain Corollaries: An Exploratory Study." *American Sociological Review* 21: 709-16.

Stebbins, Robert

1971 *Commitment To Deviance.* New York: Greenwood Press.

1988 *Tolerable Deviance.* Toronto: McGraw-Hill.

Sudnow, David

965 "Normal Crimes: Sociological Features of the Penal Code in a Public Defender Office." *Social Problems* 12: 255-74.

Sutherland, Edwin H.

1924 *Principles of Criminology.* New York: J.B. Lippincott.

Sutherland, Edwin H. and Donald R. Cressey

1955 *Principles of Criminology* 5th ed. New York: J.B. Lippincott.

Sydie, Rosalind

1987 "Sociology and Gender." pp. 315-63 in M. Rosenberg et al. (eds.), *Introduction to Sociology* 2nd ed. Toronto: Methuen.

Sykes, Gresham M. and David Matza

1980 "Techniques of Neutralization: A Theory of Delinquency." pp. 207-16 in S. Traub and C. Little (eds.), *Theories of Deviance* 2nd ed. Itasca, IL: F.E. Peacock.

Szasz, Thomas S.

1961 *The Myth of Mental Illness: Foundations of a Theory of Personal Conduct.* New York: Dell.

Tanner, Julian

1988 "Youthful Deviance." pp. 323-59 in V.F. Sacco (ed.), *Deviance: Conformity and Control in Canadian Society.* Scarborough: Prentice-Hall.

Taylor, Ian

1982 "Moral Enterprise, Moral Panic, and Law-and-Order Campaigns." pp. 123-49 in M. Rosenberg et al. (eds.), *The Sociology of Deviance.* New York: St. Martin's Press.

1983 *Crime, Capitalism and Community: Three Essays in Socialist Criminology.* Toronto: Butterworths.

Taylor, Ian, Paul Walton and Jock Young
1973 *The New Criminology*. London: Routledge and Kegan Paul.

Taylor, Steve
1982 *Durkheim and the Study of Suicide*. London: Macmillan.

Tepperman, Lorne
1977 *Crime Control*. Toronto: McGraw-Hill.

Tepperman, Lorne and Michael Rosenberg
1991 *Macro / Micro: A Brief Introduction to Sociology*. Scarborough: Prentice-Hall.

Thio, Alex
1983 *Deviant Behavior*. New York: Harper and Row.

Thomas, Charles and John R. Hepburn
1983 *Crime, Criminal Law, and Criminology*. Dubuque, IO: William C. Brown.

Thomas, Jim
1982 "New Directions in Deviance Research." pp. 288-318 in M. Rosenberg et al. (eds.), *The Sociology of Deviance*. New York: St. Martin's Press.

Thomas, Lewis
1979 *The Medusa and the Snail*. New York: Viking Press.

Thomas, W.I.
1966 *On Social Organization and Social Personality*. Chicago: University of Chicago Press.
1967 *The Unadjusted Girl*. New York: Harper and Row.

Thomas, W. I. and Florian Znaniecki
1918 *The Polish Peasant in Europe and America*. Chicago: University of Chicago Press.

Thrasher, Frederick M.
1927 *The Gang*. Chicago: University of Chicago Press.

Tomaselli, Sylvana
1986 "Introduction." pp. 1-15 in S. Tomaselli and R. Porter (eds.), *Rape*. Oxford: Basil Blackwell.

Tomaselli, Sylvana and Roy Porter
1986 *Rape*. Oxford: Basil Blackwell.

Truzzi, Marcello
1975 "Lilliputians in Gulliver's Land: The Social Role of the Dwarf." pp. 97-111 in F. Scarpitti and P. McFarlane (eds.), *Deviance: Action, Reaction, Interaction*. Reading, MA: Addison-Wesley.

Turk, Austin
1985 "Law, Conflict, and Order: From Theorizing Toward Theories." pp. 254-69 in T. Fleming (ed.), *The New Criminologies in Canada: State, Crime, and Control*. Toronto: Oxford University Press.

Turkle, Sherry
1984   *The Second Self: Computers and the Human Spirit*. London: Granada.

Turner, Bryan S.
1988   *Status*. Minneapolis: University of Minnesota Press.

Warren, Carol A.B. and John M. Johnson
1972   "A Critique of Labelling Theory from the Phenomenological Perspective."
       pp. 69-2 in R.A. Scott and J.D. Douglas (eds.), *Theoretical Perspectives On Deviance*. New York: Basic Books.

Warren, Carol A.B. and Barbara Ponse
1977   "The Existential Self in the Gay World." pp. 273-89 in J.D. Douglas and J.M. Johnson (eds.), *Existential Sociology*. Cambridge: Cambridge University Press.

Weber, Max
1949   *The Methodology of the Social Sciences*. New York: The Free Press.

1978   *Economy and Society*. Berkeley: University of California Press.

Weeks, Jeffrey
1986   *Sexuality*. London: Tavistock.

West, W. Gordon
1984   *Young Offenders and the State: A Canadian Perspective on Delinquency*. Toronto: Butterworths.

Westley, William
1953   "Violence and the Police." *American Journal of Sociology* 49: 34-41.

Wieder, D. Lawrence and Charles W. Wright
1982   "Norms, Conformity, and Deviance." pp. 258-87 in M. Rosenberg et al. (eds.), *The Sociology of Deviance*. New York: St. Martin's Press.

Wilensky, Harold L. and Charles N. Lebeaux
1958   *Industrial Society and Social Welfare*. New York: Russell Sage Foundation.

Wilkins, James L.
1970   "Producing Suicide." *American Behavioral Scientist* 14: 185-201.

Willis, Paul
1977   *Learning to Labour: How Working Class Kids Get Working Class Jobs*. London: Saxon House.

Wilson, Thomas P.
1971   "Normative and Interpretive Paradigms in Sociology." pp. 57-79 in J.D. Douglas (ed.), *Understanding Everyday Life*. New York: Basic Books.

Winick, Charles
1964   "Physician Narcotic Addicts." pp. 261-79 in H. Becker (ed.), *The Other Side*. New York: The Free Press.

Wiseman, Jacqueline P.

1970 *Stations of the Lost: The Treatment of Skid Row Alcoholics.* Englewood Cliffs, NJ: Prentice Hall.

Wrong, Dennis

1961 "The Oversocialized Conception of Man in Modern Sociology." *American Sociological Review* 26: 183-93.

Yablonsky, Lewis

1959 "The Delinquent Gang as a Near Group." *Social Problems* 7: 108-17.

Yarrow, Marian R., Charlotte G. Schwartz, Harriet S. Murphy and Leila C. Deasy

1955 "The Psychological Meaning of Mental Illness in the Family." *Journal of Social Issues* 11: 12-24.

Zijderveld, Anton C.

1968 "Jokes and Their Relation to Social Reality." *Social Research* 35, 2 (Summer): 286-311.

1971 *The Abstract Society.* Garden City, NY: Doubleday.

1983 "The Sociology of Humour and Laughter." *Current Sociology* 31, 3 (Winter): 1-100.

NAME INDEX

SUBJECT INDEX

vs. functionalism, 125
and jokes, 194
self, view of, 128-29

Tituba, 71, 73-74
Total institution, 147-48
Tourette's Syndrome, 144-45
Transactional model of deviance, 134-38
Transvestite, 49

Unadjusted Girl, The, 99
University of Chicago, *see* Chicago
   school of sociology
US, social theory and social change in,
   216-20

Valium, 86, 88, 96
Value strain, 110, 163, 217
Victimless deviance, 174

War Measures Act, 13, 168
White-collar crime, 171-72
Women's Christian Temperance
   Union, 142

XYY chromosome theory of deviance,
   27-28

Youth culture, 108
Youth gangs, 102-104
   anomie theory of, 109-14
   as folk devils, 107-108
   labels for, 107
   organization of, 115
   as reaction formation, 110, 111

Zones, urban, 100-102